INLAND PASSAGE

INLAND PASSAGE

ON BOATS & BOATING IN THE NORTHEAST

David W. Shaw

RUTGERS UNIVERSITY PRESS
New Brunswick, New Jersey, and London

Library of Congress Cataloging-in-Publication Data

Shaw, David W., 1961–
      Inland passage : on boats and boating in the Northeast / by David
W. Shaw.
            p.   cm.
      Includes index.
      ISBN 0-8135-2541-1 (alk. paper)
      1. Boats and boating—Northeastern States—Guidebooks.   2. Inland
navigation—Northeastern States—Guidebooks.   3. Northeastern
States—Description and travel.   I. Title,
GV776.N75S53 1998
797.1'0974—dc21   *97-43067*
                                                                                            CIP

British Cataloging-in-Publication information available

Design by John Romer

Manufactured in the United States of America

For Harold Foster, a good friend
and boating mentor, without whom
much of this book would
not have been possible

Contents

Acknowledgments

No book of this type would be possible without the help of many individuals and organizations, all of which played a small part in the making of it through the generous sharing of information over more than a decade of work. The old salts on the waterfronts, the professional captains, and the countless skippers of recreational boats who gave me advice when I needed it all deserve thanks, as do the special people at marinas who gave me a break on prices for goods and services when I could barely afford a box of mac 'n' cheese.

Special thanks must also go to my many editors, all of whom supported this book by granting me permission to reprint articles that appeared in their publications. I'm particularly grateful to my agent and my editor at Rutgers University Press for believing in the book and helping to make it a success.

And, apart from my wife, Elizabeth, who had the courage to set me free when I needed to fly, my deepest gratitude goes to Harold Foster, to whom this book is dedicated. He sold me the little sloop that liberated me at a difficult time, and guided me through the many intricate workings that go into all the systems a boat requires to function properly, and that almost always need fixing. He believed in my abilities as a sailor enough to give freely of his time and his vast knowledge, and for that I am forever in his debt.

INLAND PASSAGE

Introduction

The water, particularly the sea, seems to possess a special kind of magic, a magnetism all its own. You can see it come alive at every point where the water meets the land. From our spot on the shore, each of us feels the pull of the water's deepest mysteries. Imagine a solitary soul perched at the end of a jetty, eyes locked on the distant horizon. An old man with a fishing rod, his skin wrinkled and weathered, the wind tousling his gray hair as he casts. Lovers on the boardwalk on moonlit summer nights, their backs turned to the glimmer of the arcades and restaurants as they look out at the waves.

And then there are the sounds of the sea. The murmur or roar of the waves against a beach. The moan of a fresh breeze in the rigging. The clap of thunder during a summer squall. The patter of rain on the deck above while you rest quietly in your berth. These sounds evoke a sense within, a feeling that there truly is a connection to the water we all share together.

Water makes up most of our bodies. It covers more than two thirds of the earth, and it moves in time with the moon and the sun, responding to a pull far stronger than any human ingenuity can muster. Water flows in tides and rivers. It shapes the beaches and rocky shores. It even drives the engine behind the atmosphere and influences weather systems that bring life, and sometimes disaster, to entire continents.

For some of us, the passive admiration of water simply can't satisfy. It's not enough to stand on the land and look out at the shimmering ocean. We have to get much closer to it, so we can feel at one with what is arguably the most powerful element in the world. In our boats we can form a tight bond with the water; we swim in it, ski on it, taste it in our mouths, see it froth white in a wake, or fly in sheets of spray over the windward bow like a curtain of diamonds. Out on the water, free from the chains of our lives on land, the world appears perfect, its wrongs somehow made right. For those of you who share with me this special feeling, we know that this is as close to perfection as we can get. After all, that's why we own boats, to capture that feeling with each new watery passage.

A boat, no matter how large or small, can take you places in mind and body. It's more than just an object; it's alive in a way most inanimate things can't hope to match. Whenever I can, I get out on my boat and go see what I haven't seen before, and when I can't be close to the water, I write about it. The stories in this book will carry you off to wonderful, beautiful ports, though not to the balmy distant land of tropical breezes. These stories stick closer to home here in the Northeast, where the United States and Canada were first settled and colonized.

The stories will transport you through the pages of history and make you part of the rich tapestry of the past, if only for a little while. They'll take you into the workings of nature that shaped our waterways, and introduce you to some interesting characters whose lives were shaped by life on the water. Together, the stories will help you to appreciate and understand our waterways. They will draw you to the water where you find so strongly within yourself a feeling of mystery and awe, even if you don't have a boat of your own.

The Passage of Nature's Time

CRAFTING THE SHAPE OF NORTHEAST WATERS

It's not just children who ask questions of the most obvious kind, like why is the sky blue? It's just part of being human, I guess, that ever-present state of wondering about what you don't know and the eternal desire to find out once the question breaks the surface of deep, abstract thought to emerge into a conscious form. But on the water, it's easy to forget all but the moment at hand. In this moment, charged with the task of making the passage through vast waters, an intense focus develops. The state of the wind and sea, the location of the boat, the set of the tide and its unseen influence on the course you must make good all require skilled attention.

Indeed, the business of piloting a boat demands great concentration, even though it might look easy when observing an experienced skipper. The joys of being there—just you in the arms of nature—take hold of your mind and convey it to an almost cosmic level. That's why it's so often the case that the boater familiar with his or her home waters ceases to see them. It's also why questions of the most obvious kind are seldom asked.

While I was sailing my little sloop through the waterways of the Northeast, a most arduous task to undertake alone, I fell into that trap. I was too busy with the present to really think about the basic and most simple question of all: why do our waterways look as they do? When you're on the water, it's not generally a time for delving deeply into these kinds of questions, at least it isn't usually for me. But when I came home from my voyage, which took me from Barnegat Bay up the Hudson River to Lake Ontario and the St. Lawrence River via the Erie Canal, then up and down the coast to Maine, I found myself transported back to the places I'd seen time and again on those cold winter days when the north winds rattled the windows of my office.

I'd seen places rich in human history, places where George Washington's men had strung a heavy chain across the Hudson near West Point to stop British ships from traveling upriver. I saw vestiges of the old locks from the original Erie Canal, desolate yet beautiful reminders of the handiwork completed by an army of Irish immigrants hungry for work and willing to dig for their daily bread. Old forts, like the one at Oswego, New York, little coastal fishing towns that dated back to colonial times, these places strung out on a watery path that tens of thousands of mariners had sailed before.

But as I thought about the grand scenery of the Highlands on the Hudson, the vast inland sea of Lake Ontario, and the varied coastline all the way to Maine, I found that my mind kept returning to the question of how these places received their individual physical identities. The following story is the result of weeks researching the various forces of nature that created our watery playground. My studies took me into the arcane and often complex, but in the end I unraveled some intriguing mysteries and found the answers I wanted. Now when I sail, in the back of my mind I know what I'm seeing and why, and that increases my appreciation for the tremendous diversity of the cruising grounds of the Northeast.

COASTAL EVOLUTION

In 1992, I left my home waters of Barnegat Bay, New Jersey, and began a four-year voyage through the waterways of the Northeast. I learned much about the history of the places I visited: the Adirondack lakes, the Hudson River, the Erie Canal, Lake Ontario, the Thousand Islands, and the coast from New Jersey to Maine. The story of the European explorers and missionaries and the indigenous peoples they met, the pioneers pressing westward, the times of war and the industrial development of our nation linked to these waterways represents the human side of things—man's attempt to conquer a pristine continent and harness its resources.

Yet during my voyage another story revealed itself. As I traveled, I found myself wanting to understand why New Jersey's shore looked so different from Maine's. Why was much of the Hudson River really an estuary? What created harbors on the western end of Long Island's North Shore, Narragansett Bay, Buzzards Bay, Plymouth, Boston and Gloucester? Why did bays disappear east of Cape Ann and reappear at Portland? Why did dunes, pine barrens, and salt marshes exist in one place, and rock ledges and headlands in others?

I failed to find answers until I looked beyond human history to discover the natural events that shaped the land. When I did, the answers to my questions surprised me. Discovering the natural history of these familiar cruising grounds unfolded a tale far grander than the puny imprint of humanity.

The natural history of our waterways and lands helped chart our direction as a nation, encouraging fishing in Maine and farming in New Jersey, and deciding the outcomes of wars and the location of industries. It made us who we are as Americans and Canadians, and, as boaters, provided us with one of the most unique cruising grounds in the world.

The story I am about to tell will focus on my coastwise voyage, as well as the Hudson River. Let's begin in New Jersey, where I have cruised for years and where I set off from Manasquan Inlet in 1992 on my waterborne odyssey.

NEW JERSEY

Barnegat Bay, salt marshes, and pine barrens on the mainland, Great Egg Harbor, Cape May, the Atlantic Highlands, and Sandy Hook comprise the seascape New Jersey boaters enjoy. Barrier islands protect the backwaters and form a relatively straight outer coast of 127 miles. New Jersey's small tidal range lacks the power to punch many inlets through the barrier islands, so few exist. It also accounts for the largely unbroken shoreline. On busy summer weekends, boats crowd the bays and head offshore on fishing trips. All this because of natural events long ago that shaped the shore—and continue to alter it.

In geological time, the Jersey shore exists in a state of transition, striving to become one with the mainland, and succeeding little by little. The barrier islands move shoreward two feet or more every year. The tide brings in fine silt suspended in the water and deposits it in the bays, which, from a geologist's view, are considered lagoons similar to those found behind coral reefs. They are not bays in the scientific sense of the word. The mud flats reach a level of high tide and become marshes growing outward toward the sea. Birds, shell- and fin fish, and insects inhabit the tall grass clumped among the shallows and the lagoon beyond the wetlands. The entire system moves as if alive like the life it supports. Looking forward through geological time, in a mere blink, the barrier islands and the lagoons behind them will disappear.

The observant boater can't help but notice how flat New Jersey is, and the angler, venturing far offshore, can't help but notice the gentle slope of the ocean floor. The flat land and sea floor form part of the ancient Atlantic Plain. It stretches from Newfoundland to Florida and around the Gulf of Mexico. It is comprised of two parts, the continental shelf and the coastal plain. From Long Island the coastal plain extends 2,000 miles to the south. Offshore, the continental shelf, once above sea level, runs nearly flat at depths usually less than 600 feet until it abruptly descends to the abyssal depths of the sea.

However, to the northeast, no coastal plain exists. The Atlantic Plain takes on a much different character in New England, derived from a complex network of natural forces. But I'm getting ahead of the story.

Figure 1. Spaceborne image of New Jersey and its magnificent coast. New York City, Long Island, Delaware Bay, and parts of Pennsylvania, including Philadelphia, can also be seen. COURTESY OF NASA

New Jersey marks the point of transition along the Atlantic Plain. Southward the coastal plain gives the East Coast its characteristic flatness and explains the presence of barrier islands.

The coastal plain comprises as much as 60 percent of New Jersey, and much of the land lies within 100 feet of sea level. This flat, gently sloping land meeting the sea makes New Jersey's coast and the waterways what they are. The next time you cruise along the outer shore and admire the barrier islands, consider that they are as young as 5,000 years, are temporary, and were formed as a result of the waves meeting the coastal plain. Waves built the low ridges and washed along the shore, carrying sand parallel to the beach to create these beautiful, low islands. Wind created the rolling dunes. Tides and winter storms cut inlets and filled the land behind the ridge with shallow water. A look at the coast from above Barnegat Bay to Sandy Hook provides a picture of how the rest of the Jersey shore will appear someday when the beach completes its migration to the mainland.

As I made my way up the coast from Manasquan for the first time, I marveled at the purple hills of the Highlands and wondered how and why they had formed. They didn't seem to belong on the otherwise flat beach. Without getting too technical, they are what geologists call a cuesta, a formation that developed when erosion reduced land around the more erosion-resistant strata. The Highlands sit atop a formation of porous sand dating back 135 million years. The hills exist because the hard, sandy strata absorbs rainwater, all but eliminating the erosive impact of runoff. The Highlands sit on a giant natural sponge.

The logical explanation for the presence of the Highlands was just one mystery solved on my journey. I found it awesome to consider the power of nature. In relation to the earth's 4,600 million-year history, human history becomes insignificant.

THE HUDSON RIVER

In its youth, the Adirondacks formed a mountain range some geologists believe towered as high as the Himalayas. From these great heights over seventy-five million years ago, a river flowed from its Adirondack headwaters between the Catskill Mountains and the Taconics and carved what later became the Hudson Valley. Its waters ran swiftly and eroded the spectacular gorge of the Highlands above Haverstraw Bay. The young Hudson ran far deeper than it does now and flowed 120 miles beyond the modern-day coast to the sea, which was as much as 330 feet lower. In their current locations, the dozens of yacht clubs and marinas along the Hudson River would sit high off the water on steep slopes. This would seem something of a paradox. How could the river run deeper in the past? Isn't it like the Colorado or the Mississippi? Why would the marinas of today stand high and dry?

Consider an even stranger occurrence. The Hudson River ran behind the Palisades, which formed when molten lava flowed up from a rent in the earth's crust and created a basalt dike, through Sparkill Gap, past Paterson and Millburn, New Jersey, and emptied into the Atlantic south of Staten Island. How could it do that?

The answer to the latter question remains unclear while the answer to the former question about the marinas is a little easier to understand. When the last of the glaciers receded 10,000 years ago and freed all that trapped water, the sea level rose and submerged the old coastal plain that had extended to the edge of the current continental shelf. The Hudson River was literally drowned and transformed into an estuary. The sea rolled in and reshaped the Hudson, along with land across the globe, thirty percent of which was formerly covered in a mile-high ice sheet. It no longer must fall to the sea as in the past, and hence much of its power no longer exists, making it quite unlike the Colorado or the Mississippi. Those marinas I enjoy sit at sea level, of course; deep in the river's past they would naturally find themselves stranded.

In my days of cruising New Jersey and New York waters, I often heard NOAA (National Oceanic Atmospheric Administration) weather reports using Hudson Canyon as a reference point. For me, the idea of a canyon far offshore seemed strange, an abstraction I couldn't understand. Scientists had trouble explaining the canyon as well. It drops 9,000 feet and reaches a maximum depth of 15,000 feet. For years, no one could figure out how it formed. Had the sea level dropped that much to enable the river to cut the trench?

The amazing canyon stands as a stark reminder of the Hudson's youthful power. On its journey to the sea, it carried sediment that built up near its mouth and boiled down the steep slope at the edge of the continental land mass in underwater avalanches (turbidity currents) that cut a gorge 160 miles beyond the lip of North America toward Bermuda. It gave the Hudson a total signature of 894 miles.

Imagine how different the East Coast would look were the sea to rise again, as it did 10,000 years ago. The rise of the past obliterated the Hudson and the former coast, and similar incredible changes would happen now. Glaciers cover 10 percent of the earth's land surface and, excluding ground water, they hold 99 percent of the planet's fresh water. If the continental glaciers of Greenland and Antarctica melted, some experts predict the sea level would rise more than 200 feet, submerging the vast majority of the low coastal plain, and most of the islands of New England. The great natural bays east of Long Island would still exist in a drowned state, but no mariners of today would recognize them. What once were islands and headlands would become reefs and ledges.

Of course, nobody expects the glaciers to melt, even with global warming and the long-established certainty that sea level fluctuates. Scientific data suggests the ocean will rise about three feet in the next century, not much of a concern. In fact, rather than melting as a result of global warming, some scientists predict that the glaciers will grow with the added precipitation as the earth warms up, if it really is warming. (Glaciers grow when snow accumulates on top and turns to ice.)

If the glaciers grow again, sea level will drop and the coastal plain will increase in size. A new ridge of barrier islands will form farther out. The complexity of global systems can stagger the mind, and many mysteries still stump the brightest earth scientists.

The plain truth remains that nobody knows why glaciers formed in the Arctic 2.5 million years ago and in their final push south along the present coast reached Long Island and northern New Jersey. Most experts expect continental glaciers to return again, though they haven't figured out why. They staged a modest comeback just seconds back in geological time. Between 1450 and 1850 the earth cooled enough to start continental glaciers growing again in what was called the "Little Ice Age." This mini-Ice Age caused the hard winters the early settlers endured. In the 1970s, another cooling trend occurred and the glaciers grew again after a long hiatus, then stopped as temperatures increased during the 1980s. Glaciers represent a deep, unsolved mystery, one that shaped our present coast and the very nature of life today.

LONG ISLAND

After I explored the Hudson River, Lake Ontario, and the Thousand Islands, I turned the bow of the boat around and cruised up the North Shore of Long Island. As primarily a New Jersey boater, I found the presence of rocks unnerving, though eventually I got used to them. When I passed under the Throgs Neck Bridge into Long Island Sound, I felt as though I'd entered a strange land, altogether different from New Jersey. It seemed my home state represented a demarcation zone and this was true, though I only knew it through my observations of the obvious at the time. The coastal plain disappeared. I had reached the land of past glaciers.

Long Island, the largest isle off the continental United States at 118 miles in length, offers boaters a degree of diverse cruising grounds difficult to find elsewhere. The bays on the North Shore and the east end of the island, and the long barrier islands and lagoons behind them on the South Shore, make the cruising ground unique. Unlike New Jersey, Long Island has a more robust connection to the sea by virtue of its location and size. Commercial fishing, though in a sorry state today, played a big part in the island's history. Farming thrived as it did in New Jersey, though for different reasons. Had it not been for the last Ice Age, fishing and farming would not have been important on Long Island.

Interestingly enough, however, glaciers did not form the entire island. It would exist without glaciation. As I ventured into Manhasset Bay, I had in the back of my mind the notion that the glaciers created it and the other bays on the North Shore. But, contrary to popular belief, the bays on the west end of the North Shore and the long bayless straight stretch to the east, existed more than 100 million years ago. At that time the sea level was much lower, and what would later become Long Island was a low ridge or cuesta about ten to twelve miles wide with its northern limits at the same location as the present North Shore. With all the glacial deposits removed, the island would shrink to a quarter of its current area, but even so, a small amount of the ridge would still jut above sea level. I doubt the island would have its present name, though.

Streams and runoff eroded valleys in the cuesta long before the glaciers came. When the ice sheet finally reached the cuesta it lacked the erosive power it had farther north. Its contribution to the formation of Long Island was the deposition of enormous amounts of debris carried inside and in front of the ice. If these valleys weren't present prior to the Ice Age some of the Northeast's most popular cruising destinations would not exist. The character of the North Shore was almost the same before the glaciers and the subsequent rise in sea level submerged much of the ancient core of the island.

Long Island Sound was a lowland formed in the same way as the lowlands of New Jersey, as streams eroded the weaker strata around the cuesta and the oldland to the north. It was part of the old coastal plain when surf broke against what now is the far edge of the continental shelf, and its current underwater topography was also virtually unchanged during glacial times.

While cruising up the coast, I admired the inhospitable beauty of the high bluffs. As the sound widens, the sweep of the wind increases and waves build. The surf cuts into the cliffs, forming shallows at their feet as the land retreats from the power of the water. I noticed a rather abrupt change from deep water to the shoals on my way into Mattituck Inlet. These shoals constituted a platform of eroded glacial deposits carved from the Harbor Hill terminal moraine which formed when the glacier halted.

Of the four ice ages, the last one stretched farthest south. Its leading edge nosed up against the ridge described earlier. Even glaciers have to stop sometime. Their edges contained stagnant or weak ice that tended to stop when running against a resistant landform, as some geologists suggest was the case with Long Island. The ice left behind two moraines (boulders and other debris carried by glaciers): Harbor Hill moraine to the north, which spans most of the North Shore, and the Ronkonkoma moraine which runs through the middle of the island. At the east end, the remnants of these moraines form the flukes or fishtail of Long Island. Looking at the charts, I had wondered how those enormous bays at the east end of the island formed. When the sea level rose, water flooded the outwash plain between the two moraines.

At first glance, the outer coast of Long Island appears almost identical to New Jersey's. And it is. Post-glacial barrier islands and lagoons formed in the same way described earlier. The same marshes, dunes, pine barrens, rich farmland, and low rolling hills exist in both places. However, unlike in New Jersey, the presence of these features resulted from the vast outwash plain of the glacier that formed south of the moraines. The striking similarity between the South Shore of Long Island and the Jersey shore resulted from the presence of the gentle slope from the beach to the relatively flat sea floor beyond. The same shore-building processes occurred in both places. Likewise, in contrast to New Jersey, the steep slope of the partly submerged cuesta on the North Shore accounts for its deep bays and wave-cut bluffs. Thus, Long Island ranks as an intriguing place for boaters and students of earth science.

With Long Island astern, I continued my voyage east. Behind me were lands shaped by formations millions of years old and reshaped by glaciers young in geological time. Now my boat would lead me into lands and waters not on the fringe of the great ice sheet, but deep within its former domain. My voyage through the natural history of the coast was just beginning.

EAST TO CAPE ANN

On busy summer weekends, boaters parade in and out of the marinas along the Connecticut coast to cruise on Long Island or Block Island sounds. As I joined the other mariners on my way to Maine, my thoughts often wandered to questions about why the lands on both sides of Long Island Sound looked so different. Why were long stretches of high bluffs absent in Connecticut? While many accessible harbors exist there, why were great bays like Narragansett nonexistent? And why did boaters encounter more shoals along the mainland?

As I have already explained, Long Island's North Shore presents a steep slope to the sea. The descent to the submerged lowland between the ridge of Long Island's ancient core, now buried under glacial deposits, most often presents a steep fall to water depths generally greater than those found off Connecticut.

No rivers of any consequence flow off of the island's North Shore. In contrast, rivers meander their way through Connecticut to Long Island Sound, creating harbors at their mouths which often have adjacent deltalike shallows. The gradient of the water depths leading from shore lacks the plunge found across the sound along Long Island. The presence of rivers in one place and their absence in another doesn't fully explain why each side of the sound features a unique topographical personality; the slope of the land meeting the sea determines it.

Along most of the New England coast a belt of coastal lowlands fronts the ocean. In Connecticut, the land and valleys lie close to sea level atop a solid layer of erosion-resistant metamorphic rock that ranges from 250 to 600 million years old and which comprises the bulk of the New England coast. Throughout most of New England, only about twenty feet of soil rests on the bedrock. Broadly speaking, the coastal lowland represents the gentle slope at the edge of the hilly, interior upland to the north.

When you're cruising along the Connecticut shore and stopping for the night at the mouth of one of the state's rivers, consider two important natural forces that determined the location of your slip or mooring. First, the Connecticut shore is part of an ancient plain which glaciers didn't greatly alter. The major rivers flowed basically along their present routes through the lowland from higher inshore terrain.

When the ice sheet advanced across this plain, it did not change much of the relief, other than to reduce it somewhat by leaving deposits in the valleys. The weight of the ice at its southern edges failed to sink the land very much. Farther north, the weight of the ice sank the land as much as 1,200 feet, but I'll get to that later. The important consideration remains that not much crustal sinking occurred in Connecticut, nor did the sea drown much of the shore.

As the sea level rose after the last glacier receded, it did not flow far inland to reach the higher hills of the upland. If it had covered the Connecticut lowland, which ranges from six to sixteen miles in width, the shore would have presented a steeper slope. Bays and islands would have formed, and the present lowland area would resemble a mini-continental shelf a little like that off New Jersey.

However, unlike the flat continental shelf that stretches offshore south from New Jersey, the Connecticut Valley would create a depression in the sea floor and the valley walls would form an enormous bay—much like the Chesapeake. The dip of the submerged lowland of Long Island Sound and the ridge of Long Island would create a bottom on a grander scale, more like the Gulf of Maine. The submerged present coast of Connecticut would no doubt support abundant fishing, and most of the major cities in the state would not exist since humans tend to build and farm on lowlands and coastal plains, leaving the rougher upland territory alone.

These crustal sinking and drowning processes sparked my imagination. What if sea level does rise? Would the Connecticut shore look more like Maine? All evidence suggests that it might, though the prospect of a dramatic rise in sea level appears remote.

As I cruised past Block Island, I recalled my walks along the high clay cliffs and the long spit of Sandy Point. The ebb and flow of the glaciers over the land left huge deposits of debris, but only in certain places along the New England coast. Block Island is one of them.

Block Island, Martha's Vineyard, Nantucket, the Elizabeth Islands and the isthmus of Cape Cod mark the visible edge of the advance of the ice sheet in its various stages. The cliffs of the outer islands stand as remnants of the same terminal moraine that formed Montauk at the east end of Long Island, and the same post-glacial shore-building processes created the barrier islands and sand spits. The moraine on Long Island's North Shore stretched across the sound to form the islands of southwestern Rhode Island, the Elizabeth Islands that hem in and create Buzzards Bay, and the high relief of Cape Cod.

Like Long Island and Cape Cod, some of these islands would rise above sea level today even with the removal of all glacial deposits. Of course, they would be much smaller. They rest on sedimentary submerged banks or cuestas up to 135 million years old and represent the higher vestiges of an ancient coastal plain that stretched about 200 miles off the coast of Maine. It's hard to imagine that surf broke on the lip of North America so far from the present coast, but evidently it did.

The many draggers I saw offshore and their distant predecessors who ventured to the formerly rich fishing grounds of Georges Bank off Cape Cod and the Grand Banks off Newfoundland owe much to the natural forces that depressed and drowned New England's coast. The cuestas of the old coastal plain and the glacial deposits that added to their breadth and height created an ideal habitat for fish.

As many as 90 percent of all fish live on the world's relatively shallow continental shelves; the deep sea remains a marine desert. The cold northern waters and the offshore shallows made possible the lustrous history of fishing in New England, though today the story lacks the glow of the banner years when record hauls of cod, haddock, and yellowtail flounder were taken for granted.

Along the coast of Rhode Island to Point Judith, including Fishers Island, lie the remains of a moraine and its outwash plain. The long stretch of beach with no good harbors derived from these glacial deposits. A large part of Rhode Island sits atop a huge section of granite, an igneous rock type (rock that solidified from a molten state) that forms the west side of Narragansett Bay.

I mentioned earlier that metamorphic rock comprises most of New

England's bedrock. Metamorphic rocks were, as their name implies, changed as a result of exposure to heat and pressure from an igneous or sedimentary state. The presence of so much granite in Rhode Island stands out in sharp contrast to the rest of the coastal region and largely explains why most of the coast lacks natural harbors.

However, Rhode Island's granite abruptly ends at Narragansett Bay. This prime cruising ground formed from erosion and glacial carving, to a lesser extent. The softer carboniferous sandstones, shales, or slates underlying Narragansett Bay couldn't last like granite, or the wedge of metamorphic rock almost one billion years old on the other side of the bay. The bay formed between these two erosion-resistant bedrocks as the softer rocks gave way. Although no such stark examples of igneous and metamorphic bedrock borders exist in Boston and Casco bays, both basins formed in a similar manner from the erosion of softer rock types in relation to their harder neighbors.

When the glaciers advanced over the rock formation just described—really a small upland—two ice lobes branched off around the slightly elevated and resistant topography. One filled Narragansett Bay, the other Cape Cod Bay. The upland between the fingers of ice divided it. The glaciers eroded little of the old Cape Cod drainage basin but more of Narragansett Bay. Both would keep their relative shapes had the glaciers never come. But they would stand far from the sea on the now submerged coastal plain, as would the rest of the present coast.

Of course, the deposition of moraines added size to the preglacial terrain of southern New England's outer lands. What fascinated me was that the land appeared tougher than I had previously thought. The glaciers, while of paramount importance, played a far smaller role in shaping the coast than I had supposed. The two most important contributions it made to New England's coast—beyond the land of the moraines—was a depression of the earth's crust and the subsequent rise in sea level that drowned the coast to progressively higher levels the farther northeast I went.

When I emerged from the Cape Cod Canal, I couldn't help but notice the long, sandy arm of the Cape to starboard, nor the shoal water marked on the chart. Much of the sixty-five-mile Cape sits atop an ancient bank. However, east of Truro, the land didn't exist before, or even just after, the glaciers. The enormous sand spit formed in postglacial times, perhaps as recently as 5,000 years ago, due to the same shore-building processes that created barrier islands through wave action and northward currents.

Put another way, Cape Cod is a giant version of Sandy Hook; both grow with the passage of time. For example, Sandy Hook has grown one mile since 1764. The key difference between the two lies with the glaciers. Sandy Hook builds from sands created from sedimentary rock of the coastal plain. The fist of Cape Cod builds from debris of the outwash plain that stretches out beyond the lip of the moraine running along the shore.

However, the hooking in of both landforms reflects the natural tendency of spits to extend from the land into open waters of wide bays. Regardless of how the building blocks for the land came to rest in one place or another, the fine grains of sand respond in exactly the same manner when exposed to the power of the sea.

Far in the future, both spits will erect a continuous bar to the mainland. The bays will fill and ultimately disappear as the shoreline seeks equilibrium. In learning about the formation of the coast, one thing above all else became evident: Nature, which on the surface seems disorderly and all powerful, exists in a state of delicate balance.

DOWN EAST FROM CAPE ANN

Just as I wondered why few harbors exist on the east end of Long Island's North Shore, or along much of Rhode Island, I questioned why the coast east of Cape Ann offered little shelter until Casco Bay. Portsmouth, New Hampshire, a submerged river valley, provided refuge, as did Kennebunkport and York.

But why did such a stark contrast exist between that stretch of coast and the rugged headlands and deep bays filled with islands to the east? Aside from the headlands, its river harbors reminded me of Connecticut, and for good reason. The two shores share a significant characteristic: they're both plains.

The answer to the mystery, once revealed in the light of scientific discovery, remained no less intriguing or complex. The reason why the coast between Cape Ann and Portland looks as it does stems from the postglacial rise of the earth's crust and the presence of a narrow coastal plain unrelated to the one south of New Jersey.

When the ice pressed the earth's crust downward, then melted, the weight decreased and disappeared. The crust rebounded slowly but couldn't keep up with the more rapid rise in sea level. So the sea inundated the present coast east of Cape Ann. Marine deposits have been found in the clay laid down at this time eighty miles inland and at heights of 500 feet above present sea level. Gradually, the coast reached its present height. It has made land that has both emerged and drowned at different times—an interesting paradox.

I found it strange that in spite of the ice's power to make the land

and ocean rise and fall, it had failed to significantly alter the preexisting topography built from the bedrock. The ice failed to cut away more than the top, weathered layer of most rock in New England, though in mountain valleys it did create some magnificent sculptures.

Somes Sound, a fjord penetrating Maine's Mount Desert Island, marks the only place on the coast where glaciers created a landscape of consequence. This occurred for the same reasons the ice shaped the mountains: when channeled in a valley, the ice took on greater power. Otherwise, it simply rode along over mountain tops on its way south.

Back to the coast from Cape Ann to Portland, the preexisting plain rose up from its submerged state when the earth's crust stabilized and the sea stopped rising in post-glacial times. It merged with the outwash plains of inland valleys and the fringe of the drowned coast to create a bayless stretch with arms or necks of land reaching into the ocean.

To the east of Portland, the ice pressed the earth's crust farther down. Deposits in glacial lakes tilt to the north at increasingly acute angles the farther into glacial domain you go. Evidence suggests that to sink the old coastal plain, which now lies under the Gulf of Maine, the crust would have had to sink 1,200 feet.

The offshore shoals and islands were once high ridges. The deep basin in the gulf extends to 1,200 feet before rising in the shallows of the offshore banks. It is similar to the submerged lowland between the ancient ridge of Long Island and the plain of the Connecticut shore, and it formed in the same way as streams and run-off eroded softer rock.

The important consideration for boaters is that the abundance of ledges interspersed with deep water occurred because the entire gulf once was a system of hills and lowlands, and the lands that now make up the coast were highlands. When the crust sank and then rebounded, and when sea level rose, the ocean met with a mountainous region, submerging the lower relief of the old coastal plain and creating a very steep slope to meet the sea. It's not far off to say that all the wonderful bays and islands of the Maine coast were once the summits of inland mountains laced with deep valleys that now comprise one of the most enchanting cruising grounds in the world.

The next time you cruise Maine waters, imagine that everything you see was first a mountain region 200 miles from the sea. After that, ice covered it, then water. The marinas you visit are located on shorelines that were once alpine slopes, and at another time were deep underwater. As the coast matures, it will become straighter. The waves will wear away the islands and headlands, beaches will form as rock turns to sand and the deposits will gradually fill the bays as bars form across their mouths and the silt suspended in the water settles on the bay floors. The present coast exists in a youthful state, which explains why few beaches mark the shore. But far ahead in time—so far in the future human beings may no longer inhabit the earth—the coast of Maine will grow old, its landward retreat halted in a state of equilibrium that nature seems to require.

It seems humans could learn a lesson from a study of the earth. The animals and plants that we share the planet with are part of something bigger than life itself. The earth truly appears to live as well, only on a scale hard to imagine. That drive for harmony, so apparent from the workings of the earth, reminded me of why I went to sea in 1992, and why I longed to escape the inharmonious, frenetic, and often mean-ingless shuffle of life in suburbia. I, too, sought harmony, a sense of oneness with the planet denied me on land.

In taking the leap of faith to leave behind a conventional life, I was able to attain my own equilibrium. I came to appreciate that humanity's inner drive to find it, though so often buried in lives without contem-plation, was as natural as the earth itself, part of a process older than human civilization, older than time.

Offshore, 1995

Any wise mariner knows that large protrusions of land into wide bod-ies of open water represent a danger zone that prudence dictates a firm hand on the helm. The forces of wind and water pile into these points, known as headlands to some, necks to others, and capes to almost everyone. The most feared ones, Cape Horn and the Cape of Good Hope, stand in infamy among sailors, both at present and in the past. But you don't need the tip of a continent to create some pretty rough water; a small headland will do just fine.

Up and down the coast, I encountered many a headland, par-ticularly in Maine, which seems to be a land of necks, as the Main-ers call them. They jut into often turbulent seas made all the worse with tidal currents spawned from the rise and fall of the ocean to as much as twenty feet or more every six hours at the farthest points east in the United States. In New Jersey, the average boater can go a whole season without encountering a headland. Only at the north and south ends of the state will you run in with the conditions associated with a cape.

The necks of Maine all formed in a similar manner, which we have looked at in the previous story. But the headlands of New Jersey, Sandy Hook, and Cape May, each formed from an entirely differ-ent set of natural forces.

CAPE MAY CHALLENGE

Navigating around headlands and sand spits is a common part of cruising along the Northeast coast. Most states are endowed with at least one cape. New Jersey has two.

In the state's northern waters, Sandy Hook juts from the mainland like a pinkie. It's more a spit than a cape, but still significant. At the other end of the 127–mile coast, Cape May stands as a prominent, beautiful, and sometimes dangerous part of the seascape. Visible from outer space, these two features give New Jersey waters character. But contrary to popular belief, their origins aren't due to identical natural forces.

Sand carried by waves headed north along the shore built Sandy Hook, and it's still growing. When the Sandy Hook Lighthouse was built in 1764, it stood about 500 feet from the tip of the hook. Now it's more than a mile from the northern edge. Published reports estimate that the annual buildup of sand equals one ten-ton dump truck dumping its load every eight minutes all year long.

Cape May formed during the warm interglacial periods, hot spots in the Ice Age, which melted large amounts of the glaciers to the north. Deposits carried in the meltwater flowing to the sea and outwash from the mighty Delaware River built the cape. The process reversed itself, after sea levels rose 10,000 years ago when the Ice Age ended.

Little by little, the sea eats the cape; it continues to erode, and people are partly to blame. Jetties built at Cape May Inlet have robbed Cape May of sand and bloated Wildwood's beach to the north.

Capes have killed boats and crews for centuries with rough water, hidden shoals, and swift tidal currents. That's why so much effort has been made to plant lighthouses at their tips to warn mariners of the dangers. To reduce the perils of the largest capes in the Northeast as well as cut passage time, sea-level canals were dug through Cape Ann, Cape Cod, and Cape May.

Henry Hudson was among the first to experience the challenges of navigating around the Northeast's capes. Back in 1609, after crossing the Atlantic, Hudson sailed south to Virginia, keeping well offshore. Then he turned northward, taking the *Half Moon* inshore, and wandered around in search of the Northwest Passage and all the loot such a discovery would bring.

When he sailed into Delaware Bay, he ran aground in the choppy shoal waters off Cape May. An account of the voyage reported sighting many of the 150 islands in the neighborhood, sometimes called the Cape May keys, and shoals "three leagues off." Hudson almost lost his rudder in those shallow waters after bouncing off the sandy bottom.

Unwary boaters today experience similar unpleasantness. And even the experienced sometimes come to grief. The Cape May ferry ran aground last year on an uncharted shoal which grew large enough to cause trouble.

Another explorer, Cornelius Jacobsen Mey, landed on the cape in 1623. At the time, Cape May Point was an island and settlers called it Cape Island—not very creative but logical. In 1869, the cape was re-named after Mey.

Delaware Bay enjoys a nefarious reputation. The wind howls, tides race, and shoals abound. Off Cape May, Eph Shoal and Prissy Wicks Shoal compel mariners to head well out to sea, just like the shoals off Cape Cod.

The run from Sandy Hook to Cape May can be challenging because only a few first-rate inlets along the way afford easy access to the shel-tered waters behind the barrier islands. In 1908, work began on the inland waterway to provide a safer route. But not until 1942, the year the Cape May Canal was completed, could mariners avoid the haz-ards of New Jersey's famous cape.

Cape May Inlet, one of the best on the East Coast, leads into Cape May Harbor. It's a veritable roosting place, both for boats bound to or from Chesapeake Bay via the C&D Canal at the head of Delaware Bay, and for migratory birds which land in the area to rest before head-ing on their way.

Situated on the same latitude as Washington, D.C., the cape has long been a blend of the South and the North. In the 1850s, Cape May was among America's leading resort areas. Southerners used to ride steamships to the resorts on the cape before the Civil War ended the party. Boaters visiting the cape today find a much quieter place, one rich with Victorian homes to admire, rolling sand dunes, and plenty of good fishing.

The shoals off Sandy Hook, too, attract anglers by the thousands. Any Jersey or Long Island boater knows the fleet will be out on nice, and not so nice, summer weekends. The smaller of New Jersey's head-lands is a very popular place. In the past, the stretch of beach between Sandy Hook and Manasquan was a killing ground for shipping. Some reports indicate that fifteen ships a year sank there prior to 1845. It still can be dangerous, though it's no Cape Cod or Cape May. More often, however, the Hook serves as a refuge for mariners who hide be-hind it during strong southerly and easterly winds.

The swift tidal currents carved a natural channel through the many shoals in the area. Dredging helped nature along. Long before dredging, though, the natural channel just off the Hook, now known as Sandy Hook Channel, was the gateway to New York Harbor. (Actually, a previous channel, Gedney, was used to cross the sandbar, which is just a little farther off the Hook than the present channel in use today. It, too, was carved through a natural gutter in the sand.)

In the late 1800s, the Hook became a key strategic point. Gun batteries were built on the shores to protect New York from aggressors, and weapons were tested there. In World War II, approximately 18,000 military personnel called the Hook home. During the Cold War, missiles stood ready for launching against the Reds.

At the crack of dawn during boating season, the muted sound of powerboats underway fills the air around Sandy Hook and Cape May. These headlands steeped in history and blessed with natural beauty are home to the thousands of boaters who appreciate them.

Offshore, 1996

The nor'easter of December 1992 that lashed the coast and caused millions of dollars in damage acted as an impetus behind a new Army Corps of Engineers initiative to build up the beaches in the northern part of New Jersey, particularly around Sea Bright which was hit quite hard. When the big wind came and drove enormous waves before it, Route 36 in the vicinity of Sea Bright became a canal. Water washed over the seawall, across the highway, and proceeded inland with unrelenting fury. The storm damage made it obvious to most people that the beach, diminished as sand migrated northward with the current, sorely needed replenishment.

The Army Corps executed a mammoth project involving the harvesting of sand from the ocean floor and dumping tons of it along the beaches. A mighty effort, but will it work? It may, if only temporarily. Human ingenuity has tried time and again to tame nature, sometimes succeeding, often failing, and almost always hatching unforeseen consequences as a result of the tampering with natural systems we still don't fully comprehend.

Up and down the coast, jetties and bulwarks built to control nature line just about every section of beach. The preserves of Island Beach mark a notable exception. Here, the forces of nature that built the shore continue to work unimpeded, and as a result the observant soul can see in action the power that so often remains hidden deep in abstract theory or the dusty pages of a dry textbook. Tuckers Island, famous for its disappearing act in the early days of the twentieth century, seems to be making a comeback.

THE RETURN OF TUCKERS ISLAND

Back in 1524, Giovanni da Verrazano broke his habit of sailing far off-shore, deciding instead to "fetch" the coast of New Jersey (as they used to say in the days of sail). Although he had made earlier landfalls to the south, he had missed the Chesapeake and Delaware bays entirely. This time, fair weather and steady soundings led him confidently in-shore toward the (future) Garden State.

In his account of the voyage, Verrazano noted the presence of Barnegat Bay, which he viewed from Barnegat Inlet. A little while later, he also discovered New York Harbor, though he didn't stay long due to a sudden squall.

Despite the short duration of his visits, Verrazano was quite taken with New Jersey and New York. He regarded both places among the prettiest he had encountered on the East Coast. His log describes the sweet smells of flowers and trees wafting offshore, plentiful fish and fertile lands. In its natural state, unsullied by works of European civilization, the coast must have resembled a kind of Eden.

Today, most of the Jersey shore looks much different than it did in Verrazano's time. High-rise condos, beachfront bungalows, jetties, and bulkheads line the beaches down much of the 127 miles of outer coast. For the most part, the natural beauty Verrazano noted in his log no longer exists. But not everywhere. To be truthful, New Jersey isn't all glitz.

If Verrazano suddenly emerged from a time warp and found himself off Little Egg Inlet, he would see that at least down here the barrier islands look much the same as they did 471 years ago. Most of the land for miles on either side of Little Egg Inlet was set aside years ago to form nature preserves. No jetties or other structures designed to control the shore-building processes were built. The area remains largely unaltered from its natural state.

As a result, Little Egg Inlet provides a unique opportunity to observe the natural movement of the sand; and there is indeed motion. In their natural state, these sandy islands shift and grow as if they're alive.

Waves, winds, and tides propel the sand. The beaches, sand dunes, sandbars, and inlets come and go no matter how we try to stop the cycle with jetties, dredging, and other methods. We may make a little headway at stabilizing the beaches, but nature always wins in the end.

Years ago, Little Egg Inlet's neighbor, Beach Haven Inlet, began to shoal very badly. You would cruise along in ten to twelve feet of water and suddenly the depth would shoal to three or four feet. To some of the people who live and boat along this part of the Jersey shore,

Figure 2. Aerial view of the New Jersey shoreline south of Long Beach Island. Tuckers Island is the small sandbar near the top. PHOTO BY KEITH HAMILTON, STUDIO-9, WARETOWN, NEW JERSEY.

the slow demise of Beach Haven Inlet—now completely closed to navigation—was seen not as an elimination of a passage into the bay, but as the return of an island that had existed there earlier this century.

The island, known as Tuckers Island, was once quite substantial—possibly three or four miles long. A chart from the 1800s clearly defines its location south of Long Beach Island. Today, however, no Tuckers Island appears on the charts, and for very good reason. It disappeared around the middle of this century.

Legend has it that Tuckers Island, New Jersey's own little Atlantis, has emerged and vanished many times since the first settlers arrived. Back then, the rich fin and shell fishing in the bays and offshore attracted people to the protected waters behind the barrier islands. Farming was by far the more important industry in New Jersey, but maritime activity bustled as well and the people of Tuckers Island were part of it. At least when the island was there.

By the early part of this century, Tuckers Island was a popular resort, complete with a hotel and other amenities. It was also home to a small number of permanent residents.

But as the century progressed, the island began to disappear. Grain by grain it was carried away, suspended in the tidal currents. Naturally, the residents objected. But they could do nothing to stop the cycle. Eventually, the sea reclaimed Tuckers Island.

That may well have been the end of the story. When an island disappears it seldom comes back. However, nature never stops working, and for the same reasons the sand left, it now has begun to return. The sandbar that once was a resort remained submerged at low water for years. Now it rises above the waves at low tide. The reemergence of Tuckers Island has attracted people's attention. They seem surprised that nature could replace what it took away.

Had you stood on Tuckers Island and gazed out to sea, it would have probably struck you as inconceivable that the land might someday disappear. We may intellectually understand that barrier islands are temporary. But imagining the demise of Tuckers Island when you are standing right on it tends to defy our natural tendency to believe in the permanence of our natural surroundings.

Even though we understand how the power of nature sculpts geography, when we see it in action during the relatively short scope of a single lifetime, it takes on a tangible element. We see the dramatic impact of storms, floods, earthquakes, and volcanoes. But the less obvious natural processes that created the shore are harder to discern, particularly when people interfere out of their own sense of what is good for the shore.

Seventy-five years ago Tuckers Island was a resort. Now it's a sandbar. What will it be like in another hundred years? Will summer homes line the shores of a reemerged Tuckers Island? Human nature being what it is, people will surely want to build there again if the island continues to grow.

But who can say if it will keep getting bigger? Nature could always reverse its present island-building project.

But one thing is certain. Leaving the sand free to move has, at least in part of New Jersey, provided a rare glimpse at the shore-building processes that usually occur so slowly they almost seem nonexistent. And had we hindered the movement of the sand near Little Egg Inlet, we might never have seen such a fine example of nature slowly shaping our world. Tuckers Island might have been lost forever.

Offshore, 1995

Engineering the Waterways

When the first waves of European settlers came to the Northeast, they set about reshaping the land to suit their vision of what the New World should look like. Every elementary school student learns about how forests were slashed to make way for fields, how the prairies were transformed from seas of grass to the farmland that still remains the breadbasket of the nation, and how cities grew up throughout the country. Roads, railroads, airports, bridges, tunnels, suburban sprawl; it's all part of the development and shaping of America. These efforts that have gone on from the start represent the constant pressure to build, build, and build some more. The process is likely to keep on going. Human beings just can't leave things alone. It's as if we must change what's there to give ourselves a sense of identity and a feeling of control.

Along the waterways, the hands of human intervention have not been idle, either. In fact, the frenzy of canal building in the nineteenth century, the establishment of huge ports, dredging channels, shoring up waterfronts, these efforts have shaped the setting of our cruising grounds as surely as the forces of nature have shaped them. Some might say the development has permanently marred the beauty of our waterways, and they would be right in many cases. Others, however, might point to the many projects that have made our waterways safer and easier to navigate, and they would also be right.

Perhaps the most intriguing episode of people taking it upon themselves to challenge and tame nature to reshape the waterways lies in a little known chapter of the East River's history. As any boater who has gone through the notorious gut of Hell Gate knows, the East River today still requires a good deal of attention. It's a fast-flowing, turbulent, and very busy waterway that connects the west end of Long Island Sound to the upper portion of New York Harbor. It's no place to fool around.

I went through there once with a twenty-five knot southerly wind blowing against an opposing three to four knot tide. Such conditions create havoc with the water anywhere they crop up, and on the East River, with the buildings acting like funnels to increase and concentrate the wind gusts, the waterway can turn into an enormous cauldron of boiling eddies, standing waves three to five feet high, and cross currents that set the boat in precarious and sometimes frightening ways.

Imagine, then, what it would have been like to navigate a steamboat or sailing vessel through the East River when it was full of reefs and large rocks scattered about, often right in the middle of the channel. The East River was a killing ground, quite literally, and toward the end of the nineteenth century, everyone had had enough of the mayhem and set in motion one of the most fascinating projects in the history of New York Harbor.

BLOWING UP THE EAST RIVER

In some ways, history is an endless thread of events stretching back through time. In New York Harbor, that thread stretches back nearly half a millennium to the arrival of Giovanni da Verrazano in 1524 and Henry Hudson in 1609. The bitter end can be seen every day in the rusty tankers and freighters—massive ships carrying a good portion of the world's economy—that steam up and down Ambrose Channel in the invisible wakes of da Verrazano and Hudson.

Yet throughout the early years of New York's growth, the booms in commerce, war, mass immigration, the passage from sail to steam and finally to diesel, a strange paradox existed. Ranked since its discovery as one of the best natural havens on the East Coast, New York Harbor possessed two disturbing flaws: the East River's notorious reefs and currents, and the bar off Sandy Hook. For more than 300 years, these hazards sank ships and killed sailors, frequently transforming the harbor into a graveyard.

In 1851, engineers finally began a project to make New York Harbor safer for ships. It started, then fizzled, then started again, eventually dragging on until 1918 and costing more than $6.5 million—a huge amount of money in those days. (To put that figure in perspective, the entire Erie Canal cost just over $7 million in 1825, the year it opened for business.)

With its deep channels and disintegrated reefs, today's New York Harbor owes its relative safety to the efforts of the people behind those ancient shovels, steam drills, and dredges. It's an unglamorous chapter in the frequently romantic tale of the harbor. At the same time, it would be hard to imagine a change of more significant consequence to the thousands of boaters who have since cruised the inside route along the mid-Atlantic coast.

The passage through the turbulent tidal straits known as the East

River—aptly dubbed Hell Gate by the Dutch explorer Adrian Block—twists its way between Long Island and Manhattan. In the days of steam it wasn't unusual for dozens of groundings to occur every month in the East River. Given the fact that few city folk, or even sailors for that matter, knew how to swim, it isn't surprising that many such groundings ended tragically. Among the lethal underwater obstructions that claimed hundreds of victims were pyramid-shaped Pot Rock in mid-channel at Hell Gate, Hallets Point Reef off present-day Astoria and Flood Rock south of Ninety-second Street.

Despite the perils, the ships still came. The short route to and from Long Island Sound saved time and money. Just eight years after Robert Fulton tried out his steamboat on the Hudson River in 1807, an adventurous Yank from Nantucket, Elihu S. Bunker, powered his sidewheel steamboat through Hell Gate and took the shorter inside route from New York to New Haven, making his the first steamer to complete the passage.

One year later, in 1816, Bunker, who was an inveterate thrill-seeker, tried what he called a "novel and interesting experiment" that led to "moments of breathless anxiety." Not content to slip through Hell Gate at slack water, he piloted another steamer through against the full force of the tide. Twice the current stopped him. But on his third try, Bunker finally did steer the vessel through, setting another record as the first steamer to beat the rips at Hell Gate. Before removal of the reefs in the narrow channel, the current could run up to ten knots when water funneled through the tight, deep passages between the reefs.

Not everyone, though, thought Hell Gate a fun place to toy with steam. As boatyards launched increasingly large ships that often drew anywhere from twenty-one to twenty-three feet, the rocks of Hell Gate and Sandy Hook bar threatened to reduce New York's shipping traffic. At low water, the bar at Sandy Hook shoaled to twenty-four feet, requiring ships to enter and leave on a rising tide. And the multiple dangers of Hell Gate spoke for themselves.

The situation irritated New York's merchants to no end. When the Erie Canal opened in 1825, New York ranked as the nation's fifth largest port. Fifteen years later, as a result of the inland passage the canal created with the Great Lakes, New York was the nation's busiest seaport. The financial stakes soared, and all that money depended on the safe shipping of goods in and out of the harbor. By 1845, the navigational tribulations compelled New York's merchants to plea for help from Congress, but their cries went unheard on Capitol Hill.

An entry in a list of wrecks provides a glimpse at the human cost of the situation that so troubled the merchants. "In November, 1849, the sloop *Dispatch* of Cold Spring Harbor, Long Island, struck Pot Rock going through Hell Gate. . . . Captain John Mahan killed by blow from the tiller." The entry involves just one man, but it's indicative of the hazard the untamed East River represented through most of its history.

Frustrated but not defeated, a group of New Yorkers drummed up enough cash to privately fund an effort in 1851 to blast the top off troublesome Pot Rock, which was only eight feet below the water's surface. Everyone assumed brute force would work best: the bigger the bang the better the results. Seventeen tons of explosives later, Pot Rock was still undented. Eventually, those involved realized that the massive explosions did nothing more than obliterate schools of unlucky fish.

Work stopped, and the Civil War came and went. Then, as the nation lurched into Reconstruction, merchants and mariners again eyed the East River and New York Harbor as unfinished business. In 1866, John Newton, who later became a brigadier general and Army Corps chief of engineers, found himself engaged to reduce the hazards at Hell Gate to below twenty-five feet of the water's surface. To accomplish his objective, Newton came up with a practical idea that left Pot Rock and its brethren defenseless.

Previous attempts to blast Pot Rock involved placing charges on it and setting them off. Instead, Newton copied the miner's technique of drilling holes into the rock and detonating the charges inside. The trapped force of the explosion would break even the toughest structure. A special drilling scow was outfitted for the task and Pot Rock succumbed, eventually dropping to twenty-five feet below the water's surface.

Newton didn't quite know what to do about Hallets Point Reef and Flood Rock, which represented almost twelve acres of solid obstruction. If it were even possible, it would take a fleet of drilling scows years to do the job. Yet his bosses expected results, so Newton devised a demolition tactic untried on reefs and tested it on Hallets Point.

Newton and his advisers concluded the only way to get rid of the rocks would require digging tunnels into them to detonate tons of charges deep inside in a single, massive explosion. The idea seems similar to mice eating holes into a Swiss cheese, then loses all mouselike similarity with the terrific blast that follows the excavation.

The first step involved the construction of a 310–foot cofferdam to keep the East River out of the dig at Hallets Point. It wasn't easy to dam a reef, but the idea worked. The men then sank a thirty-three-foot shaft into the bedrock and tunneled into the reef. In 1876, five years after work started, Newton blasted Hallets Point Reef into rubble

Figure 3. The cofferdam at Hallets Point was designed to keep water out of the dig site during the re-engineering of the East River between Long Island and Manhattan. PHOTO COURTESY OF ROBERT M. VOGEL.

with twenty-five tons of high explosives. Ships now had twenty-six feet of water under their keels. Grapple boats didn't finish picking up the pieces until 1882.

Even bigger than Hallets Point Reef, Flood Rock served as Newton's grand finale. Again, swarms of workers built a cofferdam and dug four miles of tunnels into nine acres of solid rock to plant about 141 tons of dynamite. They hacked and blasted for nearly a decade. Finally, on a fall day in 1885, Newton waged the last battle of his nineteen-year war against a formidable natural barrier. The charges exploded under the East River, destroying the reef and sending a shock wave up the Hudson River that observers felt more than forty miles away at West Point.

The triumph over the East River's hazards didn't eliminate peril; it just reduced it to a tolerable degree of "breathless anxiety." And the passage through the shoals in lower New York Bay still remained a problem. Pilots have guided ships into upper New York Harbor since 1694, when the first regulations requiring ship captains to engage them took effect. A heavily laden ship could easily break its back if it hit the sand during a storm, and many did, both with and without the guidance of pilots.

Before the completion of Ambrose Channel, pilots sometimes used the old East Channel, which followed roughly the same course. But most followed the twenty-five-mile Main Ship Channel. The ability to dig and maintain Ambrose Channel, three miles shorter than the Main Ship Channel, existed long before Congress funded it or it bore the name of physician-engineer John Wolfe Ambrose, who lobbied lawmakers for eighteen years to appropriate the money. He died well before the first inbound liner used the channel in 1907, but his name lives on through time.

Until 1967, Ambrose Lightship stood as a beacon for ships off New York Harbor. That year, the lightship weighed anchor and steamed away from its station for the last time. Off Sandy Hook, Ambrose Tower stands in the ship's place, a practical and needed aid to navigation, and a reminder of Ambrose and the other characters in the harbor's history.

The harbor bustles now as it has in the past, and as it always will. The procession of ships never stops. In making a passage through the harbor and East River, boaters join the countless mariners to travel these waters throughout history. They become part of the nautical continuum, and the cruise becomes all the richer for the presence in mind of ghostlike companions from days gone by.

Offshore, 1995

With the East River subdued, though not entirely tamed, the merchants and owners of shipping companies turned their attention to the bothersome Sandy Hook sandbar. Although the wide waters of lower New York Harbor look deep to the novice, any experienced mariner knows that they're full of shoals dangerous to shipping, and, sometimes, to small craft as well. The East River project arguably was by far the most dramatic engineering feat in the harbor's history, at least from an aid to navigation standpoint. Nevertheless, the sandbar also has a story, not of wrecks and death, though these indeed did happen, but a tale driven forward by the ever increasing size of the ships built in the late 1800s and the need to carve out a path for them to the piers along lower Manhattan and Jersey City, Port Newark, Hoboken, and many others.

DEFEATING SANDY HOOK BAR

The Sandy Hook bar in lower New York Harbor ranks as one of the most notable natural features of the area. For almost 400 years skippers of seagoing vessels have carped about it.

Unlike major rivers such as the Mississippi, the Hudson River sits at sea level and lacks the power and surrounding lowlands to create an extensive delta. It can still get into mischief, though. The ebb tide pumps through the Narrows and quickly loses its oomph, depositing sediment suspended in the water to form the many shoals that dot the lower harbor. North-flowing currents along the New Jersey coast add to the clogging effect.

In the 1600s, the shallows didn't pose much of a danger or inconvenience. But over time as ships grew larger the bar went from a minor irritation to a downright pain. It threatened ships and crews in the event of groundings during unsettled weather, and the purses of wealthy merchants as well. It even indirectly influenced the outcome of the Revolutionary War.

In 1781, George Washington's troops had the British army bottled up in Yorktown on the fringe of southeastern Virginia. The British fleet sent to reinforce General Cornwallis took days to get out of New York's upper harbor over the bar because the huge ships-of-the-line could only exit near the top of the flood tide. As a consequence, they arrived too late to make a difference in the battle.

New York Harbor during the early to mid-1800s literally teemed with craft of all sizes and shapes. Barges from the Erie Canal, packet ships from Liverpool and other European ports, coastal schooners, paddlewheel steam ferries, lighters, all of these vessels played a part in making the port the busiest in the nation.

During this period, ships entering and leaving the lower harbor followed Gedney Channel and the Main Ship Channel with a maximum depth at mean low water of only twenty-four feet; these routes favored the western waters of the bay. There also was a little-used path through the shoals known as the East Channel, but it was only sixteen feet deep.

The first major effort to deepen the approaches to New York Harbor began in the early 1880s in response to the hue and cry from shipping companies with ships drawing twenty-five feet. At least two feet below the keel was required for safety. The Army Corps of Engineers faced a daunting task in their efforts to find a contractor capable of dredging Gedney Channel to a depth of twenty-eight feet for nearly a mile across the bar.

Because dipper and clamshell dredges used in protected waters were considered inadequate for the open sea, new technology was needed. As the expression goes, nothing new comes easy.

In 1885, the first contractor to win the bid on the dredging job proposed a new technique called hydraulic plowing. Essentially, the process entailed blasting the bottom of the channel with water jets which would stir up the sand with the hope that the ebb tide would move it away; it didn't work. So, the contractor tried sucking the sand up to the surface of the water with giant pumps, still hoping the ebb tide would move it out to sea. No luck.

The next contractor tried clamshell dredges, despite the fact that the Army Corps had already concluded these wouldn't work. The dredges looked like marine versions of modern earth movers, with two hinged jaws used to grab big piles of sand and plop them into scows. Turns out the Corps was right; another method had to be found.

The next attempt involved the use of a "hydraulic excavator" that would suck a mixture of seawater and sand in suspension through a pipe and deposit the solids into huge bunkers aboard a scow. The sand sucker seemed great in theory, but it didn't work very well, succeeding only in lifting about five percent solids through the system at one time—too slow to have a significant impact. However, some progress was better than none, and the work continued, albeit with delays due to breakdowns and bad weather.

By 1886, the short length of Gedney Channel had been dredged to a depth of twenty-six feet. That same year, Congress gave the green light to continue the work on the Gedney and the Main Ship channels to deepen both to thirty feet. Another contractor stepped in, and using a fleet of hydraulic excavators and other vessels completed the work in 1893.

The economic stakes in making the port accessible to the ever-larger ships were very high. Nearly 5,000 ships called in the port in 1890 and rang up a grand total in sales volume from imports and exports in excess of $877 million.

The late 1890s marked an intriguing period in maritime history. The age of sail had pretty much come to a close. The once-great clippers no longer roamed the sea. Swift-sailing packet ships making the transatlantic run from New York and Boston to Europe had been replaced with faster, more reliable ships with steam engines driving screw propellers instead of unwieldy paddlewheels.

The Industrial Revolution in the United States was well underway, and the common man found money left after paying for the basics. In all, it was a time of prosperity and luxury was the rule of the day.

The shipping industry, in response to the larger number of people capable of paying for pleasure cruises, as well as the rich rewards of winning contracts to carry mail and highly perishable cargoes to and from Europe, went into a building spree of megaliners that became the queens of the sea. Ships such as the *Oceanic*, *Adriatic*, *Mauretania*, *Lusitania*, and scores of others came on the scene shortly after the turn of the century. These liners drew thirty to thirty-five feet of water in most cases.

If New York was to remain a hub of maritime commerce, the channels had to be deepened even further. This point was certainly not lost on John Wolfe Ambrose, a prominent engineer active in improving the docks and channels of the upper harbor, as well as the construction of elevated railroads in New York City. Ambrose became the squeaky wheel, adding his voice to the many others demanding action from Congress.

In 1899, the same year Ambrose died at the age of 61, Congress passed legislation mandating the dredging of deeper approach channels to a depth of forty feet (later to forty-five feet), but they didn't say where to put them. It was up to the Army Corps to figure that out.

Blocking off Gedney and the Main Ship channels seemed unthinkable. The dredges would choke off traffic as effectively as the shoals, and the overall approach along the old route topped at about twenty-five miles, rather long for a ship in a hurry. The East Channel, however, if it could be deepened to forty feet, presented a much more direct shot straight into the upper harbor, so that's where the Corps decided to put its efforts.

Work started on the East Channel, later renamed after John Ambrose, in 1901. But as with the previous project, progress was slow. Only one contractor bid on the job, and he had problems, not the least of which was his death in 1905 or 1906. The Corps had its own dredges working, but they faced a long task in clearing a channel seven miles long to a depth of forty feet. Things looked grim, especially since a fleet of megaliners was almost completed and in some cases, already afloat, such as the *Oceanic*, which was launched in 1899.

The dredging went on at fever pitch throughout 1907, dropping the depth to thirty-eight feet. That September, the *Lusitania* showed up to become the first inbound liner to use Ambrose Channel; it drew thirty-two feet. A tight squeeze, but the ship made it across Sandy Hook bar.

The work continued on till 1913, and it seemed that all boded well for the future. Ambrose Channel was and still is one of the busiest stretches of water in the world.

Today, with the advent of container ships that draw forty feet or more, the same old problems have again surfaced to create a stir in the port of New York. Some ships can't even get into the upper harbor; others must leave at the top of the flood tide, just like those tardy ships-of-the-line back in 1781.

Last year, Congress passed the Water Resources Development Act, legislation aimed at resolving the dredging and other issues related to the port. Plans call for dredging more than five million cubic yards of material from channels throughout the port. The development plan is expected to cost roughly $130 million.

Problems solved? As the Sandy Hook bar has shown, it's not going away and neither are the giants of the sea that carry approximately $20 billion in commerce into the port every year. It comes down to the classic conflict you learned about in English as a kid: human spirit against nature, and you know who always wins in the end.

Offshore, 1997

Cape Cod hooks outward from the mainland like a giant finger to create the largest cape of the Northeast Coast. It's a beautiful place with rolling sand dunes, scrub pine, ponds, cranberry bogs, and little cottages with gabled roofs spread along its shores. As you stand on the beach and gaze at the beautiful Atlantic, it's easy to forget just how dangerous the waters off the cape can be. Outlying shoals, riptides, steep and confused seas, and fog have spelled doom for vessels since the first explorers sailed the length of the East Coast as far back as 1524.

Today mariners no longer must face the challenge and danger of Cape Cod because of a concerted effort to build a sea level canal across the isthmus. The canal itself presents boaters with a number of dangers, though. When the swift current of the canal opposes the prevailing southerly winds, the waterway can get as nasty or nastier than the East River. In fact, many world cruisers have commented that the stretch at the Buzzards Bay end can get as rough as any waterway on earth. Hyperbole? Maybe. Sailors are like fishermen; they tend to exaggerate. But from personal experience I can tell you, the Cape Cod Canal is no picnic.

Still, without it, the path from New Jersey and southern New England to down east Maine would be far more dangerous for the recreational boaters who regularly make the trip. The canal, for all of its faults, is a godsend. Few boaters who use it, however, know the full story behind it. It's a tale worth knowing, and it will add to the casual appreciation of the waterway.

MISSION (NEARLY) IMPOSSIBLE

The year 1914 is as important as any in the history of canals. In that year, on the eve of the First World War, a long-dreamed-of passageway finally connected the Atlantic and Pacific oceans, and eliminated the need for shipping traffic to make the perilous voyage around Cape Horn. The Panama Canal got most of the press that year, but there was also good news for mariners who traveled New England's waters.

That same year, another important canal—though not one with locks—opened for business on the Massachusetts coast. It was a sea-level channel thirteen miles long through the isthmus of Cape Cod. At the time, the Cape Cod Canal was only fifteen feet deep and had a bottom width of just 100 feet—not very impressive dimensions compared with its Central American counterpart. Nevertheless, the history of the Cape Cod Canal tells an important story about human nature, Yankee ingenuity, and America's past.

The canal's story begins with a petty controversy that merits at least a brief look. Certain sources credit no less a figure than Myles Standish (way back in 1623) as the first person to dream up the idea for the canal. That the colonists eventually established trading posts on the Kennebec River, in Hartford, and on the current site of the canal stands as a matter of record. However, the Pilgrims had a tough time after arriving in Plymouth in 1620; only fifty of the 102 immigrants survived the first winter. If Standish considered a canal in 1623, he must not have spent much time pining over it.

Life in Massachusetts Bay Colony didn't improve much until 1625, when in June of that year William Bradford, one of the first governors of the colony, wrote a friend in England to say the colonists "never felt the sweetness of the country till this year." With things on a more even keel and with the new Dutch trading post established in 1626 in New Amsterdam, it seems likely that matters of trade led to the first real considerations for the canal. No doubt as the colony grew, the idea for a canal must have appeared sensible to anyone with an ounce of brains.

Meanwhile, small boats made their way up two rivers, the Monument and the Scusset, that cut into the isthmus at its narrowest point, and a brisk trading business thrived. Goods shuttled back and forth between Buzzards Bay and Cape Cod Bay over the land—up to thirty feet above sea level—separating the watersheds. At the time a lock canal was thought feasible to create a safer, faster inside route for coastal trade. The first step forward, or rather, nonstep, occurred in 1697 when the General Court of Massachusetts appointed people to view the prospective canal site.

Nothing much happened.

But in 1776 the military importance of a safer inside passage along the coast prompted George Washington to send an engineer from the Continental Army to see if building a canal across the cape would be feasible. The fellow reported to Washington that the army could build the canal if the British let them (which was unlikely) and if resources were available (they weren't).

More than a century later, just as Washington had envisioned, the canal served as a safe channel in time of war. Ships used the cut to keep away from German submarines offshore during both World Wars. In 1944, 18.5 million tons of cargo were shipped through the

Figure 4. Aerial view of the Cape Cod Canal, showing the bridges that span it.
COURTESY OF U.S. ARMY CORPS OF ENGINEERS, NEW ENGLAND DISTRICT.

canal, setting a record that stood for more than forty years. That the canal played an important role during World War II is indisputable.

The canal remains an important commercial waterway. In 1986, 20 million tons of cargo passed through it. In 1994, approximately 6,000 commercial vessels carrying 13.5 million tons of cargo, and 11,000 recreational craft made the transit through the canal. Clearly, it's still a busy place.

All of which begs the question: if it was deemed so important a waterway at such an early date in American maritime history, why wasn't it built when scores of other seemingly more difficult canals were finished in the first half of the nineteenth century? Two notable examples are the Erie Canal in 1825 and the Chesapeake and Delaware Canal in 1829, both of which had state support. Most other canal projects were privately funded and failed for a number of reasons. Usually economics was the main cause; the tolls that could be collected amounted to less than the sum invested to build and maintain the waterways.

Yet despite the financial and engineering difficulties of building canals, the rough, muddy roads encouraged waterborne shipment of goods. By the early 1800s, the nation began a grand push to create an inland passage from Cape Ann to Florida, and into the heartland. Piece by piece the links came together, except for the Cape Cod Canal. Today, the Army Corps of Engineers, which manages the canal, calls it "The Gateway to the Intracoastal Waterway." It remained just about the last link (the Cape May Canal wasn't completed until 1942) and yet arguably one of the most important parts of the ICW, so why the delays?

In one word: money. However vital it may have been, unlike New York and Maryland and Delaware, which supported canal building, Massachusetts did little more than grant charters to private companies interested in the Cape Cod Canal project. Every one of those firms failed to get the job done for a variety of economic and technological reasons. Ground was broken several times, but the hapless entrepreneurs inevitably came up short. The state legislature presumably believed that if people wanted a canal badly enough, sooner or later they'd build one without government funds, and sooner or later one of the companies would succeed. Or perhaps the prevailing view held that if ships had sailed around the cape since the 1500s they could continue doing so. Shortsighted? Or merely the usual state of affairs for the day?

Meanwhile, shipwrecks piled up on the shoals off Cape Cod at a rate of one every two weeks in the 1880s. But few besides the merchants and mariners seemed to care.

Imagine then, the kind of character who would step up to the crap table and throw the dice on a project no one had been able to get off the ground for more than 250 years. Enter August Belmont, an entrepreneur with an ego almost as large as his bank account and a reputation for finishing big jobs, such as building the first part of the New York subway system in 1904. Based on studies indicating tolls would generate significant profits, Belmont bought and reorganized the Boston, Cape Cod and New York Canal Company—which held the charter on the canal project—and began to make the canal a reality.

Belmont's advisers, like earlier and later engineers, toyed with the idea of a lock canal to eliminate the swift currents that resulted from a five-foot difference in the tidal range between Cape Cod and Buzzards bays. But ice would clog the locks and close the waterway in winter—an unacceptable consequence—and so a design for a sea level channel was chosen. The swift current would keep it ice free. The plan called for a waterway with a bottom width of 100 feet, a surface width of 200 feet and a depth of twenty-five feet at mean low water. It would cost nearly $13 million to complete.

In the spring of 1909, schooners loaded with granite from quarries in Maine set sail for Cape Cod Bay. Meanwhile, at the construction site, crews began building a 3,000–foot breakwater. On the other side of the isthmus, two dredges in Buzzards Bay started digging an approach channel and immediately discovered enormous boulders left behind from the last Ice Age. Divers planted charges and blew them up—a very slow process. Similar blasting occurred on land.

By 1910, twenty-six vessels were on station in Buzzards Bay, including ten dredges. Crews completed work on the Buzzards Bay Railroad Bridge in September of that year, and the Bourne and Sagamore drawbridges respectively in 1911 and 1912. As two huge dipper dredges Belmont had built for the canal project pushed toward each other from each bay, steam shovels and dynamite cleared the way on land. Temporary railroad tracks were built along the route to enable locomotives to haul away train loads of debris. Earthen dams kept the waters at each end contained until work was finally completed in 1914. The canal opened with a controlling depth of only fifteen feet, but was dredged to twenty-five feet by 1916.

It remains an ironic twist of fate that an idea that made perfect sense for more than two centuries should prove an initial failure once it came to fruition. Despite the presence of the shorter route, not enough ships used the canal to make it pay. Traffic increased as Belmont deepened it during those first two years of operation. By 1916, more than 4,500 vessels transited the canal carrying 3.5 million tons of cargo. Still, the figures didn't bode well for the future, and just one year after it opened Belmont made his first offer to sell the canal to the United States government.

Ships stayed away for good reason. The narrow waterway allowed for one-way traffic only. Moreover, the 140–foot slot between bridge spans proved too small, and ships, caught in the swift current, regularly crashed into them. Finally, the entrance channel in Buzzards Bay twisted through Phinney's Harbor behind Mashnee and Hog islands (now connected by dikes) and posed a challenge to the best of pilots. (A finger of deep water marks the old Belmont canal channel on the chart close ashore to Wings Neck.)

During World War I, the federal government took over operation of the canal after a U-boat attack off the cape pointed toward the waterway's strategic importance. However, when the war ended and the government wanted Belmont to take the canal back, he refused and instead ordered it closed. Eventually, at the request of the governor of Massachusetts and in recognition of the canal's importance to trade, Belmont relented. By the time he died in 1924, Belmont had lost about $5 million on the waterway. The government eventually agreed to pay $11.5 million for the canal and, in 1928, assigned responsibility for it to the Army Corps of Engineers.

Charged with making the waterway of use to mariners instead of a hazard to transportation, the Corps identified the main problems and set about correcting them. The great public works projects resulting from the Great Depression in the 1930s presented a perfect opportunity for the Corps to get funds to proceed with the work. The passage of the National Industrial Recovery Act in 1933 led to an appropriation of $4.6 million to replace the two bridges and make other necessary improvements on the canal.

Swarms of workers, thankful to have jobs, replaced the notorious drawbridges with two fixed high-level spans with 135 feet of vertical clearance, and a lift railroad bridge of the same height. They finished the bridges in 1935 and got to work on the canal with an additional influx of cash from the Rivers and Harbors Act.

Approximately 40 million cubic yards of material were removed as workers widened and deepened the channel and lengthened it to 17.4 miles, which includes the present approach starting at Cleveland Ledge Light in Buzzards Bay. Dikes helped reduce maintenance dredging, and secure mooring basins were built. When improvements were completed in 1940, the waterway took its place as the world's widest sea level canal, sporting a surface width of 700 feet and a minimum bottom width of 480 feet. The controlling depth was extended to thirty-two feet.

Shipping increased over the decades and the canal became a very busy place. In the 1970s, the corps installed a ship traffic control sys-

Figure 5. Aerial view of the thirteen-mile-long channel through the isthmus of Cape Cod. Buzzards Bay is toward the south at the bottom and Cape Cod Bay is toward the north. COURTESY OF U.S. ARMY CORPS OF ENGINEERS, NEW ENGLAND DISTRICT.

tem that enabled them to monitor vessels in the canal with radar and closed circuit television cameras. With additional upgrades in the 1980s, the data now goes into a computer which generates maps of the landmasses, aids to navigation, and channel limits, and provides a continuous update on vessel positions, speeds, and headings.

After more than three centuries have passed and tens of millions of dollars have been spent, the dream of so many to see an easily navigable canal across Cape Cod has come true. It took vision and courage for Belmont, plus a healthy yen for profit, to provide the impetus behind the construction of the Cape Cod Canal. Think for a moment if Belmont hadn't come along when he did. Would any canal have existed for the government to later improve?

It also took the fat checkbook of the United States government, opened in part by circumstance, to finance the final project and make it successful. If it had not been for the Depression and the public works projects it prompted, would pleasure and commercial craft have the benefit of the present canal?

Today, as recreational boaters, it's easy to take the convenience of the Cape Cod Canal for granted. Doing without it seems unthinkable. Yet it quite possibly might never have been built or improved, and the long and treacherous passage around Cape Cod would be a fact of life for any mariner venturing up and down the coast—a mini-Cape Horn ready to sink the unwary.

Offshore, 1995

> Navigating an inlet in poor conditions can pose a big danger to small craft. The waves meeting an outgoing tide stack up in steep, short patterns, often breaking across the opening that leads to safety. Shoals frequently form seaward of the entrance, adding to the danger. A boat caught on the face of a breaking crest can broach, which means it turns sideways to the wave, setting it up for a capsize. An inlet can scare even the most experienced skipper, and some are worse than others.
>
> New Jersey and the South Shore of Long Island comprise inlet land in the Northeast. South of New Jersey, however, extending all the way to Florida, the running of inlets is common. New Jersey enjoys the dubious reputation for playing host to one of the worst inlets on the entire East Coast: Barnegat Inlet. The efforts to stabilize it and make it safer have gone on for decades. Most recently, the Army Corps of Engineers executed a project in the early 1990s which seems to have worked. But how well? What do the local boaters think of Barnegat Inlet now that the work has ended?

BIG, BAD BARNEGAT INLET TAMED?

Larry Polizzotto, a New Jersey boater for more than thirty years, got a bit more adventure than he cared for on a recent trip out of Barnegat Inlet. He was aboard a twenty-three-foot center console Wellcraft. But in the inlet's eight-to-ten-foot breakers he'd probably have been more comfortable aboard a battleship—if it drew less than the ten-foot dredged depth of the channel.

"It was scary, to say the least," said Polizzotto, a boat salesman at Ocean Beach Marina. "All I could see were walls of water. We had to surf through. Timing on each wave had to be perfect to avoid a broach."

Located about fifty miles south of Sandy Hook, Barnegat Inlet was known as one of the worst on the East Coast. With a stiff easterly wind against an ebb tide, the place can scare the pants off the most experienced boaters, and it can be big trouble for unwary neophytes.

"We've seen seventeen-to-eighteen-foot breaking seas at the entrance in bad conditions, but it's nothing to get eight-to-ten-foot breakers," said Coast Guard Lieutenant Mark Wilbert, commanding officer of Station Barnegat Light. "No question about it. Barnegat Inlet can be a very scary place."

It used to be even scarier.

Ken Nutt, master of the fifty-five-foot *Captain Bill*, operates his party fishing business out of Barnegat Harbor. Since the early 1970s, he's used the inlet almost every day from April to December. Before an Army Corps of Engineers project was completed in 1992, Nutt said it was much worse.

"I recall several drownings due to capsizes every year before the improvements were made," he said. "Believe me, the inlet used to be far more dangerous than it is now."

But is it really safer for small craft?

"Even after all that money was spent to improve the inlet, I still would say that an inexperienced boater should not use it about half the time. It still has some treacherous conditions a novice wouldn't be able to handle," Polizzotto said.

He added that when he sells boats to first-time buyers, he tells them not to be afraid of Manasquan Inlet, up the coast, after they get a little experience under their belts. But he warns them to watch out for Barnegat Inlet.

According to the Coast Guard's Wilbert, no fatalities have occurred in the inlet or in its immediate vicinity over the last few years. Collisions, however, occur often, he said.

This may be a problem caused more by traffic than by the inlet's treachery. Wilbert said that on a typical summer weekend, thousands of recreational boats use the inlet. Narrow Oyster Creek Channel leading to the inlet from behind the barrier islands is always full of heavy boat traffic at peak times, when the bulk of accidents occur.

"We have a tremendous amount of congestion in the channel. This year, we had a particularly large number of capsizings and collisions due to wakes, swells, and current," Wilbert said.

He hastened to point out that most boats get through with no problem. "I don't want to come off as an alarmist about the inlet," he said. "But people really need to respect it."

The Army Corps of Engineers has been trying to make Barnegat Inlet safer since the early 1940s, when the original federal inlet project was completed.

This involved the construction of two jetties which converged near the entrance to form an arrowhead-shaped configuration.

The design didn't work well. The channel through the inlet tended to shoal and move about considerably due to wave action and tidal currents. Nutt recalled that, upon leaving the inlet, he followed a treacherous channel south before turning east. That isn't the case today.

In the mid-1980s, recognizing that the inlet had some serious problems, the Corps set about trying to solve them. Gary Rohn, the Philadelphia

Figure 6. Aerial view of Barnegat Inlet. Narrow Oyster Creek Channel leads boats into and out of the inlet. The Barnegat Inlet lighthouse sits along the channel, visible near the top. PHOTO BY KEITH HAMILTON, STUDIO-9, WARETOWN, NEW JERSEY.

districts chief of civil works project management, was the engineer and project manager for the new work done.

Rohn said the arrowhead-shaped jetty configuration failed to create an adequate tidal flow through the inlet to flush out the channel. The new project, involving a nearly mile-long south jetty parallel to the north jetty, was supposed to solve the problem.

Work on the jetty was completed in 1991 at a cost of $39 million. About 495,000 tons of stone were used. Dredging of the new channel was finished in 1992 at a cost of $2.1 million, removing 175,000 cubic yards of sand from the inlet.

"We believe the new channel is a lot more stable than it had been from a shoaling and location point of view," Rohn said. "It moves less than it did."

While many of New Jersey's inlets have come and gone, Barnegat has been around for a long time, though not always in the same spot. In 1524, Giovanni da Verrazano, discoverer of New York Harbor, sighted Barnegat Inlet. His account describes the beauty of the Jersey shore in glowing terms. He didn't take a longboat through the inlet, or he would have had a darker view of the place.

Was more than $40 million worth of jetty and dredging worth it?

Recreational boaters may still have a tough time of it under certain conditions, but that's the case with any inlet on the ocean.

Nutt and other captains are sure the inlet is safer, though not fully tamed. "It was a definite improvement and has saved a lot of lives," Nutt said. "Me and all the other captains, we used to get a sickly feeling in our stomachs knowing we had to go through there. Now we don't."

Offshore, 1996

Mile zero of the Intracoastal Waterway starts at the northern end of Barnegat Bay. Known among local boaters as the "ditch," the New Jersey section of the waterway, which stretches south to Florida and the Gulf of Mexico, has for years been the subject of much derision because of its shallow depths and many low fixed bridges that prevent large sailboats from using it. Still, the state owes much to the presence of the waterway since it does bring hundreds of shoal draft sailboats and powerboats to the coast during the annual spring and fall migration of cruisers headed to and from northeastern ports.

Without the Point Pleasant Canal, however, the northern end of the Intracoastal Waterway wouldn't exist, and the upper reaches of Barnegat Bay would be much different. The area once supported cranberry bogs, freshwater fin and shell fish. It was a sleepy place far off the beaten track. Its contrast with the present couldn't be more stark.

Since the mid-1800s, there were many who wanted to see a sea level canal dug from the Manasquan River to the head of Barnegat Bay. Others thought little of the idea, wishing to preserve their own little piece of paradise. But the push for development and more convenient access to the sea among local fishermen finally won out. The canal became a reality, but it had a rocky start and caused some rather interesting things to happen to Manasquan Inlet.

THE POINT PLEASANT CANAL'S DIFFICULT START

On busy summer weekends, thousands of boaters pass through the Point Pleasant Canal outbound or inbound from the sea via Manasquan Inlet. This enormously convenient two-mile landcut puts the ocean within easy reach for tens of thousands of boaters in upper Barnegat Bay. At peak times you'll see an unbroken procession of vessels in the narrow channel.

If you're in a boat during those busy times on the canal, you'll find it resembles a waterborne version of the Garden State Parkway at rush hour. Wakes wash around plenty in there, and the tidal currents are swift.

But that's all local knowledge, a "been there, done that" for boaters who use the canal all the time. It's got its pitfalls, but we'd sure miss it if it disappeared. It's become part of the landscape, part of the scenery . . . almost. The Point Pleasant Canal isn't a picture postcard.

Much used, taken for granted, that's the Point Pleasant Canal, gateway to the Intracoastal Waterway. (The Cape Cod Canal also claims this name, but in technical terms, it's most appropriate for the Point Pleasant Canal.) But if the canal seems lackluster and utilitarian, taking a look back at its history puts a new shine on the waterway; it lets you see the common in the light of the past.

Back in the early 1800s, there was an opening in the sand off Toms River known as Cranberry Inlet. It was a key entry for boatmen in the bay, evidently less treacherous than Barnegat Inlet. Then, as inlets often do, Cranberry packed it in and closed for business.

That gave impetus to a movement to breach the small neck of sand between Bay Head and the Manasquan River. A canal would create a northern passage to the sea for the bay, a fine alternative to Cranberry Inlet.

The original plans for the canal drafted in 1833 called for a completely different route than the one eventually chosen. Engineers proposed improving a channel to Cook's Creek near the mouth of the Manasquan River south to Cook's Pond, Silver Lake, Maxon's Pond, Twilight Lake, and finally to Scow Ditch in Bay Head. Tidal gates were also proposed.

However, the plans in the 1830s came to nothing, and so did those that came up in 1903, which proposed using the same route. In 1908, New Jersey began to actively construct its portion of the ICW, and that at least set the stage for digging the canal. The present route was chosen for several reasons, including the need for fewer bridges, and development along the original route made building the canal there unfeasible.

Finally, after delays mostly due to an almost perpetual lack of state money for the project, work began in 1916. Then World War I came along and put a quick end to it. Things got going again in 1920.

Dredges began digging the ditch on the Bay Head side and slowly worked their way northward toward the Manasquan River. During those early years of the 1920s, boaters from the bay side used the canal as a docking area. The townspeople swam and fished there.

On December 15, 1925, in the mid-afternoon, the last dredge-load of land was removed from the ditch and the waters mingled. The opening was greeted with celebrations, but not everyone made merry.

Despite what all the engineers said to the contrary, it was a common belief around the waterfront that the canal might do some strange things to the local terrain, and it did. By the spring of 1926, Manasquan Inlet was closed.

The opening of the canal had siphoned waters out of Manasquan River into the upper bay, greatly reducing the flow out the inlet. In only a few months one of the best inlets on the Jersey coast was lost. The canal became a road to nowhere; its building had negated its purpose.

In 1929, passage of the Manasquan Inlet Bill in the state legislature made funds available to reopen the inlet. Two years later, the inlet was back in business. With the construction of a proper inlet with jetties to stabilize it, the tidal flow improved dramatically in the Manasquan River. In fact, almost too much.

The original canal was built on a right-of-way 200 feet wide. The channel was 100 feet from shore to shore, with a depth of eight feet at low water; it had no bulkheads. Instead of an almost one-way drain for the Manasquan River, the canal became a two-way tide race at maximum ebb and flood.

The swift currents gradually ate away the supports on the old Route 4 Bridge, which was eventually replaced with the Route 88 Bridge. Engineers tried reinforcing the pilings, then replacing them. Nothing worked very well, however, and they eventually dumped tons of rocks around the base of the bridge, hoping to trap sediments.

In theory, the rock dumping was a great idea. It meant the bridge would last and the state would have no need to build another one. For boaters, execution of the idea had some very unpleasant consequences.

The huge rocks created white water around the base of the bridge. At times when the flood opposed a snapping southwester, conditions were often too much for small craft to handle. Collisions and other accidents began to occur with alarming frequency at or near the bridge.

The problems got worse as more and more boat traffic came through over the decades. Boaters had to wait until the early 1970s for the present Loveland Town lift bridge to go up north of its swing bridge predecessor, and the mid-1980s for the present Route 88 lift bridge to replace its notorious predecessor.

Though the canal got off to a slow start, and a rocky first couple of years, it's had a positive impact on the towns, the local boating businesses, and most of all on the recreational boaters who can enjoy the best of both worlds. Time on the bay or the broad Atlantic, it's all just minutes apart because of a two-mile landcut.

Offshore, 1996

The Intracoastal Waterway was in the making, or at least in the thinking, as far back as when the early settlements sprang up in Virginia.
But the real work didn't begin in earnest until the twentieth century.
The last link of the inland passage wasn't completed until 1942—a
seemingly long overdue date, but one like so many others that depended not so much on an idea but on the necessity of getting the
job done to meet a specific objective.

The last link, the Cape May Canal, became reality because of
the violence of warfare. It was only the forces of an outside foe that
made funding available for the project, and, when it finally did begin, it was shrouded in secrecy.

DIGGING UP THE CAPE MAY CANAL

Every spring, marinas along the Eastern seaboard see an influx of pleasure boats on their way up the Intracoastal Waterway bound for cruising grounds in New England or the Great Lakes. Their passage north
often takes them through waterways of historic note. The Cape May
Canal at the southern tip of New Jersey marks one of the most intriguing, which may come as a surprise to any boaters who have passed
through it.

The canal isn't beautiful, nor is it amazing from an engineering perspective. It didn't take nearly 300 years to get it built, as was the case
with the Cape Cod Canal. Its construction didn't plug up a major inlet, like the Point Pleasant Canal accomplished in 1926, just a few
months after the completion of the waterway connecting northern
Barnegat Bay with the Manasquan River. (The inlet was reopened after jetties were built to enhance tidal flow.)

At first glance, it's a pretty boring canal. Basically, it's a three-mile
ditch connecting Cape May Harbor to Delaware Bay, a convenience
for cruisers who would otherwise have to navigate around the nub of
Cape May Point. It would hardly seem worth mentioning, apart from
the fact that it was the final link in the Intracoastal Waterway. But a
little digging revealed a story worth telling, especially in the context
of the wider picture of American history.

During World War II, the inside passages along the East Coast
became extremely important. German U-boats sank dozens of ships
offshore and even prowled into Portsmouth Harbor to map and photo-
graph the U.S. Navy's installation there for a raid that never materi-
alized.

Cruising offshore meant the possibility of career-ending confron-
tations with enemy submarines, and so ship masters took the inside
routes whenever they could. A record number of cargo vessels passed

through the Cape Cod Canal in the war years, lumbered down Buzzards Bay, Long Island Sound, then out to sea along the New Jersey coast on their way to Chesapeake Bay via the C&D Canal. The only problem? Off New Jersey the ships were sitting ducks, particularly off Cape May far out in Delaware Bay to avoid the shoals.

Sue Leaming, eighty-two, a lifelong resident of Cape May City, vividly remembers the days early in the war. "Sub watch towers were built, so were gun batteries to protect the ports," she said. "You couldn't take pictures of your kids on the beach because the military thought you might be a German spy, and every window facing the ocean had to be blacked out."

Leaming's father-in-law, Spicer Leaming, owned a bit of land near Spicer's Creek called the blueberry patch, where he grew vegetables. The surrounding terrain was low, much of it marshy. But people farmed there just the same.

In 1941, officials from the Army Corps began roaming around Spicer's blueberry patch. They said they needed the land for a special project important to winning the war, and Spicer, along with other residents, sold parts of their property to the United States.

It took a war and loss of life to make funding available for the canal. But, like many other canals throughout the Northeast, many people had thought of the idea long before the actual structure became a reality. The Army Corps had been actively tinkering with plans for the waterway as far back as 1935. Preliminary surveys were taken the following year, but nothing happened after that until it became obvious that the canal was needed to save lives and cargo.

Work funded almost entirely by the United States Navy quietly began on the Cape May Canal in 1942. It was undertaken as an "emergency wartime measure . . . in response to the mounting tide of submarine attacks on allied freighters and tankers along the New Jersey coast, which threatened to strangle the flow of oil to the industrial Northeast," according to official Army Corps records.

A strict news blackout ensured that no reports in the papers would reach the Germans, who, it was feared, might send commandos ashore to disrupt the construction. After the war ended, it became known that German submariners had on occasion landed on U.S. soil, so the fears hadn't bordered on outright paranoia.

"I wasn't conscious of the papers writing about the canal," Leaming said. "It was one of those things that sort of just appeared all of a sudden."

Local residents often stopped to watch the dredge at work. It looked strange to see it in the middle of farmland, as if it didn't belong. Work finished within the same year it started and the canal opened in 1942, playing a vital role in keeping ships safe from unfriendly submarines. Part of the project involved digging a canal through Spicer's Creek; Spicer's blueberry patch, of course, became part of local history.

Leaming had a friend, now deceased, who worked on the canal. When the last dredge full of sand was removed to open the waterway to Delaware Bay, the water rushed in with unexpected speed. "The barge they were on started to rock and pitch. The men aboard it had to hold on real tight," she said, adding that the force of the water "really surprised everyone because they thought it would just sort of run in slowly."

The original channel in 1942 was only 100 feet wide and twelve feet deep. Over the years, tides and wake action eroded the banks to a width of 300 feet. In 1982, the Army Corps began a project to shore up the banks, placing riprap in spots and constructing a gabion revetment, essentially a row of rock-filled wire baskets that eventually fill in to create a sturdy barrier.

The Army Corps estimates the cost of the fifteen-year project, which is expected to be completed this July, at roughly $5.5 million. Records of what the Navy spent to build the original canal remain somewhere in their cavernous archives.

"A lot of boats come through on the canal," Leaming said. "But it really didn't have much of an effect on people around here."

Offshore, 1997

THE DITCH

Last year, part of the Intracoastal Waterway officially disappeared, though only temporarily. Sound crazy? Not if you're from New Jersey.

In the vicinity of Somers Point along a channel known as Broad Thorofare, which leads from Great Egg Harbor if you're headed north up the ICW, markers 239 to 246 have gone. The channel there had become so shallow the Coast Guard didn't want unwary boaters steaming along, eyes fixed on the markers, only to run aground. They removed the aids to navigation, which in this case were hardly helpful at all since there was little water to float much more than a rowboat.

The missing link in the Jersey ICW, often called the "ditch," means boats must cross the wide mouth of Great Egg Harbor Inlet. This is okay in settled weather, but there is no protection from the surge brought in on the heels of a stiff nor'easter or easterly. With wind opposing tide, the alternate route could pose a danger to small boats. To head north and rejoin the ICW past Longport, a twenty-five-foot fixed bridge at Margate blocks the way for tall vessels, like sailboats.

At Stone Harbor, between ICW markers 417 and 419, the depth of the channel is approximately 1.9 feet at mean low water. Running that in anything but a small runabout will cause great merriment at the prop shop.

Just south of Barnegat Inlet, buoys 44 to 45 and 72 to 74 mark a channel with 3.7 feet at mean low water. Compared to the other two examples this is a veritable trench, a deep-water canyon.

What's going on? Isn't somebody supposed to keep these channels clear? Of course.

The Philadelphia District of the Army Corps of Engineers is responsible for dredging Jersey's ICW and they're very well aware that there are some pretty shoal spots along the route behind the barrier islands. However, they can't dredge until the state of New Jersey identifies suitable disposal areas for the sediment, and that hasn't happened yet with Broad Thorofare and Great Channel, though according to Jerry Jones, operations project manager at the Army Corps' Philadelphia District, dredging is expected to occur by October.

"We wanted to dredge there last year and this year, but no disposal areas have been identified by the state of New Jersey. The state is aware of the problems, but funding limits have restricted their ability to address them. We're hopeful that this dredging season we'll be able to take care of both those areas, since the voters of New Jersey approved a bond issue last November which will make funding available for projects like these," Jones said.

It all comes down to money and politics, and that's often way beyond the control of the Army Corps, particularly at the district level. The much-expected dredging of Tuckerton Creek to make the Seaport Museum which is under construction there accessible to excursion boats from Atlantic City as well as cruising recreational vessels won't be happening soon—because of money and politics.

According to a report in *Press Plus, The Press of Atlantic City Online*, Rep. H. James Saxton R-3rd, recently received in a letter from Franklin Raines, President Clinton's director of the Office of Management and Budget, stating that "the Tuckerton project was impressive but funding was not anticipated to be available to fund all of the worthy projects."

That's political-speak for no dice to Tuckerton, at least not for now, despite the fact that access to the Seaport by water is a vital element determining its success and that more than $2 million has been raised to begin constructing the museum. The Army Corps has submitted a proposal through channels to headquarters in Washington for the project in FY99. But since decisions at the Corps level on which projects actually get done are based on the commercial importance of a given waterway, and since Tuckerton is by no means commercially important when compared to other waterways, odds are slim that the dredging project will go through unless Congress authorizes an addition to the Corps budget for it.

If funding for the Tuckerton Creek project is approved, the Army Corps plans to dredge a channel six feet deep from the Marshelder Channel that connects to the ICW to the mouth of Tuckerton Creek. The depth would hold at six feet into Tuckerton Creek and would achieve depths of around three feet at downtown Tuckerton near the dam. The total project is 3.75 miles in length and will cost approximately $800,000.

At Manasquan Inlet, the political power to land the bucks to dig proved successful, but only due to a congressional addition to the Corps budget. The Army Corps routinely dredges at Barnegat Inlet, one of the most shoal-prone inlets on the East Coast, and at Cape May, one of the most important ports on the East Coast in terms of pounds of fish landed. In other words, Cape May is commercially important, and without regular dredging Barnegat Inlet might close, wasting the $45 million spent to reconstruct the south jetty and to do other work there as well.

Manasquan, despite the presence of a small commercial fishing fleet, kept getting passed over in the budget food chain. It's primarily a recreational-use inlet, so the bucks didn't flow to keep the channel between the jetties clear until New Jersey legislators got extra funding for the project. The inlet hadn't been dredged since 1978. Last year the Army Corps removed approximately 35,000 cubic yards of sediment.

Because the channels tend to shift position from year to year along New Jersey's ICW, it creates confusion among boaters. Where you found good water last season may not be in the same spot this year. Jones said the Army Corps is studying how to best mark and maintain the channels, with input from the Coast Guard.

The fight for dollars to dredge isn't confined to New Jersey, not by any means. Shallow, seemingly unimportant waterways such as the Royal River leading to Yarmouth in Maine, have faced similar delays. It seems even on the water, politics is inescapable.

Offshore, 1997

Old Tales of Inland Passage

In most every place you can find the past mingling just under the surface, only slightly hidden from the eye in the rush of the present. Life, however much it seems to change, nevertheless remains fairly constant in the more important realms. People feel the warmth of the sun, the bite of the wind, the hunger from a day's work the same way they have always felt these things, and it's that sameness, the link all human beings share with one another over time that makes us whole, part of the long line of lives that have in some way indirectly touched our own.

Life along the shore and aboard the boats and ships that make up the spiritual and physical elements that go into the seascape is no different. It evolved into its present form through the efforts and trials and victories that others experienced long before us. A glimpse into times past, the people and places that together create a sense of the coast, has always fascinated me. The stories are there to find, like a prized seashell in a wide expanse of barren sand, and I have over the years looked for them—with some success.

The stories you will find here cover a wide range of topics. The Cold War and its paranoia, which seems a little crazy today, touched the lives of anyone old enough to recall how uncertain life was during those decades. The days of shipwrecks, those who caused them and those who tried to prevent them. The men and women who worked to carve out a living in the best ways they could whether it was building boats, running rum, or tending a neighborhood bar. Each has a story worth telling, and collectively, the tales will transport you through time and enhance your appreciation of what went on along the coast long before fleets of fiberglass sport fishing boats and sleek motorsailers dotted the horizon on busy summer weekends.

The first story takes you deep into the Cold War. New Jersey, the site of at least fifteen Nike missile bases built to defend New York City and Philadelphia, was also the site of what was once thought of as a vital link in the early warning system for continental defense. Offshore the military built a tower, fixed radar atop its heights, and waited for the worst. The men who served on this tower would have shaken their heads in disbelief had they known that thirty years later their symbol of American know-how would rest at the bottom of the sea, haunted by local divers down for a look at the past, and by the ghosts of a small unit of men who died one stormy night.

THE TEXAS TOWER TRAGEDY

Eighty miles southeast of New York City and sixty-five miles east of Barnegat, New Jersey, the gray swells of the Atlantic once broke against a tower. It rose up from the sea on three hollow steel legs, and on its two-deck structure seventy members of a special United States Air Force unit hovered around radar screens in search of Soviet bombers and missiles that never came. Airmen on two towers northeast of the harbor also kept watch.

Built in the late 1950s and known as Texas Towers for their resemblance to oil rigs, these early warning centers seemed a good idea at the time. World War II and Korea still burned fresh in the minds of the citizenry, and the threat of nuclear war was frighteningly real.

So school children learned how to duck and cover under classroom desks, and some parents dug bomb shelters in the backyard. Meanwhile, bored airmen sat sixty-five miles off the coast of New Jersey, watching ships slowly steam across the horizon and tired sea gulls rest on the rails. The hysteria of the time helped justify the more than $20 million spent to build Texas Tower No. 4 off New Jersey, and another $40 million for two others off New York and Cape Cod. Plans called for construction of two additional stations, but they were never built.

As so often happens, war, or fear of it, spurred technological innovation. The offshore Texas Towers stand in history as forerunners of inshore platforms, such as Ambrose Light Station, that replaced lightships off ports up and down the coast during the 1960s.

Two months after the completion of Texas Tower No. 4 in 1957, land-based units with sufficient range became operational, making the tower obsolete as a radar warning system. Also, as an offshore platform, the design was far from perfect; the legs were sunk in mud and fine silt, and engineers predicted trouble. Yet now that it had its towers, the Air Force refused to abandon them. Its stubbornness had tragic consequences in January, 1961. The following fictionalized account is based on fact. I've used as little literary license as possible. The names of the two characters are part of public record.

SEPTEMBER, 1960

William Smythe, a tall man, brawny from years of farming, railroad work, and professional diving, plunged into the sea off Barnegat, New

Jersey. His diving partner, a man with whom he'd worked on raising the *Normandie*—one of the more exciting moments of his life—followed him in as the Navy boat moved a short distance off.

Above the two men, Texas Tower No. 4's rusty legs stretched upward to meet the triangular bottom of the lower deck, which blackened the water around them in shadow. They followed one of the legs down and began inspecting the structure for damage. It was a long, arduous, and risky job. They'd been poking around and taking underwater photographs for four days, and Smythe, who was sixty-one and ready to retire, wanted nothing more than to get home. He loved diving, but after thirty years of taking risks he was ready to spend more time with his wife at their home in Montauk, Long Island.

Although the huge swells left behind from Hurricane Donna no longer surged around the tower, the divers saw plenty of evidence that a big storm had passed through recently. Many of the braces that supported the tower had broken, bent, or cracked. The men assigned to work on the tower called it a "wobbler." In high winds, its massive bulk sixty-seven feet above the sea danced back and forth on its tripod; the disturbing movement acquired its own momentum, and it took nerve to stay cool.

"The noise of the metal flexing goes straight to your bones," one airman had told Smythe. After he'd heard the tower groan first hand, Smythe figured the man had it right. The sound struck as deep as marrow.

USAF Captain Gordon T. Phelan, commanding officer of Texas Tower No. 4, sat back in his chair and surveyed the diver standing in front of him. He glanced at the photographs spread out on the desk and shook his head.

"How much do you think it'll cost to repair?" Phelan asked.

Smythe gave an honest answer: "Ten million or so." He knew the Air Force wouldn't pay half the initial building cost to fix a tower nobody seemed to want anyway, and he wondered how the Air Force and the Navy, which supervised construction and repair, planned to respond. "The damage is real bad, Captain," he said, looking him straight in the eye. "The next bad storm will likely bring the tower down."

Phelan folded his hands in front of him, covering up some of the photographs of the damage. "It won't if we can fix it. In the meantime, say nothing to the men about what you saw down there. We'll get a crew out right away to repair the worst of it."

"Yes, sir," Smythe said, and walked out of the captain's office.

An hour later, Smythe and his partner boarded a helicopter for home. As the aircraft banked to port, he looked down at the tower.

Seventy brave men in the middle of the sea . . . on a fool's errand, he thought.

NOVEMBER, 1960

Smythe watched Texas Tower No. 4 loom into sight. From his vantage point in the helicopter, the tower looked almost pretty, bathed in sunlight, alone in the broad ocean. The thing seemed somehow defiant in its puniness. It didn't belong, but neither did humans belong swimming underwater or flying around in helicopters. Seen that way, the tower seemed as natural as any other human exploit, though Smythe considered the tower's mission a sad one. The aircraft touched down on the landing pad, and after formalities with Captain Phelan, Smythe walked to his quarters to wash up for dinner.

On previous trips, the tower had hummed with activity. Now, with all but twenty-eight of the seventy men evacuated as a precaution in case storms battered the weakened structure, the place resembled a ghost town. Though nothing ever was silent on the tower, a quiet sense of gloom pervaded the rooms. Smythe thought of Thanksgiving dinner with his wife, kids, and grandchildren, but the teary good-bye earlier that day pushed all cheer away.

It's only till mid-January, he told himself. Only till then and his part in repairing Texas Tower No. 4 would be finished.

JANUARY, 1961

Sunday, January 15, dawned stormy and cold, and didn't get any better. The approaching nor'easter packed winds of fifty knots with gusts over seventy-five; it would soon hit them with all its power. Seas built to prodigious heights by early afternoon, showering spray against the windows of the tower. Ice coated everything.

Phelan frowned. He'd refused the Coast Guard's offer to evacuate the men by helicopter. The supply ship had come the day before, and knowing the storm was on its way he could have ordered everyone off the platform with little fuss. A moment of doubt crossed his mind, but vanished almost as quickly as it came. He had his orders and that was that—whether the tower was safe or not. At any rate, he thought, as the tower wobbled and metal groaned, twenty-twenty hindsight never did anyone any good. He stood up from his desk and took the next logical step to save the tower: jettison equipment and building materials from the flight deck, just in case a chopper could get through.

Smythe worked with the rest of the men to clear the flight deck for an aircraft landing they knew none of them would probably live to see. They tried to rid the rig of all that weight to lessen the wobble as the gusts of frigid air hit the tower. The men all knew the two lifeboats were now impossible to launch, that an aircraft or ship rescue would have to wait. Many men silently blamed Phelan for not ordering them off long before.

The flight deck cleared, all they could do was wait until daybreak, when help would come after the storm passed through. The men sat together listening to the sounds of the blow mingled with the sounds of the tower twisting apart. Each man made his memories a companion, and, as the hours ticked on, hoped the night would end happily.

ENDNOTE

That night, Texas Tower No. 4 collapsed into the sea and sank in 190 feet of water, killing all twenty-eight men aboard, including Smythe, who was due to retire in two days. Captain Phelan should have ordered an evacuation of all personnel before the storm hit, but the blame rests with many others as well. A Senate Preparedness Sub-Committee investigated the disaster and uncovered "multiple errors" which ranged from faulty design to the Navy and Air Force's failure to "heed danger warnings."

The work on inshore tower technology went on, as did the Cold War. The Texas Towers disappeared along with lightships, and inshore light platforms became common. But the story of the men who died on a lonely tower during a violent January storm off New Jersey remains largely forgotten.

Offshore, 1995

Pilots, not the ones who fly the friendly skies, but those who guide ships safely in and out of port, have been part of life along the coasts of the world for thousands of years. They're experts with the local knowledge even the best of captains will lack when approaching a strange harbor. Not surprisingly, the first pilots to work in North America started in the Northeast, though not in Boston or up on the St. Lawrence River in Quebec. New York City bears that distinction, among many others.

PILOTS ON THE WATER

In the mid-1800s, along the shores of Raritan and Sandy Hook bays, sleek schooners with clipper bows put smartly out to sea with rough and tumble crews eager for lucrative wages. Their masters weren't looking for fish in the fashion of their New England cousins at Gloucester but for the commission paid to pilot a ship into or out of harbor.

Up and down the Eastern seaboard, in the busiest ports of the nation, these pilot boats sailed in any weather, and many paid dearly for their courage. It wasn't uncommon for them to sink in storms and collisions or to break apart on bars and ledges.

Today, power vessels have replaced those schooners, and swift launches have likewise taken over the oar-driven yawls that used to ferry pilots to the awaiting ships. But while the technology has changed, the pilots' mission hasn't in more than 300 years. In fact, it was in 1694 that New York officials formed a group of local captains to assist masters in navigating the harbor.

The Sandy Hook Pilots, comprising the New York and New Jersey Pilots associations, is the oldest of the more than fifty groups of state-licensed pilots operating in the United States. The organization is a little-known cadre of seamen (and a handful of women) who hold an important place in the maritime history of New Jersey and New York, and as professional mariners serving the merchant marine today.

A fiercely competitive, independent spirit among the various pilot companies marked the early days of what later became the Sandy Hook Pilots. At the first sight of a ship, pilot boats from Long Island and Sandy Hook set sail in a frantic and often dangerous race to get offshore first and claim the commission. The drive to win the prize led many skippers to press their boats too hard in severe storms. The voluminous list of death and disaster contains gruesome entries such as this: "Robert Mitchell, a pilot aboard the *E. K. Collins*, ran aground in a gale during the winter of 1836 and froze to death before rescuers could reach him."

The need for pilots increased rapidly as steam replaced sail and developments in ship construction led to bigger and bigger vessels. The deeper drafts of these huge steamships required the presence of a helmsman with local knowledge to avoid groundings and other unpleasantness in what remains a challenging harbor to navigate. During the mid-1800s, the harbor teemed with traffic—possibly more than present levels considering the lack of bridges and tunnels to relieve the burden on the waterway. It was the pilots' job to minimize the number of accidents.

By the 1860s, seventeen competing pilot boats employed forty-two New York pilots, and four New Jersey boats employed thirty pilots. It was not unheard of for a pilot boat to sail as much as 600 miles offshore in search of an inbound ship, a reflection of just how determined the masters of the pilot boats were to stay in business.

The competition bred an aggressive nature among the pilots, and they built the fastest boats they could to beat their competitors to the ship. They learned from experience how to sail for speed and their skill

combined with their determination to win made them excellent racers. They did for a living what the millionaires aboard their palatial
yachts did for sport. In 1851, a Sandy Hook pilot, Captain Richard
Brown, won the Queen's Cup with the schooner *America*, which was
built based on designs of the pilot boats. The Queen's Cup, of course,
thereafter became known as the America's Cup.

(The Gloucester schooners also raced each other home from the
fishing grounds to get the highest price for the fish in their holds.
America's yacht racing tradition sprouted from very real economic im-
peratives, and the crews who raced the yachts of the rich often learned
their skills in fishing, and a lesser number in piloting.)

Yet, despite the pilots' skills, an inherent flaw existed in the pilot-
age system. The pilots lived, and sometimes died, by their own set of
rules. And with each boat the rules were slightly different. The intense
competition meant more boats than were actually needed routinely put
out to sea, sparking spirited races but also setting the stage for disaster. During the famous blizzard of 1888, nine pilot boats sank and
seventeen pilots perished. Many ships also sank, with heavy loss of life.
After that, pilots would, on occasion, refuse to sail out to ships in hazardous conditions. Such decisions created a vicious circle of sorts, causing bigger ships to go aground and resulting in more deaths.

Clearly, the system required a major overhaul. Based in part on the
high death toll during the blizzard of 1888, the New York State Board
of Pilot Commissioners in 1895 ordered the New York and New Jersey pilots to merge and pool their resources and coordinate their efforts to maximize safety. The pilots banded together, became known
as the Sandy Hook Pilots, did away with the schooner fleet and built
the *New York*, the first steam pilot boat. Not long afterward they added
the *New Jersey*, and piloting continued to evolve.

During World War II, with streams of convoys coming and going
in the harbor, the Sandy Hook Pilots were hard pressed. In January,
1945, 112 pilots guided 243 ships into New York Harbor during one
twenty-four-hour period. It must have been quite a sight.

Today, the approximately 100 members of the Sandy Hook Pilots
guide roughly 12,000 vessels in and out of New York Harbor every
year. The shipping industry generates about $20 billion in revenue for
New York and New Jersey.

The responsibility of piloting a ship carrying valuable and sometimes hazardous cargo through a difficult harbor demands an unusual
level of training. Pilots spend seven-and-a-half years apprenticing under the guidance of fully qualified pilots as they work up to larger and

larger ships. It takes another seven years to become a Full Branch Pilot capable of commanding the world's biggest ships.

No book learning can replace long hours of practice under all conditions with a variety of vessels. Nor can it impart the gut feel the pilots must have for the harbor's hydrography, aids to navigation, shifting shoals, wrecks, and other hazards. Give a pilot a chart with only the landmasses outlined and he or she will be able to draw, from memory, every detail of the harbor on a NOAA chart.

The men aboard the modern versions of the *New York* or *New Jersey*—one of which stands on station near Ambrose Tower 365 days a year, ready to put a pilot aboard a ship at any hour, in any weather—carry on their important mission like their peers in other ports. The next time you see a ship steaming into or out of a port, think of the profession's long history, and the important contributions America's pilots make to the nation every day in helping ensure the safe transport of cargoes.

SHIPPING CHANNELS: KEEP CLEAR!

The fishing always seems best in the middle of a deep channel, and when the fish are biting it's easy to lose track of your surroundings. The masters of large ships as well as members of the Sandy Hook Pilots say that recreational boats adrift or anchored in channels such as Ambrose are a common problem. Evidently, some boaters wait until the last minute to start the outboard and get out of the way of oncoming ships. Engine failure could ruin a nice day—and a nice life.

A pilot on the bridge of a ship will lose sight of a recreational boater behind the containers on deck long before the ship arrives at the place he thinks the boater was. The radar is blind at that point as well. Imagine the stress on a pilot who has just changed course, assuming he can, to avoid a guy fishing in the middle of a channel. He can't see the boater from the bridge or on radar until the boater passes astern. A ship can crush a small boat or suck it under without anyone aboard the larger vessel being the wiser.

Recreational boaters who like to fish in channels drive professional mariners crazy, but they know it's bound to continue as long as fish hang around in the shipping lanes. (Perhaps fish aren't so dumb after all?) Masters and pilots ask anyone foolish enough to fish in a major shipping lane to at least pay attention and get out of the way long before a ship passes. It will be safer for the boaters, and less stressful to the pilots and masters.

Incidentally, the Sandy Hook Pilots also reported that party fishing boats sometimes crowd channels. It's busy out there, and all mariners need to maintain a high level of consideration for others in order to avoid conflicts.

Offshore, 1995

New York and New Jersey, home of the Northeast's first pilots, can lay another claim to fame: they were also the location of the first official, well-organized lifesaving service. As any boater knows, the Coast Guard's search and rescue branch stands ready to pull the hapless out of harm's way. It's hard to imagine what it was like without these brave men and women ready to risk their lives to help mariners in distress. But for a very long time along the shores of the United States and Canada, sailors in trouble had no recourse but to rely on themselves or hope for rescue from volunteers.

USCG "ANCESTOR" BEGAN ON JERSEY SHORE

When winter gales scream out of the northern Atlantic and sweep the Jersey shore with the full fury of wind and sea, the sight inspires awe. The rumble and roar of surf breaking white on the long barrier islands can be heard well inland, and spray suspended in the wind covers cars and homes with a thick salty film mixed with grains of sand.

Few recreational boaters venture out through the inlets during the stormy season, which typically lasts until early May. But our commercial cousins don't have the luxury of time. They cast off lines and head out even in severe weather, and sometimes the Coast Guard has to go out and get them—with or without their vessel.

Before 1915, however, no Coast Guard existed, at least not in the way we know it today. That year, the United States Lifesaving Service merged with the Revenue Cutter Service to form the Coast Guard. The new service's search and rescue efforts replaced those of the Lifesaving Service, which got its inception in 1848 through the drive and determination of a New Jersey man named William A. Newell. Newell, a physician and a congressional representative, successfully lobbied federal lawmakers to appropriate funds to establish a series of lifesaving stations along the Jersey shore.

In its heyday after 1871, lifesaving stations perched on the shore at intervals of no more than three miles apart. The United States Lifesaving Service was born in New Jersey and was eventually expanded to all U.S. waters, including the Great Lakes. That an organized lifesaving system was needed seemed indisputable, though it took Newell a long time to get action. New Jersey, like Cape Cod and Cape Hatteras, was known among sailors as a graveyard. The shifting shoals extending off the long stretch of coast routinely claimed lives when the wind and waves caused ships to go aground. Between 1839 and 1848, 338 ships were dashed to pieces on the shoals off New Jersey and Long Island, according to published reports.

Often, the hapless people aboard stranded vessels clung to the wreckage within view of would-be rescuers and the safety of land, so close and yet so far. They drowned when the ships finally broke apart. Clearly, something had to be done, and Newell set the ball in motion.

What follows is a fictionalized account of the wreck of the *Ayrshire*, a British immigrant ship which drove aground on Chadwick Beach north of Island Beach in 1850. Just two years after Newell's efforts led to funding eight lifesaving stations in New Jersey, which became operational in 1849, the wreck of the *Ayrshire* not only showed the effectiveness of the rescue system; it was also the occasion of the first use, in a real rescue, of a strange new lifesaving vessel called a life-car.

THE STORY

John Maxen, chief of the lifesaving station at Squan Beach, stood in the company of his volunteer crew comprised of local fishermen and watched the storm gather strength during the afternoon of January 12, 1850. A wicked northeasterly wind cut through their heavy woolen clothing. The men huddled together near the squat little building which housed the lifesaving equipment, but they kept their eyes seaward. Inside the station was their surfboat, fashioned after the famed Sea Bright skiff. It was a stout craft developed by the fishermen of the Jersey shore to go through rough surf and to handle nimbly among the shoals off the coast, and with some modifications it made an ideal lifeboat. A traditional heavy longboat found aboard large vessels had no place in such an environment, a fact proven time and again when desperate crews of wrecked ships tried to get ashore in them during storms. They almost always died when the longboats broached to and swamped.

But there were times when even the surfboats couldn't live in the violent breakers, and Maxen feared this day might be one of them. He turned his back to the sea and the stinging wind and eyed another craft at the station, the life-car, an invention of an innovative Bostonian, Joseph Francis, who had done pioneering work in his youth on building unsinkable rowboats. Maxen had long wondered whether this walnut-shaped, metal boat would work. It was the strangest thing he'd ever seen.

It hardly resembled a boat at all. Its rounded metal shell was completely water and airtight when the single top-hatch was secured. Only four to five passengers could hide inside while rescuers pulled it along a thick hawser led from a stricken ship to land.

"It's a bad storm for certain," said one of the station's crew, a big man with a weather-hardened face and a quick smile.

Maxen silently nodded, then turned again to the angry sea.

Twilight came, and with it came disaster. Amid the fury of the storm, the lights of a ship appeared not far offshore. Although the crew could barely make out the form of the vessel, they knew that it was trapped. Nothing would turn it from the lee shore. Within moments, the ship drove hard aground.

Standing just beyond the reach of the huge breakers, John Maxen surveyed the scene. The ship was fairly close to land, about 300 yards off, but separated by an expanse of churning water. As he had feared earlier that day, this storm could kill even a surfboat.

"Look lively and rig the life-car!" he shouted.

His men hesitated, knowing the contraption had never been used in a shipwreck.

"Come on—we don't have all night!"

The crew had practiced using the life-car, often with a smattering of jokes about its ungainly appearance. No one joked now as they ran back to the station, hauled the cumbersome 200–plus-pound life-car, sand anchor, crotch, and the mortar down to the beach. It looked like a battle scene, and it was.

While some men attached the bitter end of the hawser to a sand anchor, a huge wooden cross, and buried it deeply in the wet hard beach, others readied the light lines that would be used to run the life-car back and forth along the hawser, much like a flag goes up and down a pole. Maxen rammed home a charge of powder into the mortar. When all was ready, Maxen fired.

The shot went wide and the hawser dropped uselessly into the sea. As the men worked to retrieve it, the ship's standing rigging let go. Masts and spars crashed to the deck. Maxen could only hope the sailors aboard the ship understood what he was trying to do.

Maxen fired again, and this time the shot hit the ship. The crew cheered as they saw sailors secure it. With one end of the hawser secured to the beach and held high in the wooden crotch so the life-car would ride above the waves, and the other end secured to the ship, they used light lines to pull the life-car to the vessel through the violent surf. Some passengers climbed into the life-car and closed the hatch.

"Pull hard!" Maxen shouted. Once the hatch of the life-car was sealed, the air inside would last only fifteen minutes.

Ten minutes later, the life-car was ashore with its first cargo of wet and grateful passengers.

ENDNOTE

The *Ayrshire* carried approximately 200 passengers, all of whom were rescued in the life-car, save one man who tried to ride on the outside of the craft.

At the end of its use in lifesaving operations, 1,493 lives had been saved by that life-car alone. That January 12 in 1850 marked a turning point in lifesaving along the Jersey shore, and was the precursor to modern search and rescue now handled by the Coast Guard.

Offshore, 1995

The Lifesaving Service began what today is a highly effective and much needed branch of the Coast Guard. It saved countless lives and kept many a widow's walk atop old Victorian homes along the Northeast coast empty of worried wives waiting in vain for their husbands to return from the sea. However, the advent of the service in the mid-1800s also created another indirect benefit for sailors and their ships. The presence of lifesaving crews along the often desolate beaches put an end to a little-known chapter in the pages of shore history—land pirates, or wreckers were doomed.

NEW JERSEY'S LAND PIRATES

In April, 1825, the *Franklin*, a packet ship from Charleston, South Carolina, ran into thick fog off Island Beach. Contrary to common belief, even among many mariners today, the coast of New Jersey isn't a rail-straight line of sand 127 miles from Sandy Hook to Cape May. It bows outward in the vicinity of Island Beach, and shoals extend offshore to create an ideal setting for wrecks.

The *Franklin* ran hard aground in the shallows and despite his efforts, Captain Munro couldn't free his stranded vessel. As he peered shoreward into the mist, he saw a small group of people running down the beach. Soon a crowd of approximately 200 gathered, but they weren't there to offer help. The hapless crew of the *Franklin* had run into one of the most notorious groups of land pirates in New Jersey, also known as "moon cussers" for their hatred of full moons that aided navigation and revealed their efforts to lure ships ashore with false beacons.

"They plundered everything they could get hold of," Munro later wrote of the incident, remarking that if the United States Navy felt the need to dispatch convoys to protect American shipping from pirates in the West Indies they'd do well to send forces to New Jersey, too. Munro hardly felt lucky that April. Yet, he and his crew escaped with their lives. Historians say the land pirates would think nothing of murdering crews and passengers. As the saying goes, "Dead men tell no tales."

An article published on December 27, 1834, in the *Newark Daily Advisor* lends credence to the ruthless murder of crews that sometimes took place. The paper reported that "Long Beach Island had long been infested by a band of land pirates who snarled craft with deceptive lights. Many crews were robbed and thrown overboard."

A favorite tactic among the land pirates along the Jersey shore and elsewhere on the coast involved lashing a pole with a bright lantern atop it to the neck of a mule. On moonless or foggy nights when they spied the lights of a ship making its way along the coast, they'd walk the mule down the beach to simulate the lights of a ship sailing closer to shore. Unwary captains, thinking they could get in closer to the beach, found themselves aground. The land pirates also placed haystacks on the dunes and marched round and round them with lanterns, creating false lighthouses.

For the most part the land pirates of New Jersey weren't the swashbuckling type. The cutlass and boarding pike weren't the usual tools of their operations. They were opportunistic in nature, relying more on the forces of nature to bring home the bacon.

"When a winter nor'easter picked up, the land pirates, and most of the local inhabitants of the shore for that matter would look eastward with a gleam in their eye," said John Bandstra, president of the New Jersey Historical Divers Association, Avon. "They even taught their children a prayer: 'May our ship come in the morning.'"

Of course, not everyone living along the Jersey coast from 1700 through the mid-1800s found employment as land pirates. Most, however, were very poor and, human nature being what it is, couldn't resist the temptation of carting off whatever goods they could obtain from wrecks and from the victims washed up on the beach after a bad storm. Homes were furnished with goods taken from stricken ships. A church in Stafford was built with lumber salvaged from wrecks.

"These people were dirt poor and during bad winters when the bay was frozen over and they couldn't fish or hunt, anything that came ashore was an improvement on life," said Deb Whitcraft, owner of the excursion vessel *Black Whale* out of Beach Haven. "If things needed a boost every now and then when pickings were slim, there were people to do it with false lights or any other means. I can almost understand why they did it, even though it cost many people their lives."

The land pirates at times resembled the rival street gangs of today. Whitcraft noted that during a particularly busy wreck-plundering, groups of the pirates would stash their loot in the dunes. Watchers from rival bands of pirates would then come, steal the stolen bounty, and run off with it. The land pirates and local inhabitants not directly involved with luring ships to wreck ashore were also known to let crews and passengers drown rather than attempt rescues.

The nor'easter of February 2, 1846, known as the John Minturn Storm, spelled the end of most organized wrecking ventures along the Jersey shore and the tendency of local residents to watch the people on the ships die. More than a dozen ships blew ashore during the storm and the *John Minturn*, a packet ship with fifty-one people aboard, grounded about 200 yards off Squan Beach, south of Manasquan Inlet. Thirty-eight of them died while "big-boned Jerseymen" did nothing to save the victims, according to reports.

"It was suspected that land pirates had lured some of the ships that sank in the storm to their fate, which also created an impetus behind the investigation," Whitcraft said. "But I don't think land pirates lured any ships . . . they didn't have to because it was such a bad storm."

The investigation evidently "whitewashed" the incident, concluding that no hard evidence could be found to implicate even one person for looting the dead, much less luring ships ashore at the height of the storm. However, the outcry over the charges and the loss of life provided enough ammunition for Congress two years later to authorize the first official lifesaving stations in the nation.

Eight stations were built, and more followed. Eventually, a chain of stations stretched along the shore at intervals of only three miles apart. No "moon cusser" in his right mind would try a nocturnal walk with a well-lit mule. The land pirates had to hang up their lanterns.

Offshore, 1997

Most every coastal state has supported or still supports boatbuilding. In the early days of the United States, shipping played a major role in keeping the fire behind the economy burning bright and as such made for a booming business at boatyards where craftsmen built the vessels that were so much in demand. New England is famous for its shipwrights, but New Jersey seems to have been lost in the shuffle of history. Nevertheless, it was and remains a key boatbuilding center in the Northeast, even eclipsing its northern neighbors, at least in the present.

THE BOATBUILDING HERITAGE OF THE GARDEN STATE

It's no secret that New Jersey is a major center for boatbuilding. In fact, the state has the largest concentration of firms building big production cruisers and sports fishing boats in the country. A look at the history of boatbuilding in New Jersey reveals how the state came to be such a powerful player in the boatbuilding business.

As in all things great, the start of boatbuilding in the state was small. It began with early settlers building their own boats to fish in the bays and to get them from one place to another. The western reaches of the bays were and still are fringed with extensive marshes, making a small boat a very handy thing to have. The huge expanse of the Pine Barrens, thick and often impenetrable, did not encourage the building of roads, so water travel was a necessary mode of transportation, both for people and goods.

While New Jersey during the early colonial days was not considered much of a boatbuilding center, New England was. It's an interesting contrast with the present. In the past, shipwrights at ports such as Gloucester and Essex in Massachusetts were producing vessels of all kinds at prodigious rates. Huge rafts of timber from New Hampshire were floated down to the sea and through sweat and hard work were converted to ships. New Englanders built so many good vessels that they cut into the businesses of their British counterparts across the Atlantic, displeasing them to no end as they saw money drained from their coffers by upstart Yankee entrepreneurs.

New Jersey's slow start stemmed in part from competition to the north. Why go into the boatbuilding industry if the big guys up in the northern colonies had a virtual monopoly? But there was another reason, too.

Unlike its neighbors to the north, New Jersey is not blessed with a multitude of good natural harbors. The coast stretches nearly unbroken by inlets for 127 miles. The inlets, some of which are now largely tamed through bulwarks and jetties, were wild places with swift currents and ever-shifting shoals. The geography of the state did little to encourage the birth of a prosperous shipbuilding industry.

Yet, the combination of protected bays behind the barrier islands and a ready source of cedar and pine from the woodlands along much of the shore did open the possibility for boatbuilding to exist in the state on a larger scale than a cottage industry. A few boatbuilding companies did get into the business despite the obstacles.

For example, in 1712, a fellow by the name of John Leak is known to have started a boatbuilding company, no doubt one of the first on record in the state. The firm launched its first hull that year and they've been building boats in New Jersey ever since. The company is Ocean Yachts in Egg Harbor City. (At some point, the Leak family decided, and wisely so, that Leak wasn't quite the best name for a builder of boats. They dropped the "a" in favor of a more acceptable "e".)

One key development in the early days of boatbuilding in New Jersey was the burgeoning of the risky but profitable rumrunning business. The state was home, as it still is today, to many wealthy residents who flocked to the seaside resorts that existed even back then. Not everyone lived a hard life in colonial days, and those with means liked to drink good rum at low prices.

With a ready market at hand, enterprising New Jerseyans jumped at the chance to make fast money. What they needed for the job, though, were fast boats capable of running the notorious inlets and outrunning British warships. The vessels also had to be extremely seaworthy, not only for the run down to Jamaica for their illegal cargoes, but also because of the formidable nature of the New Jersey coast with its lack of safe, easily entered harbors. Swift sailing vessels were designed and built in New Jersey expressly for the rumrunning trade. Many men made their fortunes supplying rum to the rich, or anyone else who could buy it. Others perished in their attempts, or were clapped into irons for their troubles.

Although the construction of rumrunning boats was by no means the sole impetus behind the development of New Jersey as a major boatbuilding center, the necessary attention to design, quality workmanship, sea-keeping abilities, and speed form were pretty good starting points for the state's boatbuilding industry.

Slowly, then not so slowly, more boatbuilders began to operate in New Jersey. They located in places with easy access to the sea, near inlets of South Jersey and over on the Jersey side of the Delaware River.

Eventually, whalers, topsail schooners, brigs, privateers, gigs, pinnaces, and shallops were being built along the shore and launched into Jersey waters. Boats built expressly for use in the marshes abounded, including the famed present-day "sneakbox," an ideal boat for duck hunting among the thick reeds.

As the country grew after the Revolutionary War, the boatbuilding businesses in New England still prospered, but they no longer were virtually alone in the market. New Jersey became firmly entrenched as a player in the boatbuilding game, and as it turned out, had the good fortune to continue through and beyond the end of the sailing age and the ultimate decline of boatbuilding on a large scale in New England waters.

Commercial shipbuilding, which comprised all of the early orders for vessels, declined in this century. This obviously wasn't true during World War II, but on the whole, the market began to grow lean. In New Jersey, many of the boatbuilders shifted over to the construction of recreational boats, and as the American middle class prospered during the 1950s and could afford a luxury like a boat, the state's boatbuilders accommodated them. In fact, many of today's major builders in the state started out in the 1950s and early 1960s. The advent of fiberglass, which made it possible to build production boats faster and less expensively accounts for this, and gave rise to the start of more companies in the 1970s, a decade when recreational boating really began to gain popularity nationwide.

Things went just fine until the late 1980s and the early 1990s. The state's best known boatbuilders, such as Viking, Ocean, Egg Harbor, Post, Henriques, Pacemaker, Jersey and a handful of other smaller builders focused for the most part on the high end of the market. They built, and still build, boats selling in the six- and seven-figure range. Only Silverton aimed at a more popular market and only Silverton grew large in terms of volume.

When the recession hit along with the luxury tax, the bottom of the high end market dropped out. Nationwide, more than 25,000 jobs were lost in the boating industry, and 5,000 of them were from New Jersey.

But fortunately for anyone who admires the wonderful flare of a New Jersey boat's bow, the state's boating industry survived the storm. The National Marine Manufacturers Association reports that big production boats are among the top-selling craft today and the healthiest segment of today's marine industry. New Jersey's place as a major boatbuilding center seems secure again, and a tradition rooted back almost 300 years and rerooted 250 years later should make it into the next millennium.

Offshore, 1995

JERSEY BOATBUILDING: A FAMILY TRADITION

When cruising along the coast of New Jersey on a fine summer day gentle ground swells roll in off the Atlantic. But when the wind blows up from the northeast and the waves rise, the going gets tough.

Within an hour the seemingly benign coast can become a death trap, and there's nowhere to go. Even the best inlets become nearly impassable, leaving a boat on a dangerous lee shore—unless it's specially designed to outrun breaking following seas and maneuver in tight quarters between granite jetties.

"Along the Atlantic coast we have some rugged water offshore and with that we also have some very treacherous inlets. The Jersey shore is not known for its easy inlets. That being so, when this country was founded and most transportation was by water, boatbuilders here learned pretty early how to build boats to survive some seriously heavy weather," said Bob Healey, chairman and chief executive officer of Viking Yacht Company, New Gretna, New Jersey.

That tradition still lives today. New Jersey hosts the nation's largest concentration of boatbuilders manufacturing offshore motoryachts and sport fishing vessels in the forty-foot-plus range. Viking Yacht Company, Egg Harbor Yacht Company, Ocean Yachts, Post Marine, and Silverton Marine all sprang from the rich history of boatbuilding that took root 300 years ago along the shores of creeks that run dark with the acids of cedar and bog iron through dense forests of pine to the protected waters behind the barrier islands.

Modern Jersey boats are world famous, as were their predecessors a century ago. Their hard chine (V-bottom), a bow entry sharp enough to keep from pounding while providing good stability as the V-bottom flattens out toward the stern . . . the graceful flare to the bow, the ability to cruise fast and far on large engines, these characteristics mark Jersey boats, according to Dave Martin, yacht designer for Ocean Yachts, Egg Harbor Yacht Company, and others.

The designs of today, however, evolved long before fiberglass molds replaced the woodshop, long before diesel replaced steam, and steam replaced sail. Even the early recreational boats built in New Jersey during the 1920s, which often were used to run rum, all the way through the 1950s when the likes of Henry Luhrs, John Leek, Sr., and Russell Post began to make names for themselves, can trace their lapstrake construction, round bilges, and relatively straight sheer to the Sea Bright skiff. Known generically as a Jersey skiff, these sixteen-foot boats were built to launch and land through surf off New Jersey beaches starting around 1840. Of course, as time went on the boats grew, topping out in the forty-to-sixty-foot range.

"It seems all the boats going way back took the name of Jersey skiff. I always thought that was a little over-done; a little too much was put into the idea of Jersey skiffs. They were good, round-bilge fishing boats which the builders proceeded to add amenities to, that's all. There was nothing magical, but everyone wanted to own one," said Russell Post, who founded Post Marine in 1957.

Post's realistic assessment of Jersey's skiffs, his ability to cut through the flip-flap of marketing mavens, speaks volumes. No, there wasn't anything magical. The boats built along the Jersey coast were built to bring men to the fishing grounds and bring them back in the same way as the Gloucester dory was built to withstand the fury of the Grand Banks.

In the 1920s, though, designers like E. Lockwood Haggas built rum-running boats based on the early oar-powered craft. They could hit sixty miles per hour with three 300 to 400 horsepower Liberty engines or other similarly beefy powerplants. Jersey builders were happy to take orders for these vessels and for rum chasers used by the authorities out to nab them. They churned out hundreds.

New Jersey, midway between the cities of Philadelphia and New York, was a major smuggling center during Prohibition. The runners zoomed out the inlets under the cover of night to ships waiting for them offshore, and tried to outrun the chase boats. It was a game of cat and mouse which lined the pockets of builders working both sides of the field. Since the good guys and the bad guys often obtained their boats from the same source, odds were even that either side would win in a confrontation offshore.

"These boats were fast and fuel efficient," Martin said. "The designers who built them later put the knowledge to use designing sub chasers and PT boats during World War II, many of which were built in New Jersey."

Charles Leek, a major builder of custom powerboats in the days of flappers and speakeasies, evidently never did build any boats for the rum smugglers, though he built pursuit boats. In World War II, he built seventy-to-eighty-foot sub chasers for the British Navy. With the help of his two sons, Cecil and John, the family went on to found Pacemaker.

John Leek, Sr., put in a brief stint at Egg Harbor Yachts, though, before the Pacemaker days. But he decided to leave a year after he co-founded the company in 1946 with Russell Post. Ralph and John Leek III, descendants of Charles, now run Ocean Yachts. All the Leeks are descendants of a Welsh immigrant who emigrated to the British colonies in the early 1700s and began building boats in the future New Jersey.

About the same time Charles Leek was getting his start, Henry Luhrs began his boatbuilding career. Like the Leeks, the Luhrs family traced its roots far back in American history. Among other enterprises, the family owned shares in commercial sailing ships.

Henry started out in the 1930s building and repairing boats for the local Jersey fishermen, and during World War II his yard repaired submarine patrol boats for the Coast Guard. After the war, he went into custom boatbuilding and eventually became famous as the first production builder of Jersey skiffs, introducing features such as shelter cabins with a flybridge.

Henry Luhrs Sea Skiffs was incorporated in 1952 and produced boats in the twenty-six to thirty-two-foot range. Eventually, in 1965, Henry sold the company to a large corporation and stayed on as part of its management team. His sons, Warren and John, went on to found Silverton Marine, among other boatbuilding companies, beginning in 1969 after purchasing a small independent operation on Toms River.

Earlier in the 1960s, the Healey brothers, Bob and Bill, got into the Jersey boatbuilding game. They started Viking Yachts in a small building on the Bass River deep in the pines of South Jersey and have since grown into a 400,000 square-foot facility in New Gretna, carrying on a long tradition of family owned and operated boatbuilding businesses that collectively produced some of the best luxury cruising and sport fishing boats around.

"There is an old-world standard of craftsmanship associated with boats here that speaks to what is unique to the New Jersey boat. It goes beyond the flare of the bow, the sheer lines, or chines. It's about quality, and the people who make it happen," said Mike Usina, director of sales and marketing, Silverton Marine Corporation in Millville, New Jersey.

Power and Motoryacht, 1998

A bit of grog, a mixture of rum and water, has brightened the days of many a sailor on old ships-of-the-line and many others since. Up and down the coast, you can find spots where local mariners gather to sip a drink and swap yarns. Even in the midst of tourism Meccas, if you look, you'll find these places. The Broadway Bar in Point Pleasant is one of them, a special kind of watering hole that almost ended on the scrap heap of local history.

THE BROADWAY BAR IS FULL OF FISHERMEN AND HISTORY

Have you heard that radio ad starring Dick Cavett? It's set in a truck stop—seems prevailing wisdom dictates if you want a good hamburger you go where the truckers eat. Cavett's logic can be applied to watering holes, too. But in this case, follow the fishermen to the Broadway Bar & Grill in Point Pleasant.

You'll find skippers and crews from local fishing fleets out of Manasquan there for hearty food and inexpensive beers during the morning happy hour, which runs from 7:00 A.M. to 10:00 A.M. The bar provides a welcome place to go after a long night on the water.

As the day goes on, local residents, visitors, summer vacationers, boaters, and recreational fishermen come and go. One woman we met at the Broadway Bar called it a second home, and not because of an insatiable thirst, but because of the friendly banter.

"You get to know an awful lot of people on a first-name basis. It's a nice comfortable feeling. We try to maintain that kind of close family atmosphere," says Brian DeDreux, one of the owners.

The DeDreux family bought the bar in 1991. They're carrying on a long tradition. A restaurant or bar has been located on the corner of Randall Avenue and Broadway at least since the early 1920s. Back when the town of Point Pleasant relied primarily on the commercial fishing industry, the little restaurant a stone's throw away from the Manasquan River was a very busy place.

In the 1930s, a local family by the name of Neilley bought the restaurant, changing its name from the utilitarian Inlet Restaurant to Neilley's. The family ran the place for more than fifty years. In the 1940s, after a fire destroyed the original two-story building, the family built what became known as Neilley's long bar, which derived from the very long bar set against the back wall.

The Neilley family saw the town change from a New Jersey fishing port to a busy resort community replete with boardwalk amusements and beachfront bungalows. All the while Neilley's remained a popular place among both locals and visitors—until the late 1980s when the bar became known as a pretty rough place.

That continued until the DeDreux family stepped in with a vision of turning things around. They put their money where their mouths were to do it, too. Over the last five years the family has spent approximately $200,000 on improvements which have helped revive the bar's popularity.

"When we purchased the bar, the building, the property, and the business were in need of a lot of repair," DeDreux says. "I started renovating from the floor up. We knocked down some walls and incorporated the kitchen behind the bar so we could start serving food."

DeDreux chose a simple menu offering meals made from meats purchased at a local butcher and fish fresh off the boats. He believed charging a fair price for a meal, and not increasing it during the busy season, would meet with approval among the folks in the area. You can pig out and drink up for next to nothing at the Broadway; it was a smash hit and the rest, as you might say, is history.

But besides the reemergence of one of Point Pleasant's oldest watering holes, what makes the Broadway Bar special is the decor. It's done in the nautical motif, but one which doesn't make you think, "Ah, tacky!"

In fact, people sometimes come to the Broadway Bar just to look at the thirteen intricate handmade models displayed throughout the room. The models are wooden replicas of local fishing boats still working the waters off New Jersey, and other craft native to the state. The details are so finely done even the sea gulls perched here and there on the draggers, clammers, and scallopers look real enough to snag an unwatched French fry right off your plate.

As you lift your beer glass for another swig, you'll notice those rings you leave behind appear over a collection of old photographs of life in Point Pleasant long before it became a resort. You'll see plenty of old boardwalk and beach shots, too. These old photos, which DeDreux painstakingly embedded in the finish on the top of the bar, were gifts from local residents who knew he was looking for tidbits of history to put in the bar.

"We've spent the last five years looking for artifacts to put in the bar," DeDreux says.

He's accumulated quite a collection of nautical odds and ends: shark jaws, stuffed fish, swordfish bills, bits of gear off antique boats from the area, and other things. On the walls are three paintings which have hung there since the 1950s.

Entering the Broadway Bar is a little like walking into a museum, except there's a large bar in the center of the room with tables along the walls. On hot Saturday nights during the boating season, the place really hops. Nobody pays much attention to all the details which make the Broadway Bar unique. They're too busy having fun talking and listening to the local bands.

Even at the height of the busy time at the boardwalk, the Broadway Bar doesn't lose the small-town flavor which is so apparent during quieter times when the Jersey shore reverts to a much slower pace and the local inhabitants can drive without suffering the ordeal of traffic jams. The prices stay the same; the style doesn't change, as it does at some places which seem to transform into something different when the tourists return.

"The locals really appreciate that we don't change our style when summer comes," DeDreux says. "And so do the visitors who like the local feel of the bar."

So next time you're boating near Point Pleasant, either passing through or for a visit, take a stroll into the Broadway Bar. Just follow the fishermen.

Offshore, 1996

Prized Boats and the People Who Own Them

Most every boat owner loves his or her boat, despite those times when things break and must be fixed and in a fit of frustration the idea of scuttling the old tub for a moment seems like the easiest way to go. There is a saying: The happiest time in a boat owner's life is when he or she buys the boat and when it's sold. Of course, the boater, with the check burning a hole in the hip pocket after the sale, usually goes out and buys another boat. It's a sickness of sorts, one I hope never to be rid of.

The pride that goes into the vessel almost becomes manic in its hold on the skipper's entire being. A boat, while properly termed an "it," most often is called a "she" because the craft seems almost alive, like the sea itself. The boat, whether it's a rundown old fiberglass sloop or a battered aluminum runabout, still conjures up a special feeling in the heart of its owner, a place that almost no other object, except possibly a house, can hope to compare with. After all is said and done, a boat is far more than a hole in the water into which you pour money, and lots of it. It's a reflection of the owner, his or her position in life, sensibilities, desires, successes, and so much more.

The Northeast enjoys a well-founded reputation as the birthplace for many a fine boat design. The Gloucester schooners first built at Cape Ann, Massachusetts, or the whalers from Nantucket; the first steam-powered ferry boats of the Hudson River; the surfboats of Nauvoo (now Sea Bright, New Jersey), and many, many more craft, both recreational and commercial, all can trace their roots back to the Northeast. The very fabric of much of the region is tied to the boats that came from its boatyards and later helped to build fortunes and entertain those who had finally made the big time.

The boats and their owners you'll meet in this chapter all share the love of a very special vessel and demonstrate through hard work a dedication to perfection that can only be admired. The boats themselves are mere shells, for without their owners even the grandest yacht can never take to the sea. The boats aren't typical of those that find favor in books or magazines, at least not generally. Rather, they are examples of wooden vessels ranging from a palatial commuter yacht to a stout little rowboat that crossed the Atlantic Ocean in 1896. Together, along with their owners, and the stories that go with them, the boats provide a glimpse into what makes boating such a beautiful and rewarding part of life for millions of people throughout the world.

WOODIES MAKE WAVES

Painted on the side of a wooden speedboat in the town of Lake Hopatcong, New Jersey, is a sign that reads simply, "Old Boats Restored." Down a steep hill is Wayne's Marine, one of the best restoration workshops for antique and classic wooden powerboats in the country. Seventeen years ago Wayne Mocksfield turned his hobby of restoring old runabouts into a business, and today, at forty-nine, he has more than thirty-six years of hard-won, hands-on restoration experience. Nationally known among collectors, he is one of the few craftsmen to specialize in restoring all parts—finish, leather upholstery, and engine—of the rare mahogany speedboats known as woodies. These days he finds himself increasingly in demand as the popularity of the classic wooden boats soars and owners seek expert restoration skills for their vessels.

"Interest in classic wooden powerboats really started to take off in the late 1970s," says Bill Taylor, president of the New England chapter of the Antique and Classic Boat Society, formed fifteen years ago to bring collectors of woodies together. Today the society has grown to more than thirty chapters and 2,500 members nationwide. It sponsors meetings, publications, and competitions, as well as scores of annual shows and regattas from California to New Hampshire. And not only diehard boating enthusiasts participate. Last year, for instance, the country's largest show drew thousands of enthralled spectators to admire some 100 gleaming wooden beauties as they cut through the blue waters of Lake Tahoe.

Hollywood is responsible for some of the new-found acclaim. "The movie *On Golden Pond* sparked a lot of enthusiasm when people saw how beautiful these old boats really are," Taylor says. Indeed, the first sight of an antique motorboat—even without Hepburn or Fonda at the wheel—is impressive. The sleek lines, the soft leather upholstery in the cockpit, the glow of nickel and chrome fittings all complement a runabout's aesthetic trademark—varnished Philippine or Honduras mahogany, whose subtle wood grain gleams a rich brown.

Woodies also handle well, a major attraction for owners since the end of World War I, when the technological advances in boat and engine design and the rapid economic growth in America during the 1920s made possible the advent of fast, lightweight boats that ordinary families could afford. The six-cylinder engines in woodies are capable of speeds in excess of forty miles an hour, and the planing hull makes these handsome vessels highly maneuverable.

Woodies fall into four official classifications: historic, built before 1918; antique, built between 1919 and 1942; classic, built between 1943 and 1968; and contemporary classic, built after 1968 (new replicas of older boats). Most in demand are products of the big three manufacturers: Chris-Craft, Fay-Bowen, and Gar Wood.

Over the years Wayne Mocksfield has assembled a personal fleet of woodies, some twenty vessels, including many Chris-Craft runabouts, a couple of Dodge boats, and a twenty-eight-foot Gar Wood Limousine. One of his historic prizes is a Fay-Bowen launch built in 1910, possibly the last used on New Jersey's Morris Canal, which connected Lake Hopatcong with Jersey City and Manhattan.

Mocksfield also owns one of the rarest antique boats in the world, *Mr. Benny*, a twenty-eight-foot three cockpit 1926 Rochester. Only three of these boats are known to survive. Designed by A. W. Mackerer (1895–1973), who later became the principal designer for Chris-Craft, *Mr. Benny* is noted for lines that were decades ahead of the time. Mocksfield bought the boat sight unseen from a salvager who picked it off the bottom of the St. Lawrence River eight years ago. When it arrived, "you could stick your fingers through the bottom and sides," he recalls. He and his craftsmen spent nine months simply restoring the woodwork, but today *Mr. Benny* wins awards regularly.

Growing up on Lake Hopatcong, Mocksfield began restoring runabouts with his father and uncle at age thirteen. He bought his first one in 1960, and while he worked at various jobs around the lake he watched and questioned older craftsmen working on vintage boats. He added to his fleet regularly and in 1973 bought the marina. "I couldn't make all the improvements at once, so we built the marina little by little," he recalls.

Mocksfield's business has increased along with the surge of interest in woodies. "In the 1960s, when fiberglass boats began to be produced in quantity," says Bill Taylor, "people abandoned their wooden boats and left them to rot"; some simply set the boats on fire to be rid of them. The formation of the Antique and Classic Boat Society in 1975 (its first chapter was on Lake Hopatcong) fostered an awareness that the fine old boats should be preserved, and rising values strengthened the trend.

Ranging in price between $5,000 and $150,000, woodies increase in value an average of 10 percent a year, making them an extremely attractive investment. "The days when you could find old hulks for as little as $50 are long gone now, since everybody knows how much some old hulks can be worth," explains Mocksfield. Prices rose as demand increased and the supply of hulks decreased. Mocksfield estimates that today there are approximately 10,000 to 20,000 yet undiscovered hulls still in backyards, barns, and garages. The most valued boats are more than twenty feet in length and carry on the frame the manufacturer's number, which is required if the boat is to be shown. Prized woodies now cost $150,000 or more.

In the Lake Hopatcong area, boat aficionados fortunate enough to acquire old hulks often seek out Wayne Mocksfield. "If you put together the parts of three boats that Wayne has restored for me, you'd have a total restoration," says Bob Rice of Somerville, New Jersey, who is president of the Lake Hopatcong chapter of the Antique and Classic Boat Society. "He can do everything from basic restoration to finishing varnish. I marvel at the way he turns a candidate for the fireplace into a boat that is better than the day it came from the factory."

When Mitchell Shivers of Westfield, New Jersey, bought his 1947 twenty-two-foot Chris-Craft Sportsman (the Golden Pond boat) from Mocksfield, Shivers remembers, "it had been deteriorating for years and was in derelict condition." The two men got the boat's records from the Chris-Craft archives (interestingly, its hull is cedar because mahogany was in short supply after World War II), and Mocksfield set to work replacing parts, restoring the engine, remaking the gauges, and sanding the hull and mahogany decks. "There's a mystique to working fine wood," says Shivers, "that can't be reproduced on a computer. When Wayne finished, *Spray* took best in class in a boat show."

Typical problems that Mocksfield faces in his restorations are gashes in wood that mar the finish and dry rot in planks, missing parts (he has a stockpile of used parts), broken engines, and ruined upholstery. One of his pet peeves is what he calls a mud job—when an owner attempting restoration applies too much stain, blotting out the texture of the wood grain. "We make sure to apply only enough stain to darken the wood while letting the grain show through," he explains.

Special talents are needed to restore woodies if the job is to be done right—or at all, continues Mocksfield. He points to a Chris-Craft docked in front of the marina, explaining that a longtime customer hoped to restore it himself but gave up after stripping one side of the hull, daunted by the weeks of sanding, staining, and applying ten coasts of varnish still to come. "To refinish an average seventeen-foot runabout can take as long as two hundred hours," Mocksfield says, "and the work is very monotonous. Sanding a boat takes days. When you stand there minute after minute, hour after hour, with a piece of sandpaper in your hand or a machine buzzing in your ears, you understand that this is not a job for just anyone.

"Restoring these boats takes many different skills," he adds. "You have to have a talent for working with your hands, and you have to be a jack of all trades. You've got the finish, upholstery, and mechanical work with the engine and the drive train. I've always loved this type of work—and at the end of a job, I have a work of art."

How much does all that work cost? "Owning and restoring antique runabouts is an expensive hobby," Mocksfield admits, adding that rechroming alone can cost from $800 to $3,500 and that a total reconditioning can cost as much as $40,000. Prices depend on size and condition.

Although Mocksfield's restoration expertise will undoubtedly continue to be in demand, he has some ideas of his own. "I used to live on the other side of the lake and look over here at the marina, wishing I owned it," he recalls. "These days, though, I'm ready to relax a little and not necessarily be here seven days a week. Although I've restored lots of boats, I've never actually built one." He adds with a gleam in his eye, "I've always wanted to build a runabout."

Americana, 1990

THE EVER-GREAT *GATSBY*

Gatsby is a thirty-five-ton, sixty-foot commuter yacht built by Consolidated Shipbuilding Corporation. A classic now owned by John and Audrey Callahan of Westfield, New Jersey, her story begins in the spring of 1929.

It was a boisterous and prosperous time marked by speakeasies and flappers. The slogan, "A chicken in every pot and a car in every garage" symbolized America's view of its future. No one could have imagined the calamity to come on Thursday, October 24, when the stock market crashed and irrevocably changed the American way of life. It was during these times that the commuter yacht came of age, and Mr. Fulton, a millionaire manufacturer of plumbing fixtures, fancied he'd give one to his wife for her birthday that fateful year.

Characterized by sleek lines, plumb bows, narrow beams, a plethora of teak or mahogany brightwork, and the ability to cruise at speeds in excess of twenty knots, commuter yachts were popular among wealthy businessmen. Stock market millionaires who owned estates far from the frenetic pace of Manhattan would commute by boat to a dock near Wall Street.

Mr. Fulton had no need to commute to Wall Street, but knew his wife loved cruising and a commuter yacht seemed best suited to her tastes. The Fultons laid the boat out for day trips rather than for long stays aboard. This gave *Gatsby*, which the Fultons named *June XVI* after Mrs. Fulton's birth date, a one-of-a-kind arrangement unusual for a commuter yacht.

Gatsby's forecastle was for the crew (who were only allowed to enter through a fore hatch, not through the main saloon). It now has four comfortable bunks, a galley, head, and the original icebox which has been electrified.

Abaft the forecastle is the main saloon, which is also the wheelhouse. The teak console is in the forward section of the plushly carpeted room which has the custom-made windows characteristic of Consolidated's luxury yachts. There are also two original pull-down bunks and a dining set.

Step down five stairs and you enter the master stateroom. This has a three quarters and a twin-size berth, a walk-in dressing room, and a writing desk. Beyond the stateroom is a ten-foot by twelve-foot deck. It could have been closed in and used as a cabin, but Mrs. Fulton liked the air and opted to leave it open. It was her favorite place on the boat. The original twelve-foot upholstered seat is still in mint condition as are the four rattan chairs with thick goose-down pillows.

"Mrs. Fulton used to stroll straight down the catwalk to the aft deck. She'd settle on the sofa, and when she was ready to go, she'd press a mother-of-pearl call button located on the floor in front of the sofa to let the captain know it was time to leave," says Nelson Hartranft, who bought the boat in 1968. "I thought that was pretty neat, so I left the button there when I had the boat modernized."

When the Depression came, the way of life that gave rise to commuter yachts was gone forever. Many were scrapped, converted to work boats or left to slowly rot. Fortunately, even in hard times people need plumbing fixtures, and the Fultons continued to live in luxury with *Gatsby* an integral part of their lives until Mrs. Fulton grew ill in the early 1960s.

"At that time, the boat hadn't been used much for a few years and it needed cosmetic repairs as well as modernization," Hartranft recalls. Mrs. Fulton wanted the work done but her son-in-law, who was taking care of such matters, apparently didn't want to spend any of the family fortune on the boat and dragged his feet until Mrs. Fulton died with her wish ungranted. The boat went up for sale.

To Mrs. Fulton's daughter, the boat was a tangible icon of her happy childhood. Selling it was traumatic.

"This was the boat the whole family grew up on. She wasn't going to sell to just any Tom, Dick or Harry who came along," Hartranft says. "She told the broker if she couldn't find the right buyer, she was going to take the boat out in the middle of Long Island Sound and scuttle her. She'd have sooner seen it sunk than allowed to rot away."

After months of negotiating, Hartranft convinced her he was the right buyer and in December of 1968 they came to terms. "I bought myself a beautiful Christmas present," Hartranft says with a laugh.

Over the next five years, Hartranft gradually modernized the boat—rechristened *Hart's Desire*. He had her wired for electricity, installed a shower, a water heater, an electric stove, and permanent bunks. Ultimately, though, he had to sell *Gatsby* because she was too big to handle alone.

Like the Hartranfts in 1968, the Callahans in 1973 were looking for a boat they could stay aboard in their familiar cruising grounds of Barnegat Bay, New Jersey. They admired the sleek lines, the teak, the fine details—such as the cabinets in the main saloon which were built to hold long-stemmed crystal and lined for silver place settings, the call buttons throughout the boat, and of course, the aft deck.

The Callahans haven't yet cruised extensively with *Gatsby* due to time constraints, but they hope to when time permits. (Several years after this article was published, they took *Gatsby* to Florida.) In the meantime, they take sunset cruises on the Metedeconk River, and often throw quiet black-tie dinners for four in the main saloon.

"Enjoying cocktails with friends or reading on the aft deck is one of the greatest pleasures of the boat," Audrey Callahan says. "The atmosphere is bucolic yet civilized."

But nothing comes easy. The Callahans do most of the maintenance on the teak themselves, which they say is time-consuming and costly. For the second time in sixteen years, they are completely stripping and refinishing it. And this year they will pay professionals to haul *Gatsby* to check the double-planked cedar on oak hull for rot and to repaint it. "You have to love a boat to do this," says Audrey, "but it's worth it. The boat deserves to be preserved."

The Callahans, like the Hartranfts and Fultons before them, have grown to think of *Gatsby* as a member of the family. "She's an heirloom," John says. "She'll stay in the family a long, long time."

Why *Gatsby*? An acquaintance who is an avid collector of classic cars pulled up to the dock in a 1928 Packard shortly after they bought the yacht. "He was fascinated with the boat," Audrey explains. "He came aboard and was quite taken. He observed that, like his Packard, the boat reflected the opulence depicted so well in F. Scott Fitzgerald's

Figure 7. View of the replica of the Mayflower docked in Plymouth Harbor, Massachusetts. PHOTO BY DAVID W. SHAW.

novel, *The Great Gatsby*. Then, in a burst of enthusiasm, he said, 'The only name for this boat is Gatsby!' We thought so, too."

'38 SKIDOO
The infamous hurricane of 1938 hit Long Island Sound and southern New England without warning in September, killing 600, injuring 1,754, and causing more than $300 million in property damage. The storm's eye moved at more than fifty knots, and the highest recorded wind velocity reached 183 knots. That was enough to heave boats well inland.

Only quick thinking on the part of Mr. Fulton saved *Gatsby* from certain destruction at her slip. As the storm struck, Fulton had the boat scuttled so that she would be safe beneath the raging storm surge. Afterwards, she was salvaged.

The sinking meant that *Gatsby*'s original power plants (twin six cylinder, 200–horsepower Speedways) had to be replaced by a pair of Chrysler 225–horsepower marinized truck engines.

Power and Motoryacht, 1990

SPY SPARKS A-CATS REVIVAL

When Roy Wilkins of Island Heights, New Jersey, bought a leaky A-Cat named *Spy* in 1978, he didn't know he'd spark an A-Cat restoration movement four years later. But that's what happened.

Steeped in history as rich as the businessmen who owned them in the days of flappers and Prohibition, the remaining four original A-Cats, *Mary Ann*, *Spy*, *Lotus*, and *Bat* are among the most well-known vintage racing boats on Barnegat Bay. These beamy, twenty-eight-foot, Marconi-rigged catboats carry 605 square feet of sail, double that of auxiliaries of comparable length, on a forty-three-foot mast and a twenty-eight-foot boom. They cut an unmistakable profile under sail.

At the time Wilkins bought *Spy*, *Bat* and *Mary Ann* leaked as much as his boat. *Lotus* had been severely damaged, and had sunk. It was hauled from the bottom of Toms River and left to rot outside at David Beaton & Sons boatyard in Mantoloking.

Ultimately, Wilkins' zeal for the restoration of *Spy* infected the right people. The owners of *Bat* and *Mary Ann*, not to be outdone by Wilkins, followed suit and restored their craft. Wilkins' best friend, real estate executive Steve Brick of Medford, got involved with the restoration of *Spy*. He subsequently bought *Lotus* and restored it.

A longtime A-Cat lover, Pennsylvania businessman Nelson Hartranft, saw the growing interest in the boats and commissioned construction of *Wasp*, the first A-Cat to be built in fifty-seven years. Built by craftsmen at Beaton's boatyard, *Wasp* cost about $65,000. A second new A-Cat is under construction at the Philadelphia Museum and should be launched within two years.

In 1988, for the first time in four decades, five A-Cats competed in races at Barnegat Bay: the restored *Spy*, *Mary Ann*, *Bat*, and *Lotus*, as well as the new *Wasp*. In 1982, the notion of five, sound A-Cats competing in races would have seemed ridiculous. Wilkins recalled a favorite anecdote to make the point.

"We used to go out racing with two electric Rule 1000 pumps capable of pumping 2,000 gallons per hour through the centerboard well. One time during a race, the batteries powering the pumps died. *Spy* immediately sank at the mouth of Forked River."

Wilkins told this story with a smile.

Wilkins may have been accustomed to *Spy*'s submarine act, but by 1982 he realized it couldn't continue. The huge rig set so far forward had for six decades tended to push the mast through the hull. The A-Cats were built strictly for racing, not longevity. In reality, it's a tribute to A-Cat owners through the years that all the boats didn't deteriorate into rotted hulks.

"The A-Cats were built as throwaways, just like the 12 Meter boats," Wilkins said. "There was that kind of progression. As better designs came up, the owners would throw the old boat away and build a new one."

After consulting with craftsmen at Beaton's boatyard, Wilkins realized the prognosis for *Spy* was bad. To save it would mean tearing it apart and rebuilding it from scratch. "It was either throw fifty-eight years of history away or make the commitment to restore the *Spy*," Wilkins said.

Wilkins is patient, competitive, and highly motivated. These personality traits carry over to his profession, teaching adaptive physical education for handicapped children. They also proved invaluable in realizing his goal of restoring *Spy*.

Despite a lack of funds and woodworking know-how, Wilkins chose to keep *Spy* and restore it. He rounded up two financial partners, Jim Reynolds and Richard Fruff, and made a deal with them. If they'd bankroll the restoration, he'd do as much of the work as he could, and in return, they'd each have a third interest in *Spy*.

"We hauled her out at Beaton's in the fall of 1982. We worked on her all that winter. She sat out the season of '83, and by 1984 she was ready.

"I worked an average of thirty hours a week on her during each of those winters. It was either see my family or restore the *Spy*. The choice seemed obvious," Wilkins said, again with a smile.

Wilkins, along with his close friends and with help from Tom Beaton and other craftsmen, rebuilt 75 percent of *Spy*. It was a job well done. "One of the men who used to own the *Spy* in the forties said it looks better than he's ever seen it," Wilkins said.

Spy was restored with three types of mahogany: Amazon, Philippine, and Honduran. Its planking is New Jersey white cedar on oak frame, with spruce spars and yellow pine decks with the original canvas covering. The cockpit is plywood with canvas.

There are twenty-five ribs and more than 2,000 bronze fasteners, each of which had to be capped by hand with wooden plugs. "If you don't line up the grain of the plug with the plank, they expand and split the wood. You wouldn't believe the amount of time it takes," Wilkins said.

Wilkins pointed to a beautifully carved knee at the transom. "You see that knee. That's handmade. No machine could do it. It took half a day just to do that. Nearly every fitting aboard is handmade and one-of-a-kind. We used very few power tools because they just couldn't do the job right."

After the work came the play. Wilkins takes family and friends sailing, and races *Spy* every chance he gets. In fact, he is the proud winner of the 1988 Toms River Challenge Cup, a race especially for A-Cats.

"The *Spy*'s not a light air boat. If I come out in light winds, I know I've got to be ready for some very skillful sailing. In winds over twenty knots, she's a rocketship," Wilkins said. "With a maximum hull speed of eight knots, we can usually sail circles around any boat under forty feet which drags a propeller."

© *Reprinted with permission from Soundings Publications, LLC, 1989*

THE FAIR *EAST WIND*

David and Dr. Frank Zindel have had a six-decade love affair with wooden sailboats and Barnegat Bay, New Jersey. They are among the few sailors on the bay who own rare wooden sailboats from the 1920s.

Last year marked the silver anniversary of their purchase in 1963 of *East Wind*, a one-of-a-kind, gaff-rigged sloop designed specifically for cruising in the bay's shoal waters.

As with their counterparts in the rare wooden sailboat racing community, the Zindels believe it's important to preserve the craft that illustrate a bygone era in Barnegat Bay's history. They also are willing to do arduous routine maintenance and restorative work to keep the vessel sound.

"It's a big job getting the boat ready for the beginning and the end of the sailing season," said Frank Zindel, sixty-eight. "In the spring, sometimes I wish it would rain on weekends so I could get my office work done. The boat always takes priority over my other work."

The Zindels' work isn't over when snowstorms buffet *East Wind* in the slip at Cedar Creek Marina. Once a month throughout the winter, David Zindel of Ocean City, New Jersey, or Frank Zindel of Oreland, Pennsylvania, go to the marina to check the boat's automatic bilge pump, which keeps pace with minor water seepage.

"People admire the *East Wind* when they see her at the slip or under sail, but not very many are willing to do the work to keep a boat like her," said David Zindel, sixty-six.

Built in 1928 at the request of a wealthy businessman who summered on the bay, *East Wind* is the only one left of its kind. Originally, a Manhattan-based naval architect designed four centerboard boats named for the four winds. *South* and *North Winds* were yawls, and *East* and *West* were sloops.

The whereabouts of the two yawls is unknown. *West Wind* burned in a boatyard fire years ago. "The loss of the *West Wind* was tragic, like losing a piece of history forever," David Zindel said.

East Wind hails from days when sailors wore brass-buttoned blue blazers, white ducks and shirts, and thin black ties. To board the boat is like stepping back in time. There isn't a winch or a metal cleat aboard. All heavy work, from the mainsheet to the running backstays, is done with the original mahogany blocks and synthetic running rigging. Its standing rigging is quarter-inch stainless steel telephone pole cables. The dacron mainsail runs up the mast with hoops, not on a track as with modern sailboats.

Down below is a mammoth centerboard well set amidship in the mahogany-trimmed cabin, which is big enough to sleep four people. Antique oil lamps hang on gimbles.

East Wind is twenty-eight feet from bow to stern, and has an eight-foot beam. Although its cedar planks and oak frame weigh as much as a midsize car, its narrow beam makes it tender in breezes stronger than fifteen knots, despite the boat's six-foot draft with the centerboard down. It draws two and a half feet with the centerboard up.

In 1953, *East Wind* became an auxiliary when it was equipped with a Gray Marine Sea Scout, four cylinder, twenty-five-horsepower gasoline engine. Last summer, the engine was rebuilt. A weathered bronze gearshift protrudes from the cockpit floor near the tiny mahogany wheel.

"She's as sound as the day she was built. If you use a boat as much as we do, you'll know if problems develop," Frank Zindel said. "We haul it every other year to clean and paint the bottom. It'll come out of the water on a Thursday, and we hustle like crazy to do the work and get it back into the water by Monday. It's a tough job."

As a result of the Zindels' efforts, *East Wind* has been problem free, with the exception of minor dry rot, loose fittings, and seepage near the centerboard well.

East Wind has brought joy into the Zindels' lives for more than twenty-five years. But just as times have changed, so have the brothers' needs. David Zindel has suffered medical problems which have made it difficult for him to work on *East Wind*.

"A couple of years ago, we never would have considered selling her," David Zindel said. "But we're getting on in years, and we're ready to buy a smaller wooden boat which is easier for both of us to maintain."

The Zindels worry that when they eventually sell *East Wind*, the new owner will not have the commitment to cherish and preserve the boat. "We're going to be very particular about who buys her," David Zindel said.

© *Reprinted with permission from Soundings Publications, LLC, 1989*

Figure 8. Sailboat in the waters of the St. Lawrence River among Thousand Islands. PHOTO BY DAVID W. SHAW.

TALE OF THE *FOX*

On a foggy morning this August, *Fox* once again put to sea. The *Fox* isn't a sleek motoryacht or a sailboat. It's a rowboat just over eighteen feet long. But the *Fox* is steeped in history, which goes back to a historic moment in small boat voyaging, and extends through a century to an eventful day just months ago.

The story begins back in 1896 when a wealthy newspaper publisher, Richard Fox, put up a $10,000 prize for the first person or persons to cross the Atlantic in a rowboat. No rudder, motor, or sails could be used.

Frank Samuelsen and George Harbo, two clammers from the Atlantic Highlands, decided to give it a try. They admired the sea-keeping abilities of the famed Sea Bright Beach skiff, designed and built locally by the Seaman family. It was a round-bottomed, clinker-built craft used by fishermen off the beaches just south of Sandy Hook.

It was well known as a fast, seaworthy little craft capable of being launched or landed through heavy surf. Today's lifeboats share some of the same design features. Samuelsen and Harbo worked out a deal with William Seaman, the boatbuilder operating the business at the time, to construct a skiff based on a modified design thought more suitable for the transatlantic passage. The design shares most of the characteristics of a Sea Bright Beach skiff, except the transom was removed, making it a double-ender. It also included watertight compartments forward and aft, and special handrails mounted on the bottom that would enable the crew to right the boat in case of capsize. It's a good thing they added the handles. During a storm off England, they needed them to right the boat after it capsized.

Working along with William was his son, Harold, age thirteen. Together, they built the *Fox* in their shop at Branchport. At the time, the builder couldn't have known his craft would make history, and that seventy-nine years later Harold would play a major role in keeping the story of the *Fox* alive.

Samuelsen and Harbo set off on June 6, 1896. Sixty-two days later, after rowing 3,250 miles, they reached Le Havre, France. They endured storms, exhaustion, and may have been stalked by a giant shark. In the end they won a place in history and the *Guinness Book of World Records* as the first adventurers to successfully row across the Atlantic. They also won the ten grand, which in our vastly smaller dollars today amounts to approximately $500,000.

On their way back from Europe aboard a steamer, with the *Fox*, Samuelsen and Harbo saw just how lucky they'd been. Storms far more fierce than those they'd experienced on the row battered the ship, which finally ran out of coal about 250 miles off Sandy Hook. The captain wanted to burn the *Fox* for fuel, but instead Samuelsen and Harbo rowed off, evidently in a storm, to get help ashore.

Rescuers came, and that's about the last exciting thing to happen with the *Fox* for nearly the next eighty years. Over the decades, the boat was lost; no one knows what happened to it.

Also over the years, Harold Seaman grew up and kept messing about in boats. He was a charter member of the Long Branch Ice Boat and Yacht Club, founded in 1901. Known and loved by members, he went by the nickname, "Pappy."

The impetus behind what happened next is unclear. But in 1975 members of the club decided to build a replica of the *Fox*. Perhaps it was Pappy's direct link to the original craft that made it seem like a good idea. Pappy was ninety-two at the time, and no one but him knew all the fine details that went into making *Fox* such a special boat.

Donald Godshall, who was and still is a skilled boatbuilder, with Pappy looking over his shoulder, worked with about twenty members of the club on nights and weekends to build the new *Fox*. They followed the original blueprints and used cedar and oak, plus copper rivets, just like the original. The only modern material was an occasional dab of epoxy.

Frank Samuelsen's great-granddaughters, Laurie, Nancy, Mary, and Sharon, christened the boat when it was launched at the club in May 1975. As it rested at the dock, a huge forty-six-star American flag flew from a tall pole in the stern, just like the original one carried across the Atlantic. It was as if a link had been formed with 1896.

In July, members of the club rowed *Fox* 130 miles from Long Branch to Mystic Seaport. They left on Friday and arrived Tuesday morning, July 8, after rowing an average of forty-two miles a day.

The following year, the *Fox* made an appearance at the Jersey Coast Boat Show held in Asbury Park in February. It spent time back at Mystic Seaport on display, and for the last eight years it's been on display at the Twin Lights of Navesink Museum.

But, on the one hundredth anniversary of the historic crossing, it just didn't seem right to leave the *Fox* in dry dock. The Long Branch Ice Boat and Yacht Club retains ownership of *Fox*, so members made arrangements to retrieve the boat and make it ready for a celebratory voyage from the Shrewsbury River to the Statue of Liberty.

Even after so many years out of the water, the *Fox* remained sound, requiring only minor caulking and a paint job. On August 3, with the help of about seventy club members and supporters of the event, the

Fox put to sea. In addition to celebrating the crossing, the row would raise money for Ronald McDonald House in Long Branch.

Through thick fog and a foul tide, chase vessels shuttled fourteen two-person crews to the boat for their turns at the oars. Struggling against the tide wiped out seven crews in a matter of miles. Chase boats brought in fresh reinforcements, and they pushed doggedly on.

Off the Verrazano Bridge, five-foot rollers piled up against an ebb tide. A slow, steady rain fell. Joe Gervolino, one of the oarsmen, recalled what it was like.

"We were out in the shipping lanes, fog was moving in, it was rainy and choppy. It really gave you a taste of what even a good day must have been like for Samuelsen and Harbo. It was quite impressive out there."

The exhausted crews never made it to the Statue of Liberty, though they did raise $1,000 for Ronald McDonald House. Thick fog swept in and the ebb tide would run for hours. Continuing would have risked crew safety.

The *Fox* still resides at the yacht club, where members can enjoy it. It will go back to the museum, eventually, so thousands can admire its lines and hear the tale of the *Fox*.

Offshore, 1996

Life on the Waterfront

For most of us, life along the waterfront is something we can only glimpse. We travel to the shore for a day at the beach, a stroll on the boardwalk, or dinner at a seaside restaurant. Even the boaters, at least most of them, anyway, venture to the shore when time permits, and there's precious little of it. The majority of the days and weeks are spent away from the water in the heart of suburbia or in the big cities where money can be made to pay the mortgage and the grocery bill, and to put the kids through college. And to pay for the boat.

Walk down the docks at the marinas even at the height of summer and you'll see row after row of boats locked up and snugged down. If you ask around you'll find out that most boats just sit, hardly ever leave the slip except on the weekends, and often not even then. The lucky few who live near the shore and own boats, or those with the time to stay for extended periods aboard are in the definite minority. However, everyone who takes to the waters becomes a part of life there, if only for a short while, and that time brings out the essence of why we try to spend as much of our lives in tune with all it has to offer, good and bad.

Sometimes, though, the crowds seem overwhelming, as so many converge at once to taste the joys of the water, and, sometimes, the sheer numbers detract from the experience. There are traffic jams, speeders, drunks, natural and man-made hazards, accidents. These unpleasant things remind us that no place is perfect. The water is certainly no exception. But, like life in general, happiness can be found in the acceptance of the imperfections and the working around that which we can't readily change.

The less savory aspects are also tempered by the positive; the sunset admired while at anchor; the meeting of another boater from a different part of the coast, and the sharing that almost always comes about. The good and the bad, it's all a part of the experience.

The stories you'll find in this chapter will take you to life on the waterfront with a much less romantic view than many might suppose would be worthy of mention. For boaters, the stories will ring of truth, and for nonboaters, they might even come as a surprise. But to really see the waterfront, its good and less positive faces, provides more than a glimpse into what shapes boats and boating in the Northeast.

BEATING THE TRAFFIC

Jack Roland and Charlie Murphy have solved the weekend traffic problem on New Jersey's Barnegat Bay. They go boating on weekdays or at twilight on weekends.

"It's hectic on the weekend, really hectic. You've got to be constantly on the alert for other boats," said Roland of Franklin Township, New Jersey. He and his wife, Natilie, sail a twenty-seven-foot Catalina.

Murphy and his wife, Mary Jo, from Morgan, New Jersey, like to take their twenty-seven-foot Hunter on the bay late Saturday afternoon and sail until twilight, when most boaters return to the dock.

Roland and Murphy are part of a minority of boaters in the Barnegat Bay area who regularly avoid traffic jams and overcrowded waterways by boating at off-hours. These boaters include seasonal workers with winter vocations and those who can work flexible hours. They can experience the bay in quiet isolation with nothing around them but empty expanses of water and flat stretches of shoreline. Roland is chairman of the science department of the elementary and secondary schools in the District of Union, and Murphy was, until he retired this year, a principal of a school in the same district.

"There's no strain on you when you sail here during the week because there's no one to dodge," said Roland. "You can sail in peace and quiet, and leave the pressures of life behind. It's a private bay."

According to Diane Moller, a supervisor of the Forked River State Marina, many people who live in the area seldom venture out onto the bay on weekends. "It's nuts here on the weekends," she said. "Everybody's in a rush to go nowhere."

Roland and Murphy can understand why weekend boating is appealing. "The attraction of Barnegat Bay on the weekends is the wider circle of friends available to rendezvous with on the water," Murphy said. Both Roland and Murphy said weekends are social times. Rafting together at popular anchorages, such as Tices Shoal, is fun.

Although most boaters cannot take time off from work to go boating at Barnegat Bay during the week, Murphy pointed out that sailing there at night on weekends is as pleasant as sailing on weekdays. "Even on the weekends, night sailing on the bay is terrific," Murphy said.

The Murphys like to anchor at Tices Shoal in the southern part of the bay close to the inlet to the ocean. There, they enjoy quiet dinners and picturesque sunsets over the mainland.

Marina supervisor Moller has also gone night sailing on Barnegat Bay. "At night, there's no one on the water. There's no noise. You won't see much, but if you're out there alone, it puts you in a nice mood," she said.

Both Murphy and Moller said that anyone who is familiar with Barnegat Bay can sail safely there at night. They don't advise newcomers to try it, though.

"Once you are familiar with the bay, you really don't have to worry about running aground day or night," said Murphy.

© *Reprinted with permission from Soundings Publications, LLC, 1988*

MARINE POLICE UNDERCOVER

Consider the following scenario. It might make you feel better as you navigate through New Jersey's waterways on weekends when it seems as if all the state's 190,000 registered boats are in the channel with you.

It's a busy Saturday afternoon in July on Toms River and hundreds of boaters are out. Most of them obey boating laws and heed common-sense safety rules, but one skipper thunders along, trailing a huge wake astern. He and his buddies are drinking beer. The skipper thinks it might be fun to play chicken with a sailboat headed out into Barnegat Bay, who he thinks is coming too close. First he cuts across its bow, then circles it twice. The family aboard the sailboat hangs on for dear life as their vessel rocks and rolls.

Onshore, a fellow sits on a dock with a fishing rod and a pail. He's wearing Bermuda shorts and a muscle T-shirt. Witnessing the reckless boating incident, he pulls out a handheld radio hidden in the pail. Meanwhile, the guys cool down. They slow the boat and idle out of the channel.

A few minutes later a marine police boat pulls up. The skipper thinks he got away with his horseplay and asks what the cops want. They tell him. He's cited for reckless boating, speeding in a no-wake zone, and since he is legally drunk they arrest him for boating while intoxicated.

Undercover cops ready to bust unsuspecting violators isn't what most people think of when they think of marine police. They're usually much more visible—too visible, in fact. Their boats stand out in a crowd, and that can cause problems.

"We'd get calls about violations, but the subjects could see us coming two miles away. They'd just take off and we had no way to witness the violations," said Sergeant Erich Herkloz, commanding officer of the marine police station in Point Pleasant. Effective enforcement on the water boils down to catching the violator red-handed, and that's not always easy. Posting a cop ashore in civvies has proved effective; they've dressed as fishermen, crabbers, or sun worshippers on the beach.

"Are we too aggressive? I don't think so," said Lieutenant Albert Dempster, assistant bureau chief of the New Jersey State Police Marine Law Enforcement Bureau in West Trenton. Boaters who have had a run-in with the marine police probably wouldn't agree with him. But boaters who've had run-ins with drunk, speeding, or inept skippers would probably praise the cops.

Marine police are a mere handful, compared to the number of boats they have to watch over. Only 132 cops from nine stations, with seventy-two boats, cover the huge Jersey shoreline.

Dempster says it's likely that the $8.6 million annual budget for marine law enforcement may be cut as New Jersey continues to tighten its budgetary belt. Tight budgets mean no new officers have been hired since 1989, and Dempster doesn't see any new hires in the near future, even as boating traffic continues to increase.

Since 1989 more than 40,000 additional boats have been registered, bringing the number to 190,000. "We expect to see more traffic than ever this year," Dempster said. "PWCs (personal watercraft) are particularly popular now, and they're competing for space in already crowded waters."

In 1995, eight people died in boating mishaps in New Jersey, down from twelve the previous year. Likewise, injuries dropped from 185 in 1994 to 145 last year. The bad news is the number of reported accidents increased from 279 to 352. Coast Guard officials confirmed that 1995 was a busy year for accidents.

At the end of last summer's heat wave in July, eleven accidents involving injuries occurred in northern Barnegat Bay alone. Sergeant Herkloz said on summer weekends his station receives an average of thirty calls per shift, usually complaints about speeding boats and damaging wakes.

In New Jersey, boat registrations are way up. Accidents are up. The number of marine cops is the same, but some tactics are changing. That guy clamming may be doing another job.

Offshore, 1996

NEW JERSEY ANGLER TAKES COURSE JUST IN CASE

Len Arnold wasn't typical of the students registered for a basic seamanship class sponsored by the U.S. Power Squadron (USPS) of

Watchung, New Jersey. Arnold didn't own a boat, and he had no plans to buy one in the future. His interest in recreational boating amounted to going fishing with a friend, Harry Macher. Together, they take Macher's twenty-one-foot Bayliner Capri powerboat to fish for fluke and flounder off the coast of Wildwood, New Jersey.

Arnold took the USPS course because he wanted to know how to handle a boat in case his friend's health failed while at sea. Before Arnold took the course, he didn't know an anchor rode from an asphalt road or a red nun from a flying nun. Now Arnold knows enough about basic seamanship to feel confident that he could maneuver the boat back to the dock if something happened to Macher.

Arnold, sixty, said there was a danger that Macher could become seriously ill while they were out fishing. In his late sixties, Macher is overweight and suffers from emphysema. Without a working knowledge of how to operate the boat, of navigational markers, coastal piloting or the rules of the road, Arnold feared for his friend's life in the event of a medical emergency.

"He could have died out there with me helpless to save him," Arnold said.

For Arnold, taking the course gave him the confidence he needed to get the maximum enjoyment out of the fishing trips he takes with his friend. When they're on the water, the two men like silence as well as conversation. "We're out there each lost in our own thoughts, each enjoying the boat bobbing around—the freedom of it," Arnold said.

Both men worked most of their lives in accounting careers, and they are both the treasurers of the condominium complexes in which they reside. More often than not, they talk numbers between the lulls in the conversation. "We're probably the only guys out there talking about accounting," he said.

Arnold and Macher may like to mix shoptalk with fishing but they refrain from mixing another of their delights—bourbon.

"Harry has a standard rule. No booze on the boat," Arnold said, adding that Macher doesn't allow drinking alcoholic beverages at dockside, either. Macher took a class in basic seamanship sponsored by the Coast Guard and learned that the majority of boating accidents are caused by or connected with alcohol.

Arnold strongly believes in taking a course in basic seamanship sponsored by either the Coast Guard or the USPS. "Some people go out on the ocean like it was acres of pasture and there's no one else out there but them. That's just not true," he said. "I think the most important thing to know is how to avoid collisions with other boats—knowing who has the right of way."

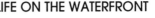

Even though Arnold now knows who has the right of way, he said he still feels apprehension about other boaters. "Now I look at the guy driving a boat and wonder if he's operating the boat because he has the money to buy it or because he has the knowledge to run it safely."
© *Reprinted with permission from Soundings Publications, LLC, 1988*

Note on the right of way issue:
Many boaters still believe there is a given right of way for particular recreational vessels, such as those engaged in fishing or those under sail. Technically speaking, based on a revision of the old rules of the road, no recreational boat operating on coastal waters has a right of way over the other. Both skippers are responsible for operating their boats in a safe manner, which means giving way even if the rules of the road say you're in the right. Recreational boats, of course, must give way to large commercial vessels in restricted channels, or elsewhere. Here you have a case where the right of way issue meets with common sense. Too often, though, skippers operating recreational craft push the limits of common sense under the mistaken impression that they have a "right of way" over another boat; they don't.

NEW JERSEY'S URBAN WATERFRONT

Barrier islands, bays, marshes, and piney mainland shores are what you'll see along most of the New Jersey coast. But one spot defies the norm—the waters of northeastern New Jersey.

Separated from the waters to the south by an island of industry, the urban waterfront lines one of the nation's busiest ports. It's an all-business sort of place, generating more than $20 billion in annual economic activity and more than 200,000 jobs.

But all business? Not quite. A fleet of approximately 1,500 recreational boats is berthed at the marinas along the Jersey side of the Hudson River, and every year more than 3,000 transients stop to enjoy the boating amenities.

Most of these facilities are relatively new, born out of a decade-long effort to clean up and revitalize New Jersey's urban shore. It's the latest chapter in the long history of an old American port.

The Newport complex in Jersey City was built as part of a $10 billion revitalization program to foster economic development. It's a sprawling development complete with luxury apartment and condo high rises, health spas, sports facilities, and Newport Mall. It also includes Newport Marina, which opened in 1989 and provides 180 slips.

Upriver in Weehawken, Port Imperial Marina also opened for business in the late 1980s with 300 slips. Both Newport Marina and Port

Figure 9. Aerial view of the state marina at Forked River, New Jersey. PHOTO BY
KEITH HAMILTON, STUDIO-9, WARETOWN, NEW JERSEY.

Imperial offer easy access to Manhattan by Path train and ferry, respectively. This is a big attraction for transients traveling through the
area who want to see the sights in the Big Apple.

Of course, not every old pier has been blasted into oblivion. Not
all the abandoned buildings, reminiscent of the London Blitz, have
been razed. Yet, progress has been made. More marinas means more
access to the urban reaches of the Hudson River for recreational
boaters.

The beauty along this stretch of New Jersey comes in both the natural and man-made varieties. The skyscrapers, the Moorish architecture of Ellis Island, Lady Liberty as she stands watch over the harbor,
and even the ships are beautiful in their own way. For ten miles above
the George Washington Bridge, the natural beauty of the Palisades,
forever preserved as parkland, enhances the beauty of the river as it
begins to widen into the Tappan Zee.

In Jersey City, just minutes from the Battery, you can find one of
the state's prettiest urban anchorages. It's a place with a unique history, a place where the present mingles with the past at the old Morris Canal basin, just north of Liberty State Park, right across from the
Battery.

You'll have to look back to 1819 to find the origins of the Morris Canal. That was the year anthracite coal gained recognition as an alternative to wood for heating purposes. Soon mines in Pennsylvania's Lehigh Valley began turning out tons of the stuff, but there was one tiny problem—how to get the coal to urban centers where demand was great.

During this time, America was crazy about canals. Many were built up and down the Northeastern coast, connecting river systems and lakes to create a waterborne highway. The Erie Canal holds a special place in New Jersey history. It was a coal artery which fed New Jersey iron foundries and other industries.

The 102–mile route from Phillipsburg to the head of Newark Bay led through the glacial hills of New Jersey's highlands, giving the waterway a meandering path. The total rise to Lake Hopatcong, whose waters fed the canal system, was 914 feet above tidewater. About 300 locks would have been needed to lift and lower boats over the highlands—unthinkable, as anyone who's locked through knows; it would have taken forever to get anywhere.

Thanks to a very bright Englishman by the name of James Renwick only thirty-four locks were eventually required. Renwick accomplished the bulk of the work with twenty-three inclined planes. He created a series of low grades and built a marine railway system on top. He figured out how to use the weight of the down-going boats to help lift the up-going craft, and used a water turbine to give power.

The pretty anchorage in Jersey City might never have been, though, had the canal been built larger from the outset. It soon became congested after it opened in 1832, just like the Erie Canal, and its original dimensions had to be enlarged. As you sit and watch the sunset turn the windows of the Manhattan skyline to gold, and look south down the harbor at Ellis Island and the Statue of Liberty, the rarity of such an urban vantage point comes home.

Liberty Harbor Marina, located in the Morris Canal Basin, or Port Imperial—under three miles upriver—are convenient fuel stops for boats passing through. Slip rates at the marinas average around two dollars per foot. Reservations are a good idea on holidays or busy summer weekends.

On the Fourth of July, the marinas are packed with transients who come to see the fireworks. Although the firing location shifts every year, the marinas are seldom without a spectacular view of the display. For many boaters, the journey to Jersey City or Weehawken every summer marks the height of the season.

Offshore, 1996

SHIPS THAT GO BUMP IN THE NIGHT

When a Sandy Hook pilot, Captain Edward Britton, boarded the *Aegeo*, a 754–foot, Liberian-registered tanker laden with 18 million gallons of oil bound for the refineries in Woodbridge, he had no idea that the trip would make news. It turns out he was the first to be let in on a big surprise, one that's left commercial and recreational mariners scratching their heads in disbelief.

Britton boarded the ship at around 5:00 A.M. on Saturday, October 5, and proceeded toward New Jersey. At about 5:30, the master of the vessel came up to the bridge and said, "I've got major problems here."

"What, a bad voyage?" Britton asked.

"No," the captain said. "I just hit Ambrose."

Pilots don't hear that kind of thing every day. Sure, tugs and tows, and plenty of recreational boats, occasionally nick aids to navigation, but how do you hit one of the most prominent navigational aids in the world?

Located about seven miles off Sandy Hook, Ambrose Light Station stands 136 feet above sea level (or at least it did by press time) and its light is visible for twenty-five miles. It's pretty hard to miss; you can see it for miles.

Britton learned that the ship hit the tower at about 4:25 A.M.—before he had boarded to bring the ship down Sandy Hook channel into Raritan Bay. Naturally, he called the authorities to let them know about the mishap. The phone rang at Coast Guard Sandy Hook. First Petty Officer Mathew Giltner, the duty officer on watch at the time, took the call and for a moment he couldn't believe what he was hearing.

"We got a call from the pilot boat on station saying that one of the legs of the tower was missing. I called my executive officer and told him."

Unsure of the seemingly unbelievable statement the executive officer said, "You mean one of the lights is missing."

"No, sir. One of the legs has a big piece missing," Giltner said.

Like the pilots, the Coast Guard doesn't hear that kind of thing every day.

"We decided this was the call of the month," Giltner said.

Back on the ship, which was diverted to Stapleton anchorage off Staten Island to await the arrival of the investigating officer from the Coast Guard, the twisted rails and bulwarks of the ship's starboard side visible in the dim light of dawn revealed that this was no minor "nick." Later, investigators discovered two one-foot holes in the vessel's bow; no oil leaked out.

The impact knocked a fifteen-foot section out of a leg supporting the tower itself, according to Petty Officer Jeff Fenn, a Coast Guard spokesman. He described the damage as extensive, so extensive in fact that repair crews weren't allowed on the tower until a structural assessment was made to ensure crew safety. The accident extinguished the light, which wasn't relit until late the next afternoon.

"We're still concerned about the structural integrity of the tower," Fenn said. The Coast Guard has hired private contractors to assess the damage and make temporary emergency repairs. A similar incident in Buzzards Bay caused $2 million in damage to a major navigational aid. It is expected that Ambrose will cost at least that much to fix.

How did the accident happen and why didn't the master of the ship, whose name wasn't released, report it immediately? Fenn said that's under investigation. He also said Coast Guard Sandy Hook reported that the light was on the morning of the "allision." (An allision is the proper term to use when describing a floating object hitting a fixed object.)

The light may have been lit that morning. However, according to official Coast Guard records, Ambrose Light was out at least fifteen times from May to October due to equipment malfunctions. The light wasn't out for long intervals, no more than twelve hours at a time, Fenn said.

"Those navigation aids are what you look for. They're like road signs. It's kind of baffling that they hit it and that it wasn't reported until later," he said, adding that any damage to an ATON, whether it's caused by a commercial or recreational vessel, should be reported immediately.

Giltner said commercial "mashing" of navigational aids isn't very common, but he's aware of hundreds of incidents involving recreational boats. The boaters hit buoys, particularly in constricted waters such as the Shrewsbury River where the current runs very swiftly, knocking off the lights and solar panels.

"The recreational boaters often don't report the mishaps, which can cause problems," Giltner said.

Fenn encourages any recreational boater who has hit and damaged a buoy to report it. The Coast Guard won't make the boater pay for the damage. "The damage is seen as wear and tear," he said.

Captain Scott Vigar, owner of the *Freespool*, a charter fishing boat out of Atlantic Highlands, got a first-hand look at the tower while out fishing for striped bass shortly after the mishap. "The tower looked pretty damaged," he said.

Like many captains of the local fishing fleets in New Jersey and the South Shore of Long Island, Vigar found the incident scary. "You'd think they'd have picked up such a large object on radar and steered to avoid it. It really makes you wonder what the ship captains are doing out there. If that oil had spilled, it would have wiped out the fishery."

Fenn said the Coast Guard has lost many men working the lightships that once stood on station off New York Harbor. "Ships used to hit the lightships more often than you'd think. This is a modern example of an age-old problem."

Offshore, 1997

THAT DAMNED RAILROAD BRIDGE

Boaters in Barnegat Bay and along the Manasquan River are united in their hatred of a structure that dates back to 1880. It's the site of accidents which have sunk boats and seriously injured people. It's also not going away, despite the fact that mariners in this neck of New Jersey would do just about anything to make it disappear, short of heaving a few sticks of dynamite at it.

The object of loathing? The railroad bascule bridge that spans the Manasquan River. If you've ever tried to get through the forty-eight-foot-wide passage after the bridge has been closed to allow a train to pass over, you know why skippers in the area would just as soon see it vanish.

"When the bridge is down on a busy summer weekend, you'll have twenty to twenty-five boats backed up on either side of it," said Petty Officer Troy Loining of Coast Guard Station Manasquan. "When it opens everyone tries to go through at once. No one wants to wait."

In short, it's a free-for-all. Hapless skippers end up playing bumper boats.

Loining knows of at least six collisions that occurred in 1996, but he said many more probably occurred but weren't reported. Other incidents included boats losing power in the swift current and ending up wedged under the bridge. One man severely injured his leg when he tried to push off the pilings after his boat was swept into the bridge; he landed in the emergency room.

On most every weekend last summer, Loining said the station received at least fifteen to twenty complaints about inexperienced boaters failing to operate their boats in a safe manner at the bridge. The bridge is a major trouble spot, he said.

Now is it fair for boaters to hate the bridge? Shouldn't boaters who'd like to see it go away just learn how to navigate this tricky patch of water with prudence? Absolutely.

"I'll be trying to get my 100–foot party boat, with a thirty-six-foot beam, through that bridge with a screaming ebb tide behind me and almost every day some recreational boater coming from the other side will try to beat me through," said Tony Bogan, general manager of Bogan's Deep Sea Fishing Center in Brielle. He operates four party vessels that run the bridge gauntlet several times a day. "Don't they realize I can't stop? Don't they realize the boat going with the current has the right of way?"

Evidently, not enough boaters in this part of New Jersey know about the unwritten rule of the road: the boat going with the current has the right of way. On western rivers, inland rules of the road make this clear, but in coastal waters the issue isn't addressed. Yet, when it comes down to brass tacks, safe boating and common sense dictate that you give way to a boat heading toward you, particularly if it's huge and riding the five to six knot current that rips there most of the time.

Bogan and many other captains have petitioned the Coast Guard and the Marine Police to keep station at the bridge on busy summer weekends to direct traffic. While sympathetic to the requests of the commercial skippers, neither the Coast Guard nor the Marine Police are in a position to act as traffic cops.

Although the troubles at the bridge can be attributed to too much traffic and boneheaded actions of certain boaters, the bridge really does pose a hazard to navigation. It's been a headache for skippers in the area for more than 100 years.

Back in the late 1890s, the railroad found that marine boring worms had a great fondness for the wooden pilings that supported the trestle. As the worms chowed down on the pilings, the railroad simply added new feed in the form of additional pilings. More than 1,500 pilings eventually were put in place, creating a damlike barrier across the river.

Thanks to the worms, the railroad finally decided to fill in the southern half of the bridge in 1905, further restricting the flow of the river. Despite complaints from fishermen and other residents of Point Pleasant and Brielle, the work was completed in 1909.

Blocking off half the river like that helped channel the current in a south to north direction on the ebb. Since the river flows east toward the ocean at the draw bridge opening, that south to north set causes a boat passing through on an ebb tide to sweep into the north side of the passage. Anyone who's unfamiliar with this is understandably going to have a problem.

Back before the Point Pleasant canal opened in 1926, setting the stage for the transformation of the area into a boating Mecca, the Manasquan River was a pretty sleepy place. The dangers of the bridge were just as real, but the problems were far less numerous.

As boating gained popularity, the incidence of problems increased markedly. In the mid-1970s, with the bridge in need of a major overhaul, there was serious talk of removing the structure and busing rail commuters in Point Pleasant Beach and Bay Head to the stop in Manasquan on the north side of the river. For a short time, boaters lived in hope that they'd finally be rid of the bridge.

But a battle ensued. Commuters got up in arms. Town councils fought the proposal, too, fearing it would hurt tourism. The thousands of boaters in the area, as so often is the case, failed to come together in great numbers to lobby for the removal of the bridge, so repairs were made and the bridge is here to stay.

"To say we're stuck with the bridge just because the railroad spent a lot of money fixing it twenty years ago is ludicrous," said Tony Bogan. "That bridge is a constant source of danger and it's getting worse every year."

Offshore, 1997

NEW JERSEY'S ARTIFICIAL REEF PROGRAM

Compared to New England waters with their ledges and reefs, and fields of glacial boulders littered across much of the ocean floor, New Jersey's underwater scenery looks like the smooth plain of a pool table. Sure, there are some exceptions like the Klondike and Shrewsbury Rocks, and the Barnegat Ridge off Manasquan Inlet. But by and large the continental shelf off the coast amounts to nothing more than a long, flat expanse of sand, clay, and silt. It's not a happy place, if you're a hungry bottom fish.

Thousands of shipwrecks dot the bottom off the coast. By some estimates as many as 3,000 ships have sunk since the early 1700s. Wrecks, of course, provide the structures that lure fish and the more popular sites attract fleets of small craft. Charter boat captains operating out of Atlantic Highlands, Manasquan Inlet, Barnegat Inlet, and Great Egg Harbor Inlet closely guard the locations of little known wrecks. They literally represent gold on the fin.

But even with the plentiful supply of wrecks the total area of structure they comprise remains minute. The wrecks break apart quickly and become mounds or humps, nothing to write home about from a fish's perspective.

Now most New Jerseyans couldn't care less about the well-being of a sea bass, blackfish, or porgy. If these critters weren't finding New Jersey a nice place to live, so what? However, with more than one million recreational fishermen in the state, which has a population of roughly eight million, anglers may not hold a majority but they certainly do possess a loud voice if they holler together.

Fish advocates back in the early 1980s pointed out to the New Jersey Department of Environmental Protection Division of Fish, Game, and Wildlife in Trenton that lots of other states with similarly flat ocean floors had seen fit to establish networks of artificial reefs. If God didn't bless the state with natural reefs, well, why not go ahead and build some habitats for the fish?

"New Jersey was slow in getting on the (artificial reef) bandwagon," said Bill Figley, reef coordinator from the DEP's Division of Fish, Game and Wildlife, Port Republic. "We weren't the last of the states to do this, but we weren't among the first, either."

In 1984, the DEP launched the artificial reef program. "It started off very slowly," Figley said. "Then it gathered momentum and it's been going strong for quite some time, with almost exponential growth. Considering that we rely solely on donations of money and materials to build the reefs, we feel the program is very successful."

Figley's not just blowing smoke. Over the last thirteen years more than 1,006 artificial reefs have been built at fourteen sites from Cape May to Sandy Hook at a cost of more than $20 million. Out of the estimated four million fish caught in New Jersey waters every year, more than 25 percent come off the reefs.

"We find twenty-three adult fish per cubic yard and 115 juvenile fish per cubic yard on the most productive reefs," Figley said. "These areas contain 200 times more biomass than the sandy bottom surrounding them."

In other words, the fourteen artificial reef sites represent oases in the marine desert, hangouts for all players in the food chain from algae to striped bass who'll drop by to chow down on bait fish before swimming on their way. "The reefs hold a lot of fish," said Vinnie Mayer, skipper of the *Tiderunner* out of Atlantic Highlands. "I can't say how many are down there, but when I take customers out to the Sandy Hook reef they catch fish and come back to the dock happy and ready for a fresh fish dinner."

The artificial reefs consist primarily of concrete from seawalls, piers, and bridges. But other interesting things also go into the reefs: Army surplus tanks, personnel carriers, subway cars, Liberty ships, tugs, barges, landing craft—just about anything big that's safe to dump can find its way into the deep to make a good home for the fish.

According to Figley, cleaning the ships and other intriguing reef makers to ensure no environmentally hazardous by-products, such as oil or floatable debris, get into the reef system costs plenty of cash. Some help comes from the Artificial Reef Association, comprised of charter boat captains and other parties, which sells T-shirts and reef charts to raise money. The New Jersey National Guard cleaned up the tanks at Fort Dix to make them safe for the environment. There's even a program to raise funds through the "adoption" of wrecks.

At least seventeen federal, state, county, and municipal agencies have contributed to the program's success in one way or another—from the United States Navy to the Atlantic City Police's bomb squad. That's a lot of people pulling for the fish, and what makes the fish happy makes recreational anglers grin.

Mayer said fishing the reefs is easy as long as you have a good fish finder to accurately locate the structures and a good loran set to record the coordinates of the best places. "You've got to be right on top of the reef to get any results. Just a little ways off and you're not going to catch fish," he said.

Many skippers find the reefs a bit tough on anchors. Dropping expensive ground tackle on a reef isn't exactly a great idea; you may well lose it if it gets snagged. Mayer makes his own reef anchors out of concrete reinforcement rods welded together and bent into hooks.

"If you get stuck, all you have to do is back the boat off till the hooks bend out straight," Mayer said. "Then you're home free and you can bend the hooks back for another day."

The DEP plans to continue with the reef program for an indefinite period of time. The work is far from over, even with 2.2 million cubic yards of material down already, which is enough to cover one lane of the Garden State Parkway for 172 miles.

"We're dealing with an immense environment," Figley said. "It's going to take a lot of effort and time to have a significant effect on an area that large, especially since we have a zero budget."

Offshore, 1997

SNOWBIRDS DOCK ON JERSEY SHORE

Fall sweeps over the Jersey shore, chasing away summer vacationers and rowdy daytrippers, and bringing in a sense of quiet.

The beaches empty out, and boardwalk businesses close up shop. The marshes teem with birds. The trees along the rivers and creeks meandering through the flat lands to the bays blaze with colors. Wood smoke from snug, warm homes perfumes the air, blending with the sweet scent of pine and the earthy odor of fallen, wet leaves.

Yes, the swimmers and sunbathers are gone. But their place is taken by the "snowbirds"—boaters from the north stopping in New Jersey on their way to points south to escape the coming winter.

Back in the dark days of the Depression, the word "snowbird" was used to describe hoboes who migrated south aboard freight trains to escape the winter freeze. Today, folks along the coast call boaters headed south snowbirds, and there are lots of them.

Snowbirds cruise down the Jersey coast from places as far away as Halifax, Nova Scotia; Montreal in Quebec, and Kingston, Ontario, arriving at New Jersey after a long journey through the locks of the Erie and Champlain canals, which end on the upper reaches of the Hudson River.

Bound for ports in warmer Southern states and the islands of the Caribbean Sea, the snowbirds show up every year as predictably as their winged counterparts, the Canada geese flying in tight V-formations and filling the air with their almost otherworldly cries.

The migration of the snowbirds begins in earnest during early October, peaks at the start of November, and tapers off by the middle of the month when the threat of serious nor'easters makes the passage down the coast very dangerous.

Ernie Utsch, owner of Utsch's Marina in Cape May, has observed the migration of the snowbirds since his boyhood. Like his grandfather, who built the marina in 1951, and his father, who took over the business and passed it on to him, Utsch sees to the needs of boaters headed south for the winter, providing fuel and a place to tie up for the night.

"For as long as I can remember, the migration of boats coming through here on their way to the Chesapeake and Delaware Canal has been part of fall. Cape May is the last good stop before the canal, so pretty much every boat stops here for an overnight stay prior to proceeding farther south," Utsch said.

The snowbird might sound like a very well-heeled breed with lots of dough to feather his or her nest. But many are just plain, ordinary Joes who have saved for years for their voyage. They don't usually own mega-yachts.

"The typical boat is a sailboat or trawler in the 40–foot range," said Dee Brown, dockmaster at Farley State Marina in Atlantic City. "Often you'll see them traveling in groups. You know, they meet another cruiser in a port farther north, make friends, and all of a sudden you've got a convoy."

New Jersey offers the snowbirds their first glimpse of the South. The coastal plain, characterized by the sandy barrier islands, the protected bays and sounds behind them, and the extensive network of marshes, starts in New Jersey. Roughly 60 percent of the state lies on the plain at less than 100 feet above sea level. It's the same story all the way to Florida.

Above New Jersey, you get into land shaped by glaciers. Rocky shores with frequent harbors are the norm. From Sandy Hook south, you get the sandy low country with few natural harbors, and inlets that can become impassable in a storm, making the offshore passage a bit of a gamble in iffy weather.

Many boats head down the Intracoastal Waterway, which begins just after the Point Pleasant Canal that connects the Manasquan River to Barnegat Bay. It can take you safely inshore all the way to the Gulf of Mexico. The inside passage in New Jersey is known as the "ditch" because of its shallow depths, but it will serve in a pinch, and farther south practically everyone uses it instead of braving the treacherous waters offshore.

At all the major New Jersey ports, such as Sandy Hook Bay, Manasquan Inlet, Atlantic City, and Cape May, the snowbirds are intent upon putting as many miles under their keels as possible. They're sightseeing on the run, anxious to keep going unless the weather really gets bad.

"They (the boaters) come in at dusk and leave at dawn," Brown said. "The casinos attract some of the cruisers, who will stay for a couple days. But for the most part they use the port as a resting place. They're kind of like the birds on their way south. They want to get where it's warm."

The Star-Ledger, 1996

All for Pleasure

The water brings pleasure to millions of people every year, and not all of them own boats. Indeed, the boaters fall into a rather small group when compared against the sheer number of folks who find themselves drawn to the waterfront for a vast array of experiences. Certainly many of the fun times require a boat to make them happen, but the boating aspect comes in as a secondary part of the overall equation.

Take the wreck divers. They often use boats to get out to the wreck sites, but they go to the water for the adventure of diving down under its surface to see what they can find. The thousands of whale watchers who flock to the piers up and down the East Coast ride swift passenger vessels offshore to observe the largest creatures on earth in their natural surroundings; the boat ride is just part of the package. Even the angler, whose boat is so important to pursuing the fish, more often than not views the craft as a vehicle, a way to get where the action is.

You'll find all kinds of water lovers on the beaches, boardwalks, and docks. They like to watch boats, swim, worship the sun. It's all for the pleasure, though, no matter how it makes itself known. That's the bond the water forms among those who find themselves drawn to it.

In the following stories, you'll get to experience the pleasure that so many find on the water in so many different ways. You'll see what it's like to speed along in an iceboat, or in a high-performance racing machine; you'll run rapids on the tributaries of the upper Hudson River and canoe the brown water in a creek off the St. Lawrence River, or dive deep into the sea to catch a glimpse of wrecks on the ocean floor. The boater has an advantage, because he or she can take to the sea, river, or lake at a whim. But there is plenty out there for the nonboater, too, and that's as it should be.

THE ICEBOATERS OF BARNEGAT BAY

Elementary school teacher Don Bottomley has a special job every January and February. He's an ice tester.

His home in Island Heights, New Jersey, faces Barnegat Bay, and on weekends when the ice is thick enough, up to twenty-five iceboats will fan out in front of it from morning until evening.

"When it's been very cold for three days in a row, I walk out and chop holes in the ice with an ax. That way, I can check the depth. Four inches is the minimum thickness," Bottomley said.

Bottomley, fifty-five, never formally races his DN Class iceboat, a trait he shares with most of the others in the Island Heights group. Typical of many iceboaters, he is involved primarily for the thrill of gliding at speeds up to forty-five miles per hour.

"In winter, we're out to just horse around, which is why we don't race. Most of us race against each other during the summer," Bottomley said.

Those who are in the racing community also enjoy casual sailing on ice, according to three-time, former iceboating world champion, Henry Bossett, of Point Pleasant Beach, New Jersey. Like Bottomley, Bossett, a sailmaker, races sailboats during the summer.

"During the winter, I look forward to iceboating on weekends just for the fun of it. In the summer, I look forward to sailboat racing on weekends. In a sailboat, I'd hardly ever think about sailing in circles just for fun, but in an iceboat I'll be there sailing in circles," Bossett said.

There is a serious aspect to the sport, however. It is essential to observe commonsense safety precautions, such as strict iceboat maintenance, wearing a helmet, goggles and warm clothes, and sailing in groups. Both Bottomley and Bossett said they go iceboating with groups of people. Often, due to the high stress put on fittings, breakdowns occur. Less frequently, an iceboat will hit a soft spot. This is particularly true over saltwater.

"We sail in brackish water, and sometimes you can hit a weak spot and go in through the ice. Everyone sails up to the hole, and we drag the boat out. Sometimes we use ladders to walk over thin ice, and occasionally we need boats," Bottomley said. Although it takes skill to operate an iceboat, both Bossett and Bottomley said that it's easy to learn. "You can sail an iceboat, initially, with a lot less skill than it takes to sail a sailboat," Bottomley said.

The DN Class iceboat is by far the most popular. Its twelve-foot hull is tapered to fit the skipper's body, and its widest point is only twenty-five inches. It weighs between forty and forty-five pounds, and fully rigged, a DN weighs a scant 120 pounds. DN iceboats sit about eight inches off the ice on a tripod of a starboard and port runner plank. These hold the skatelike runners, and a third is mounted in the bow.

This runner is turned with a tiller. DNs carry sixty-five square feet of sail, enough to blast across the ice.

"These boats attain their greatest speeds sailing upwind. As the boats move faster, they generate their own wind," Bottomley said.

If iceboating is so much fun, why aren't more people doing it? Bottomley and Bossett agree the word is spreading.

After all, Bossett, who grew up near the Manasquan River in Brielle, New Jersey, didn't discover iceboating until he went out west in 1973 to work for a boatbuilder. Now Bossett, thirty-seven, knows every iceboating spot in New Jersey He believes more people don't know about iceboating because they tend to stay away from the water during the winter. "They just don't see us out there."

© *Reprinted with permission from Soundings Publications, LLC, 1989*

POINT PLEASANT SPEED FREAKS

Offshore racing boats require a real hands-on effort to win. A driver concentrates on outmaneuvering competitors; the throttleman squeezes every ounce of speed from the engines, and a navigator plots compass courses to distant markers. Each part of the team must work together in harmony like the finely tuned machines they race.

Back in the late 1970s, Rich Troppoli of Toms River used to be a pit groupie. Point Pleasant has been a venue on the circuit every July since 1969. When the big boys of the national high-performance races came there, Troppoli found the action irresistible.

Troppoli spent time in the pits talking with the teams and salivating over the sleek speed machines. As he watched them tear across the waves, he longed to get more involved with the sport. In 1985, Troppoli's dream came true. The owner of an offshore powerboat participating in the national racing circuit invited him to join the crew as navigator, and he jumped at the chance.

"I thought I'd died and gone to heaven," Troppoli said, recalling races that took him twenty-three miles off Point Pleasant through six-to-eight-foot seas. "When you're out there and it's that rough, all you can do is try to keep the boat from breaking apart."

Sucking air in conditions like that will burn out engines. And, boats can flip, roll, and collide in the best conditions. It's not a sport for the fainthearted. Today, even with courses set much closer to shore than in the past, fatalities and serious injuries still occur. Last year at the SBR-APBA World Championships in Key West one racer died when his boat hit a wave at speed, demolishing the vessel. Three other racers were critically injured in other incidents during that event. Despite

Figure 10. Classic runabout on the water near Toms River, New Jersey. PHOTO BY
DAVID W. SHAW.

the inherent danger of the sport, the speed demon hit Troppoli hard.
He bought an old race boat and started to hone his skills. And as with
everything else, practice pays. Troppoli is the only racer in the United
States Offshore Racing Association to win the national championships
in the B-Class three years in a row. He grabbed the title in 1993, 1994,
and 1995.

Owning and racing an offshore boat takes big bucks. It's just like
racing cars or horses; you need lots of cash. Troppoli, who owns a
thriving automotive business, but is by no means a multimillionaire,
sank $250,000 into his newest boat, *Shock Wave*. He spends an aver-
age of $50,000 a year to race the national circuit.

Arnold D'Ambrosa, who owns two marinas and a restaurant in Point
Pleasant and Brielle, races three boats: *Rolling Thunder*, a thirty-three-
foot Baja, *Rolling Thunder Too*, a thirty-five-foot Jaguar, and *Toshiba*, a
thirty-five-foot powerhouse he said can hit top speeds of 130 miles per
hour. D'Ambrosa said he spends an average of $200,000 to $300,000
to do the national circuit.

"If nothing breaks, the cost to race can be as low as $150,000,"
he said. "But something almost always breaks. That's part of the
challenge."

D'Ambrosa recalled the 1990 World Championship races at Key
West. He was two laps ahead of the boat in second place as he was

speeding along on the last leg in the last lap of the course. As they headed toward a glorious finish another boat broadsided them, knocking them out of the race.

D'Ambrosa takes such things in stride, however. "It could have been worse. The accident just cracked the hull," he said, adding that the mishap caused approximately $25,000 in damage.

So why do these guys spend all that money? Surely there must be huge purses to justify the expenses, and big corporate sponsors to help defray the costs. D'Ambrosa, who has a fistful of national and world championships under his belt said no, there's no real money in the winner's circle.

There also aren't scads of large companies breaking the doors down to sponsor race teams, largely due to a lack of visibility of the sport. However, that's changing as the sport continues to grow in popularity. "You do it because you love to go fast," D'Ambrosa said. "It's exhilarating to get out there and race against the best. We don't do it for the money."

According to Troppoli, the largest purse in his class was roughly $4,000 for a national championship. In the modified and open classes, the fastest and most expensive race boats, purses only amount to around $8,000 to $10,000.

"You take a guy who's spending $250,000 to race and give him a prize of $10,000, he's just going to shrug his shoulders. He's definitely not into it for the money," Troppoli said.

Offshore powerboat racing used to be really offshore, where only spectators aboard boats could witness the action. In the mid-1980s, race sponsors got hip to the fact that they had to make it easy for spectators to get the thrill of seeing boats packed together in neck-and-neck battles for the finish. They moved the courses inshore, right off the beach.

This is quite true at Point Pleasant. By special permit from the Coast Guard, racers gather on the Manasquan River and charge out the inlet at full throttle to the cheers of more than 100,000 spectators lined up on the breakwaters and along the beach. For the first time, the event was televised on cable TV's Sports Channel New York, bringing the thrills into living rooms of fans unable to see the races in person.

"It's an incredible feeling to fly out the inlet like that," Troppoli said. "You know your friends are out cheering you on, that they can actually see the boat up close. Point Pleasant is one of the best venues on the circuit because it's so spectator friendly."

Offshore, 1996

NEW JERSEY DOWN UNDER

Tom DiMichele of Bridgewater has had the rare pleasure of visiting one of New Jersey's most unique relics from the Cold War. Although it is open to the public, few New Jerseyans ever get to see it. You can't exactly reach it with the family station wagon.

Part of a network of early warning radar stations that resembled oversized oil platforms known as Texas towers, the relic rests on the ocean floor about sixty-five miles east of Barnegat. It's been there since 1961, when it crashed into the sea during a savage nor'easter, killing the twenty-eight airmen serving as a skeleton crew.

The thirty-year-old DiMichele, an avid recreational diver for twelve years, says diving down to see the remains of the tower, which bottom out at 193 feet, is both eerie and beautiful. Before its demise, the $20 million, double-decked structure rose sixty-seven feet above the sea on three hollow steel legs.

Water from the Gulf Stream mingles with the nutrient-rich inshore waters, clearing away the limited visibility underwater to allow views of as much as 100 feet in all directions. The Texas tower can easily be seen resting at a forty-five-degree angle from the bottom, its platform carpeted with sea anemones and northern coral.

"I've gone into the old communications center," DiMichele says. "You can still see the vacuum tubes from the old radios, and wires all around. It's really sharp out there."

Over the course of a year, with the season at its height in July and August, tens of thousands of divers visit New Jersey's fascinating world down under. Like DiMichele, they come to sightsee beneath the waters off the Garden State because of the plethora of exceptional dive sites. Some divers even travel here from as far away as Virginia and Massachusetts.

A fleet of twenty to thirty charter dive boats operate out of Shark River, Manasquan, and Barnegat inlets, taking groups of divers out to the wrecks seven days a week for day and night expeditions. Hundreds of privately owned boats also take divers out.

The state is a very active dive spot, according to Ed Bogaert, chairman of the New Jersey Council of Dive Clubs, an organization representing thirty-one clubs with more than 2,000 members. Bogaert estimates that about 200,000 New Jerseyans have their basic open water certification, which provides the foundation for more advanced training.

It's the stepping back in time, entering a world few people get to see that keeps DiMichele coming back for more and more Jersey dives.

He dives the state's wrecks, jetties and inlets with fellow members of Dosil's Sea Roamers, a thirty-member dive club that meets in Hazlet.

"It becomes an addiction seeing the different wrecks," DiMichele says. "You never know what you're going to see . . . the wreck itself, artifacts, the marine life. In the summer you see tropical fish, sea turtles, and dolphins."

More than 70 percent of all diving in New Jersey occurs on wrecks. There are plenty of them, with some estimates placing the total number of wrecks at more than 3,000.

More wrecks are being added through the state's artificial reef program, which involves sinking Army tanks, Liberty ships, tugs, barges, even subway cars to provide habitats for marine life, and recreational opportunities for anglers and divers. State officials estimate that the volume of reef material dumped since the program began in 1984 would cover one lane of the Garden State Parkway four feet high for its entire 172–mile length.

The artificial reefs provide divers with weird and sometimes amusing underwater views, such as the absurd juxtaposition of lobsters hanging out in the overhead luggage racks in subway cars and fish swimming in and out of open tank turrets.

"A lot of people come from out of state to dive the wrecks. We dive the *Delaware*, the *Mohawk*, the *Algol*, the *Tolten*, the *Pinta*. These are major dive sites, very popular among Jersey divers and visiting divers," Bogaert says.

The *Delaware*, a Clyde Line steamer, caught fire off Bay Head in July 1898, and sank about one mile offshore. She lies in seventy feet of water and is often used as a site for divers going for advanced open water certification or who are part of the special wreck diving classes offered at many New Jersey dive shops and dive clubs.

In the gloom, you can see the enormous steam engine, the boilers, the prop, and other large metal pieces of the ships. Thousands of fish swim around the wreck and lobsters hide in the dark recesses along the sandy bottom. Lucky divers are able to catch their lobster dinners.

"The *Delaware* is a great wreck where you can get onto it and dig and come up with old bottles, coins and sometimes even some china," DiMichele says.

The *Algol*, called by some the best dive in New Jersey, is a 460–foot Liberty ship. She carried troops and supplies during several wars, and was taken out of mothballs in 1991 to become a permanent guest of New Jersey's artificial reef system.

The *Algol* lies off Sea Girt in 130 feet of water, the maximum depth for recreational dives. However, the vessel sits upright on the bottom, allowing divers access to the upper decks at shallower depths. The bridge is accessible at eighty feet.

The *Pinta*, a 194–foot cargo ship that sank when it collided with the freighter *City of Perth* in 1963, rests on its side in ninety feet of water off Asbury Park. Its cargo of lumber litters the sea floor. Abundant marine life and good visibility draw many divers to this spot.

Many wrecks lie right off the beach, enabling divers to reach them directly from shore in communities that allow it. Wrecks close to the beach are usually very old sailing ships and contain artifacts, fittings, and other trinkets popular among archeologically minded divers.

The Dual Wrecks off Takanasse Beach at the San Alfonso Retreat House in Long Branch consist of the steamer *Rusland*, which sank in 1877, and the bark *Adonis*, which sank in 1859. This site is popular, though access is somewhat limited.

The Manasquan wreck, as it's commonly called, is a popular beach dive. It's located in twenty feet of water about 300 yards off the beach, five jetties north of the inlet. DiMichele describes the swim out there as "tough."

Wrecks also lie off the beaches at Island Beach, Belmar, Deal, Spring Lake, and other communities. In addition to wreck diving, the inlets, jetties, reservoirs, and quarries also are popular dive spots. Each represents an entirely different Jersey diving environment and experience.

Reservoirs, such as Round Valley, are deep with rocky bottoms, visibility is excellent, and there are no currents to fight. Naturally, divers don't need a boat to reach their destination. Jetties are often used when the tides are not running swiftly to teach beginner divers about ever-fluctuating tidal ranges and currents. There is a lot of support available for those who would like to dive New Jersey waters. Dive shops and clubs are the best places to start.

"Our club was set up for new divers to join and dive with experienced divers who can help them learn the ropes," DiMichele says. "I joined for that reason eleven years ago. It's just good for new divers to know they have someone with them who has done it before and knows where they're going and what they're doing."

The Star-Ledger, 1996

MOBY KICK: WINTER WHALE WATCHING OFF NEW JERSEY'S COAST

On Christmas Day, Shannon Newman, twelve, received an unusual gift from her stepfather, Al Litwak of Manasquan. Litwak knew she had always harbored a deep interest in the sea and he wanted to give her something the average kid on the block wouldn't receive, a chance to see a whale in the wild.

In deciding on the gift, Litwak, whose business for a bio-tech firm had often taken him to Florida, recalled swimming with the manatee, whalelike creatures known commonly as sea cows for their bovine face and rotund shape. "It was almost a religious experience, swimming with the manatee," he said. "I wanted Shannon to share in something that special."

So, on an early and unseasonably mild January Saturday the two set off aboard the *Atlantis* to catch an up-close look at Moby Dick's baleen kin: humpbacks and finbacks which don't have teeth like sperm whales but large, sievelike mouths ideal for scooping up huge quantities of herring, mackerel, and small crustaceans known as krill. The *Atlantis*, a private charter fishing boat out of Bogan's Brielle Boat Basin in Brielle used for whale watching from January through the end of March, lifted to the swells as it passed through Manasquan Inlet and headed for the open sea.

The whale watchers decked out in knit caps, sweaters pulled up over their faces, heavy gloves, and foul weather gear, had high expectations. They'd come to see whales, but would the whales cooperate?

Every winter humpbacks and finbacks follow an unmarked watery highway from the Bay of Fundy and points north, a path taken for more than 200 million years, down to the Caribbean Sea where they find food more plentiful and the tepid tropical waters ideal for giving birth to their young. On their way, they like to visit New Jersey to enjoy a fishy feast and to build up strength for the long journey ahead.

"Every late December, we get a plankton bloom off the Jersey coast. The plankton attract the krill, the krill attract the herring, and the krill and herring attract the whales," said Francis Bogan, the *Atlantis*'s skipper. "There's as much as 20 percent more bait fish off New Jersey in winter than in the summer, and the whales stop here to eat. That's why they stay around."

Each species of whale has a unique personality, though all are very social (much like elephants) and they travel in pods, not herds. Most everyone has heard tales about the orca, most commonly known as the killer whale. They're aggressive hunters, traveling in wolflike packs that herd seals and other creatures together before feeding on them. Like the sperm whale, orca are toothed. You won't find any hanging around New Jersey, however.

The baleen whales, such as the finbacks and humpbacks, are far more docile with varying degrees of curiosity about whale watch boats. For instance, if you had a choice, you'd probably pass up a finback, which is rather aloof, in favor of seeing a humpback. Humpbacks are playful and inquisitive. They'll swim close to boats and sometimes poke their heads above the surface for a look at the humans, or they'll leap and slap the water with their huge flukes. They put on a great show when they're in the neighborhood.

In sheer bulk, humpbacks average forty feet in length and weigh in at about twenty-nine tons, making them larger than most recreational boats. They're small fry compared to finbacks, however, which are second in size only to the blue whale, the largest mammal in the world. (The finback ranges from sixty to eighty feet and is a hefty fifty tons.) Unlike finbacks, humpbacks show their tails when sounding (diving), their most distinctive feature. Humpbacks can be individually identified by whale watchers and oceanographers solely by markings and grooves on their tails, much like human fingerprints.

The *Atlantis* steamed northeast, passing a popular fishing ground called the Klondike, a boulder field left on the flat bottom from rock-filled glacial drift ice that settled there about 10,000 years ago. The mackerel fleet out of Manasquan dotted the horizon. A rust-streaked freighter steamed past the starboard bow on its way to New York Harbor.

Perched at the very tip of the bow was John Kontje of Belvidere. A heavy coat and a black turtleneck sweater pulled up over his jaw kept the chill off. Every now and then he scanned the horizon. The bow, he said, is the best roost on the boat for seeing whales, though some avid watchers like the upper decks.

"I've been on over 200 whale watching trips, mostly in New England and on the West Coast," he said, the wind catching his words and sending them aft. "It's really incredible to see a whale breach (jump out of the water), to hear it breathe. Humpbacks, which are curious by nature, will often swim right up to the boat. You can see them watching you sometimes."

Just then, the long columnar spout of a finback shot twenty feet in the air, looking like a diminutive Old Faithful. (Not so modest, perhaps. A spout can be spotted from as far away as four miles and emerges from the blowhole at speeds reaching as much as 200 miles per hour.) Immediately, all the passengers on the right side of the boat moved to the left side, hoping to catch a glimpse of the elusive beast. No one spoke, but everyone scanned the waters.

No more whale.

"Did you see it?" was the question of the minute. A handful of watchers said yes, but most had missed it, including Shannon Newman. Whales, despite their thirty to sixty-foot length, can play quite a game of hide and seek if they've a mind to.

Dave Barbara of Rahway has been on twenty whale watching trips in New Jersey and as he talked about whales it was plain this trip wouldn't be his last. "I've always loved whales. They're like the dinosaurs of the present. No other creature is bigger. When you see them next to the boat, it's really awesome," he said.

So, where were they?

"Sometimes it's like the fishing stories you hear. You know, you should have been here last week! The thing is you really can see quite a show in New Jersey. It's as good as other whale watching spots," Barbara said.

The whale watch boats typically run for five-hour hunts covering an average of twenty square miles of ocean. The skippers contact the fishing fleets and other whale watch vessels on the radio to get the skinny on the latest whale sightings, and they also use fishfinders, sonarlike devices that show the ocean floor and what's swimming above it. When an area looks hot, they get ready for whales.

Mostly, however, the boat cruises around. "It's definitely mellow a lot of the time. People who like to come out here really love nature, just being out on the water in winter with the seabirds," said Janine Pestel of Spotswood, a wildlife photographer. She'd been out on the Atlantis the previous weekend and said the humpbacks paid the boat a visit. "One swam right under the boat," she said.

At several points the whales did make an appearance. But they never came close to the boat. Shannon Newman looked a little dejected. Gray clouds masked the sun.

Suddenly, the water came alive with white-sided dolphin. Dozens surrounded the boat, cavorting in the bow wave. They kept pace with the boat and jumped from the waves, their backs arched, spinning and twisting in a magical kind of dance. It was just like those nature films on TV.

Shannon, and just about everyone else aboard, smiled broadly, and took in a sight most people never see in the wild. "They're really cool," she said as three dolphin jumped together in formation, then disappeared beneath the gray-blue surface of the sea.

SPOUTING OFF ADVICE

Winter whale watch boats run from the Atlantic Highlands and Manasquan Inlet from January till the end of March. Boats don't run in blizzards, nor'easters, or high winds which kick up big waves. The boats all have heated cabins, snack bars, and some have heated handrails. Snacks are basic. It's best to bring your own lunch.

Dress warmly. Heavy jackets, gloves, and hats are a must. Bring binoculars, and a camera because whales often come close enough to get some good shots. The fee is $20 for adults and $10 for children under twelve. No advance tickets are sold. Just show up at the boat. Departure time is 9:00 A.M., but be there by 8:30. You'll be back at the dock by 2:00. Atlantic Highlands trips run only on Saturdays.

Whale watch boats also run in the summer, but whales off New Jersey during the warmer months are far less numerous.

WINTER WHALE WATCH BOATS

ATLANTIS,
800 Ashley Avenue, Brielle,
Saturdays and Sundays,
(732) 528–6620 or (732) 528– 5014.

EXPRESS NAVIGATION,
2 First Avenue, Atlantic Highlands,
Saturdays only,
(800) BOATRIDE.

The Star-Ledger, 1997

The image of a lighthouse, its beam penetrating the murk of a stormy sea . . . the stuff of hyperbole, almost hackneyed in its own way. You'll find the same scene reproduced on coffee mugs, T-shirts, place mats, and greeting cards in most any tourist trap along most any spot on the coast. The lighthouse can indeed make the cash registers jingle.

Yet, there is a reason why the lonely lighthouse holds an attraction for so many of us, whether we are boaters or just love to head to the beach to watch the gulls swoop over a gray-blue sea dappled with splashes of sunlight. It goes deeper than surface appeal, a pretty image on a cup or a card. A lighthouse represents strength in weathering the elements and a gentle aspect, too, since its function is to guide weary sailors home. It brings up a feeling deep inside that no other building can match. For that reason, I have always loved lighthouses, especially the ones I can climb. Seeing the world from the top of a tower provides a perspective of the seascape hard to get in any other way. Flying in a small plane comes close, but the throb of the engine, the penned-in feel behind the windows, detracts from the view, at least a little.

From the lantern room of a lighthouse, you can hear and feel the wind whistle by, see the gulls, the ships that look like tiny smudges on the horizon. The climb often makes you sweat, and that, somehow, makes the view even more enjoyable.

The following story will tell you a lot about the lighthouses in New Jersey which you can climb yourself. It contains information about events that took place at the time I wrote the piece, but I left them in place rather than editing them out to give you an idea of the special goings-on that you may find at the lighthouses when you visit.

After the main feature story, you'll find a listing of the lights, with their basic information such as telephone numbers, hours of operation, and so forth. This should steer you in the right direction if you decide to hop in the car to check out the lights of the Garden State.

LET IT SHINE

SENTINELS OF THE SHORE OPEN THEIR DOORS

The romance of lighthouses brings people to their feet—and keeps them moving with the promise of something wonderful to see—just a few . . . more . . . steps . . . ahead.

Lighthouses are snapped by shutter bugs and tread by climbers, who pant ever skyward up twisting iron staircases to get a seabird's view of a piece of the world. From the ground or the observation deck, the timeless qualities of lighthouses transport us to days long past when clipper ships and whalers plied the oceans.

A lighthouse represents a link to the past and a reminder in the present that the sea still plays a part in life, acting as a watery highway for container ships and freighters that bring in everything from bananas to Toyotas. In New Jersey, which is almost an island, with only a fifty-three-mile border linking the state to the mainland, these beacons bejewel the shores and waters stretching from upper New York Harbor to the Delaware River.

They are among the most intriguing on the entire East Coast, according to Andy Flanagan, president of the Sea Girt Lighthouse Citizens Committee which restored and now manages the Victorian Sea Girt Light in Sea Girt.

"People from all up and down the coast and the Midwest come to see New Jersey's lighthouses because many are among the tallest and oldest in the nation. In the case of the Sea Girt Lighthouse, it's an example of a light built right on top of the keeper's home, as opposed to a tower with a separate residence," Flanagan says.

Of New Jersey's twenty lighthouses, eight are open to the public; diehard aficionados often take boats to see those that aren't. Robbins Reef Lighthouse, Romer Shoals and West Bank lights all sit in shallow water in New York Harbor, warning ships to keep clear of danger, as does Great Beds Lighthouse, opposite Perth Amboy in the Arthur Kill. Likewise, lights such as Brandywine Shoal Lighthouse, Cross Ledge Lighthouse, Miah Maull Shoal Lighthouse and Ship John Shoal Lighthouse all mark shoals on Delaware Bay.

There are a handful of other picturesque lights—Chapel Hill Lighthouse in Middletown, which is a private residence, Conover Beacon in Leonardo, and Tinicum Rear Range Lighthouse in Billingsport— which sit on land, but nevertheless are closed to visitors.

Sandy Hook Lighthouse, the oldest in the nation, dates back to 1764. Unlike more modern lighthouses, its spiral staircase is made of stone and winds its way upward along the side of the tower. The only railing is a rope strung along the walls, and at the top visitors must climb a steep metal ladder and enter the lantern room through a tiny hatch.

"It can be kind of intimidating to some people," says Fred Thies, a lighthouse enthusiast from Medford. "But you look out and get the feeling you're right in the harbor. You don't get this perspective from Twin Lights."

Built in 1849, East Point Light ranks as the second oldest lighthouse in New Jersey and is the only Jersey lighthouse still in operation on Delaware Bay. Back at the turn of the century as many as 500 ships operated along the Maurice River, dragging for oysters, fishing, and working the coastal trade routes.

"The lighthouse is in a somewhat remote location overlooking the Bay. It brings you back in time and gives you a view of New Jersey you might not expect to see, as if those old sailing ships were still around and the river bustled with a way of life that's long been forgotten," says Gail Robinson, president of the Maurice River Historical Society, which maintains East Point Light, a two-story, barnlike house with a cupola perched on top. Volunteers are currently restoring it.

New Jersey's lighthouses have a sometimes quirky history. Sandy Hook Lighthouse still looks much as it did before the Revolutionary War, despite the fact that it was supposedly used for target practice in the War of 1812. It once stood only 500 feet from the tip of the hook, but ocean currents carrying sand northward have extended the peninsula a mile and a half farther. In the 1890s, a second light shined on the very end of the hook to keep ships off the beach.

The shifting sands, ever building and eroding along the coast, toppled earlier versions of Cape May and Barnegat lights into the sea. Hereford Inlet Lighthouse was literally picked up and moved back 150 feet from its original position after a severe storm damaged it in 1913.

The live-in lights such as Sea Girt, Hereford, and East Point Lighthouse make for the easiest climbs. However, the ladders leading from the home proper up to the lantern rooms can be tough or impassable for small children or people with physical problems.

Twin Lights Historic Site in the Highlands is also an easy climb, but it's not a live-in type building, at least not in the Victorian house sense. Situated on a hill almost 200 feet above sea level, the short climb up the sixty-five stairs of the north tower affords a view from 256 feet. No other point on the mainland between Maine and Kitty Hawk, N.C., is higher.

Built in 1862, the twin towers resemble a "castle in the sky," says Yvonne Miller, of Medford, a lighthouse enthusiast and active member of the New Jersey Lighthouse Society. "You can look out across Sandy Hook and see the New York skyline and get a real feel for the surrounding land and the bay."

One of the most interesting climbs in New Jersey can be found at the Finns Point Rear Range Light in the Supawna Meadows National Wildlife Refuge in Pennsville. Situated about a mile and a half inland from the shore of the Delaware River, this wrought iron tower juts 115 feet skyward from the surrounding woodlands and meadows. It was once used as a range light to guide ships up the river. (A range consists of two lighted towers, one shorter than the other. Captains steer their ships to keep both lights in line with each other, thus enabling the vessels to stay inside the channel boundaries.)

"The first question many people ask is why is there a lighthouse on land," says Pat DiDomizio, a federal employee at Supawna Meadows. "Many people wonder if the land was filled in. It's a logical question, but it all becomes clear when they understand how a range light works."

The bird's-eye view from the lantern room of a tall lighthouse more than makes up for the effort it takes to climb the tallest of New Jersey's towers. Old Barney, at 170 feet above sea level, can tax even the most athletic of individuals. But once the climb is done, sweeping views of Barnegat Bay, the barrier islands, the inlet, and the Pine Barrens on the mainland create a panorama of beauty with a distinctly New Jersey flavor.

"I always get an almost humble feeling when I'm at the top of a lighthouse. The vastness of the world around us really becomes obvious and you realize how small an individual is compared to the land and the sea," Miller says. "There is no other building more romantic than a lighthouse, at least for me, anyway."

ONCE MORE, FROM THE TOP

Lighthouse lovers come from far and wide to climb the eight light-houses in New Jersey which are open to the public. From Sandy Hook Light and Twin Lights in the Highlands, the ocean meets the Big Apple in a glimmer of steel against a backdrop of blue. Old Barney reveals a panoramic view of the barrier islands at the south end of Barnegat Bay while the old wrought iron tower of Finns Point Rear Range Light opens up views of the Delaware River and the verdant expanse of the Supawna Meadows National Wildlife Refuge.

SANDY HOOK LIGHT, FORT HANCOCK
Located on Sandy Hook in the Sandy Hook Unit of Gateway National Rec-reation Area. For more information call (732) 872–5970. Grounds are open for daily visits; lighthouse closed to public except during special tours. Height above sea level: 103 feet; number of steps: 105; range of light: 12 miles; pic-nic facilities: yes; museum: yes. Special tours: June 14 and June 22, from 10:00 A.M. to 4:00 P.M. every half hour; limit eight people per tour. July 17, from 6:00 P.M. to 8:00 P.M.; July 31, same hours; August 14 and 28, same hours. No admission fee. Children under age 10 may not climb the lighthouse for safety reasons. The ladder up to the lantern room is quite steep.

TWIN LIGHTS HISTORIC SITE, HIGHLANDS
Located on Lighthouse Road. For more information call (732) 872–1814. Open every day from Memorial Day to Labor Day from 10:00 A.M. to 5:00 P.M. Free admission. Height above sea level: 256 feet; number of steps: 65; range of light: formerly 22 miles (decommissioned in 1949); picnic facilities: no tables, but plenty of benches with views; museum: yes.

SEA GIRT LIGHTHOUSE, SEA GIRT
Located on corner of Beacon Boulevard and Ocean Avenue. For more infor-mation call (732) 974–0514. Open from 1:00 P.M. to 4:00 P.M., June 22. Open from 1:00 P.M. to 4:00 P.M., on the first and third Sundays of the month through November. Free admission, donations appreciated. Height above sea level: 44 feet; number of steps: from the second floor landing, 12 steps and a seven-foot ladder to the lantern room (the ladder is quite steep and may be difficult for small children); range of light: formerly 15 miles (decommissioned in 1945); picnic facilities: none; museum: none, though the home is furnished with period pieces.

BARNEGAT LIGHTHOUSE (OLD BARNEY), BARNEGAT LIGHT
Located at Barnegat Lighthouse State Park off Broadway Avenue. For more

information call (609) 494–2016. Open every day from Memorial Day through Labor Day, 9:00 A.M. to 4:30 P.M. Admission fee: $1 for anyone over age 12, age 12 and under, free. Height above sea level: 170 feet; number of steps: 217; range of light: formerly 20 miles (decommissioned in 1944); picnic facilities: yes; museum: no.

HEREFORD INLET LIGHTHOUSE, NORTH WILDWOOD
Located on Chestnut and Central Avenue. For more information call (609) 522–4520. Open daily from 9:00 A.M. to 7:00 P.M. and on Saturdays from 9:00 A.M. to 9:00 P.M. Free admission, donations appreciated. Height above sea level: 57 feet; number of steps: 65; range of light: 13 miles; picnic facilities: yes; museum: yes.

CAPE MAY LIGHTHOUSE, CAPE MAY
Located at Cape May Point State Park. For more information call (609) 884–5404. Open daily June 20 to September 4, from 9:00 A.M. to 8:00 P.M. Admission fee: $3.50 for adults (one child climbing free per adult), and $1.00 per additional child. Height above sea level: 157 feet; number of steps: 199; range of light: 24 miles; picnic facilities: yes; museum: yes.

EAST POINT LIGHTHOUSE, MAURICE RIVER TOWNSHIP
Located on East Point Road, off Route 47 (follow the signs to the lighthouse). For more information call (609) 327–3714. Grounds are open for daily visits; lighthouse closed to public except during special events. Free admission. Height above sea level: 43 feet; number of steps: 30; range of light: 13 miles; picnic facilities: no; museum: no.

FINNS POINT REAR RANGE LIGHT, PENNSVILLE
Located in the Supawna Meadows National Wildlife Refuge at intersection of Fort Mott Road and Lighthouse Road. For more information call (609) 935–1487. Open for tours every third Sunday April through October from noon to 4:00 P.M. Free admission. Height above sea level: 115 feet; number of steps: 130 (the wooden ladder leading to the lantern room is quite steep and may pose difficulties for small children and persons with physical problems); range of light: formerly 8 miles (decommissioned in 1950); picnic facilities: no, though they are available at nearby Fort Mott State Park; museum: no.

The Star-Ledger, 1997

CLAYTON CANOEING: EXPERIENCING FRENCH CREEK'S WILDLIFE

I had just arrived at K's Motel in Clayton, New York, and was talking with the motel's owner, Don Lingenfelter, and the motel's manager, Linda Brown. Leaning against the counter in Don's kitchen, I asked them about the wildlife that I would be seeing the next morning on French Creek. I had been looking forward to canoeing up the eleven-mile stretch of water that meanders through the French Creek Wildlife Preserve.

As we talked, I gazed out the picture window in Don's living room, feeling the tension that accompanies city life ebb from my muscles as I watched the sun set. I remembered how the slow pace of Clayton, the friendly people, and beautiful scenery, had pleased me during my last Thousand Islands vacation. I was glad I returned.

The scenery visible through the picture window gradually faded away as the twilight became night. Don and I made plans to go out to some of Clayton's bars after I changed my clothes in my motel room. As I was about to grab my suitcase and head for my room, the shrill voice of another guest calling through the kitchen window made me turn and look outside. A woman tapped on the windowframe. I later found out that she was staying in the room next to mine with her husband and great-grandson.

"Kay . . . Kay, I hate to bother you, but—."

Linda shot Don a smile and hurried past me out the door. Don told me that Linda was used to being called Kay, the name of his mother, who had the motel built in 1949. Don said she left the motel to him when she died in 1977.

"I'll get changed," I said as I grabbed my suitcase. "I've never been to any of Clayton's bars."

Don smiled.

The next morning, I awoke excited enough about the canoe trip to diminish the effects of the night on the town, spent mostly at O'Brien's. The rooms came with coffee makers, so I perked some.

A short time later, Don, Linda, Bill Heady, the photographer, and I were motoring under the Route 12E Bridge into what Don called French Creek's flats, a wide open, deltalike waterway. We towed the fiberglass canoe behind the motorboat.

I glanced off to my left at French Creek Marina, and then straight ahead at the creek as the tall cattails and marsh grass growing along the banks began to narrow the channel. We passed some homes and

K's Motel on the right shore. And, as we followed the creek's mean-derings, signs of civilization vanished.

The sun seared through layers of alto cumulus clouds. A blue heron soared across the motorboat's bow, looking magnificent against the background of the trees and the marsh grass. The powerful smell of marsh flowers reminded me of spices.

"They hunt duck up here in the fall, and fish for bullhead after the ice goes," Don said. He also told me he used to bowfish for carp on French Creek when he was a teenager.

Don has spent most of his life in the Thousand Islands, and Linda grew up on Grindstone Island. Their company and knowledge of the area was helping to make my trip pleasant, I thought, looking past Don at two ducks we had startled from the reeds.

"Up here," Don said, pointing off to the left, "that's cowpie point." He said that cows from a farm that was once behind the point used to roam down to the water and drink. Hence the name of the point.

When we arrived at Rocky Rollaway, I got into the canoe with Linda. A path behind Rocky Rollaway, a cluster of granite rocks at the shoreline, leads to a stand of pines, a perfect camping spot because the ground there is level.

Once in the canoe, we paddled away from the motorboat. With the sounds of the engine gone, nature's music played.

The breeze stirred the reeds. The sounds the paddles made as they hit the water blended with the drone of bullfrogs and the intermittent cry of a red-winged blackbird, two common residents of French Creek. I stared over the side of the canoe at the vines swaying beneath the surface of the water, moved by the quiet but rhythmic sounds as we paddled.

We could have spent a day or two exploring French Creek, but I wanted to see more of Clayton. We arrived back at the motel by mid-afternoon.

I was famished when I got back to the motel. I walked to a diner nearby, ate lunch and headed into Clayton. To be honest, I spent a couple of hours just sitting by the St. Lawrence River watching the ships, motorboats, and sailboats, and a seaplane, which was available for flying vacationers on tours of the Thousand Islands.

Boat watching on the Seaway brought back memories of past vaca-tions on Block Island, Rhode Island. Watching boats, particularly sail-boats, has been a favorite pastime of mine for years. As I basked in nostalgia and ate an ice cream cone while ambling down the street, a beautiful woman smiled at me and said, "Hello." It had initially surprised me the day before when a boy riding a bicycle on the side-walk said, "Hi, how are you doing?" on his way by. But I began to realize that the people of Clayton are as much of an attraction as the Thousand Islands scenery.

On the Trail, 1984

AWASH IN ADVENTURE

The white water tumbling ahead of the sixteen-foot raft blended in with the snow-covered banks of Indian River, a tributary of the Upper Hudson River located deep in the heart of the Adirondacks. Tall pines on the shoreline sped past, faster and faster, until the roar of the rapids nearly drowned out the voice of the river guide, Gary Staab.

"Okay! Now we're heading into Big Nasty," Staab shouted. I stopped paddling and looked back at him over my shoulder. "This is a bad stretch of water," I heard him warning, "so when I tell you to paddle hard, paddle hard."

I again faced the rapids, wondering why that particular section of Indian River was known as Big Nasty. I knew I would have my answer soon. We were almost at the spot where the dark river turned white.

Earlier that morning, my friend John Farner and I met twelve members of the St. Lawrence University Outing Club at the guide's base in Indian Lake. There, we donned bright orange wetsuits to protect us from hypothermia if we were hurled out of the raft into the thirty-five-degree water. We talked nervously among ourselves, wondering what adventures waited for us on the river.

Two people of the Outing Club, Al and Ginny Schwartz, had rafted on the Snake and Colorado Rivers. They said they hoped that rafting in the Adirondacks would not disappoint them. It did not.

"Can I have your attention, please?" Staab asked. Everyone formed a circle around him. He looked like Grizzly Adams. He was six-foot-five, muscular, and wore a heavy beard. He wore a black wetsuit, a ski cap pulled down over his head and sneakers three sizes too large over bulky wetsuit booties.

"It's important that you listen for the guide's commands," Staab said. "He may tell you to paddle hard, back paddle, hang on, or ease up. We'll go over the strokes at Indian River." Then he explained the white-water swimming posture in case someone fell out of the raft.

"Don't panic. And don't try to swim with the life jacket on. Just spread your arms straight out," he said, lifting his huge arms, making wings of them. "Go down the rapids feet first. We'll pick you up when we get through."

We boarded army-green buses and twenty minutes later we were at Indian River, deciding in which raft we wanted to ride. Farner and I went in Staab's raft, along with Mr. and Mrs. Schwartz, and two other Outing Club members. We all picked up the raft and tramped through the snow, down a steep hill to the river's edge.

"The person up front gets the wettest," Staab warned as Mrs. Schwartz and I sat in the bow. He explained the best way to wrap our legs around the fat sides of the raft to keep balanced while surging through the white water.

"Don't stick your foot under the thwart," he said, patting the seat. "If we go over a rock, you could break your ankle."

Our raft joined the many others floating in the water near the launching area.

"Right back!" Staab yelled. I plunged my paddle into the frigid water and pushed the blade toward the bow. Mrs. Schwartz dug her paddle into the river and pulled the blade back toward the stern. The raft spun in circles.

"Okay, forward paddle everyone," Staab said, his voice easy and confident as he steered us around the first bend of the river downstream from the launching site. Once around the bend, it was as if we had entered another world—wild, rugged, pristine.

Soon we were used to the way the raft handled in the smaller, less violent stretches of white water. We were ready for the biggest rapids we would encounter on the trip: The Narrows, Big Nasty, and Harris Rift.

Shortly before reaching Big Nasty, we stopped at Blue Ledge to rest. Ice-coated cliffs of blue granite towered hundreds of feet above the river. The pines on top of the cliffs cut into the blue sky, which was sometimes obscured by banks of gray-white clouds. When we finished resting, snacking, and drinking hot chocolate, we left Blue Ledge ready for the rough ride ahead of us.

We shot the Narrows. Big Nasty was next. As we approached Big Nasty, the roar of the river and the sight of the boiling white water reminded me of some of the bigger rapids I have shot. I glanced at Mrs. Schwartz. She clutched her paddle and shot me a smile.

Moments later, the fury of Big Nasty surrounded us, hurling the raft wherever the currents were strongest. Huge waves reared up above our heads as if they were angry grizzly bear, roaring defiantly at us as we sped by. Waves broke over my head and filled my wetsuit with freezing water. My scalp ached from the shock of the cold dunkings. Icicles formed on my hair.

"Paddle hard! Left back, left back!" Staab shouted above the roar of the river. I could barely hear him. I frantically followed Staab's command, and dug my paddle deep into a wave.

On the next stroke, I dug it into air, as the raft perched momentarily on the crest of another wave. We were halfway through the rapids. I looked at the water ahead and suddenly realized why this stretch of white water is called Big Nasty. Two huge waves snarled at the end of the rapids. They were big and nasty looking.

"Paddle hard! Hard! Forward paddle, everyone!" Staab commanded.

"Paddle hard, Dave," Farner yelled to me from the seat behind mine, making sure I could hear Staab's orders. I had no time to answer.

"Here comes a big wave. Paddle hard!" Staab shouted, leaning on the long, rudderlike steering paddle.

"Yaaahooo!" I screamed above the roar of the waves. I paddled hard and craned my neck to look at the eight-foot wave we were about to punch through. The wave hit us hard. It plucked me from the bow and dumped me in a heap in the bottom of the raft at Farner's feet. The white water surged around me as I half floated in the bottom of the raft. My wetsuit booties slipped on the slick floor of the raft when I tried to clamber back to the bow seat.

"Left back. Hard, paddle hard! Forward paddle now," Staab continued with orders.

"Switch with me, Dave," Farner yelled over the noise. He slid into the bow section of the raft. I struggled to my knees, still holding my paddle, and managed to sit back up on the side of the raft.

"How did you get up here?" Mrs. Schwartz asked Farner, wondering how he had taken my place amidst the chaos. Farner grinned as we floated out of Big Nasty.

The rest of the trip had exciting moments, but none were as thrilling for me as the moment I found myself in Big Nasty's grip. The river was calm between each set of rapids, which allowed time for us to rest before shooting the next set. I was ready to relax and put on warm clothes by the end of the trip.

After we pulled the rafts from the river, the buses took us back to Indian Lake, where warm clothes and a good meal awaited us.

I was curious about how the Adirondack white water compared to the Snake and Colorado rivers. I asked Mr. and Mrs. Schwartz what they thought of the day's adventure.

"The rafts on the Colorado are much bigger, and crisscrossed with ropes," Mrs. Schwartz recalled. "You're just a passenger really. What you do is hang on for dear life. It's like riding a bucking bronco."

Her husband agreed, adding that the Colorado River was much rougher, and that they went on the Snake River trip mostly for the scenery.

"The Adirondack white-water trips are a good blend of beautiful scenery and exciting white water," Mrs. Schwartz said, pleased she had come to raft in New York State.

New York Alive, 1989

Ports of Call and
Beautiful Places

An old salt I know in Bay Head, who also happens to run a marina, told me once that most of the time the beautiful boats under his care just sit at the dock. Power or sail, it doesn't matter, he said, they sit and wait for their owners to take them somewhere, and often they never leave home waters. It struck me as quite odd, the idea of owning a boat capable of cruising long distances and yet only keeping to the backwaters of the bays behind New Jersey's barrier islands. After that conversation, I watched the comings and goings of the boats around me with an eye to proving this old gent wrong.

Yes, the boats did leave the dock. The owners piled beer and picnic lunches aboard, along with the kids, and often the family dog or cat, and joyfully set off on a cruise to some pretty spot. But when night fell, they'd be back. Occasionally, I'd notice boats that would disappear for a week, though that was pretty rare. I realized the old salt was right: most boats never go any great distance from home, and, after giving the matter some thought, it makes sense.

After all, the vast majority of people who own boats, and people who don't, for that matter, must work very hard to keep a roof over their heads, put food on the table, and pay the light bill. Leisure time is as scarce as diamonds in the modern world, and while a boat is a form of leisure for many it's not the be all and end all. The boat is just a part of the overall leisure-time equation, not its sum total.

Then, of course, not every skipper has the skill or the inclination to test the waters, so to speak, and take his or her boat into the realm of the unfamiliar and all of its challenges and potential dangers. For these boaters, it's best to keep to the safe, the sure, and the expected, which, again, makes sense. If you only have a little time on your boat, you might as well take the best shot at having a good time aboard it. I can tell you from personal experience that cruising long distances is not always fun. In fact, it can be dangerous, extremely tiring, and even boring sometimes.

Yet, even though many boats don't venture far from home waters, there are some that do. Mine has taken me thousands of miles through the waters of the Northeast, as I journeyed to and from the Great Lakes, up and down the Hudson River, and up and down the coast from Manasquan Inlet to Maine. I had the luxury of time, and, perhaps, in retrospect, the luxury of few employment possibilities that could have tempted me to stay home and earn money like most folks. I lived simply and cheaply on my little sailboat, which cost practically nothing in terms of fuel, when I needed the engine, and nothing, when I didn't.

The experience of taking a small boat long distances brings with it the joy of being free from the confines of conventional life, the same old day-to-day routine that for many means stability. It allows you to see places from a perspective on the water that compares little to seeing the same location from land. It enables the soul by giving it time to breathe, and unencumbers the mind by giving it time to think. It feeds the spirit that burns inside every person who loves to watch the clouds dance across the sky, the sun slowly set in a lightshow of reds, oranges, and the deep blue and purple accents of the coming night, who cannot find anything greater than the feel of the warm sun on the skin, the brush of wind through tousled hair. All this is part of what makes cruising long distances something worth doing for those who have the time, the means, or just the excuse to cut the ties to land and go.

The stories you will find here were mostly drawn from personal visits to beautiful ports of call I enjoyed during my journey on the sweet water of inland lakes and rivers. They were all written for the cruising yachtsman who might want to visit these places with their own boats, and so you will find some pretty hands-on information about navigation and accommodations for boats and their owners mixed into the more general facts about the ports.

For the boater, perhaps these stories will inspire a longer trip this season, one that will take you far from home waters to experience some of the greatness your boat can offer you. For the nonboater, these pages will take you to places you may not have ever been, and will provide you a glimpse into what a cruising yachtsman must think about after he or she has cast off the lines and heads off to find what awaits just over the horizon.

CRUISING THE CHOSEN PLACE

The Finger Lakes, once considered an Eden by the Iroquois, offer boaters the fruits of discovery. This region of New York attracts more than eight million visitors every year, primarily by car or trailerboat. But the two largest lakes, Cayuga and Seneca, are also accessible for cruisers from Lake Ontario and Lake Erie via the Erie Canal. The Finger Lakes offer cruisers a selection of marinas and state park dockage, small-town hospitality, historic sites and museums, a multitude of activities, and the fine dining and cultural events available in Ithaca, one of the larger cities of the region.

The Finger Lakes embody a character distinct from the Great Lakes. The Ice Age had a hand in creating both sets of waterways, but the process took a unique turn in forming the Finger Lakes. Mile-high sheets of ice rode up against the barrier of the Appalachian Plateau and carved out deep troughs in old stream valleys. The resistant plateau funneled the erosive power of the ice, cutting lakes from north to south into long narrow waterways shaped much like the outstretched fingers of a human hand. Of New York's 7,500 lakes and ponds, no others were formed in quite the same way. Cruising there feels like boating within a valley, hemmed in on either side by rolling, verdant hills and fertile fields.

It's a place steeped in the ancient history of the Iroquois and their predecessors, the pre-Iroquois Lamoka culture, the citizens of which may have occupied the land since the last of the glaciers receded 10,000 years ago. The indigenous peoples of the region called it "The Chosen Place," believing that the Creator had blessed it and left His handprint upon the land. Later, as the age of European exploration began, the deep valleys and marshes and the presence of the feared Iroquois kept the region relatively free from settlement. After the Revolutionary War, much of this land was given to former soldiers of the Continental Army and settlement began in earnest.

With the opening of the Erie Canal in 1825 and the Cayuga/Seneca Canal in 1828, the region became an industrial and agricultural center. A moderate climate also allowed the blossoming of a notable winery region. The Finger Lakes are exceptionally deep and the deepest of them seldom freeze, making conditions favorable for growing grapes. Today more than forty wineries dot the area's hills and fields and form the locus of the Northeast wine industry.

As you spend days on the lakes fishing, swimming, and exploring, and nights at anchor or tied up to the many dock sites, the past and present merge into one, a heady blend of history and recreational activity combining into a truly charming waterborne vacation.

GETTING THERE

The Cayuga/Seneca Canal branches off from the Erie Canal within the broad reaches of the 6,432–acre Montezuma National Wildlife Refuge. Flocks of ducks and geese and other migratory birds fill the sky and roost among the grass during the spring and fall. The swamp, which posed a formidable barrier to the early settlers and the gangs of Irish immigrants who dug the canal with picks and shovels, inspires awe with its natural beauty spread out in a flat panorama of still water.

The canal passes under the New York State Thruway and leads straight to Cayuga Lake after Lock 1 and the Guard Gate (sixteen-

Figure 11. Inside the bowels of a lock on the Erie Canal. PHOTO BY DAVID W. SHAW.

foot vertical clearance). Here you can stop for the night at Lockview Marina before you proceed into Cayuga Lake or follow the canal past the towns of Seneca Falls and Waterloo to Seneca Lake. Most cruisers will take the first opportunity to leave the confines of the canal system for open water, making Cayuga Lake their first stop.

CAYUGA LAKE

This lake was named after the Cayugas who lived along its shores. They were known as "people of the muckland" because of their close proximity to the Montezuma Marsh. The Cayugas called the lake "Tiohero" meaning "clear water." The name would still fit today. Cayuga is the largest of the eleven Finger Lakes at thirty-eight miles long and over two miles wide, with depths up to 435 feet.

Anglers will find an abundance of good fishing on any Finger Lake, including Cayuga. In the shallows of the weedy bottom, largemouth bass, bullheads, and carp thrive. Northern pike, smallmouth bass, lake trout, landlocked salmon, sunfish, yellow perch, and smelt swim in the deeper waters. The state requires anglers to obtain a fishing license, and five-day licenses are available.

Cayuga Lake State Park, located about four miles east of Seneca Falls at the north end of Cayuga Lake, has a boat harbor that offers dockage and a pumpout station. Water depths are five feet or less. The shallow water warms up nicely during the summer, making swimming here pleasant. The park was the site of a short-lived reservation for the Cayugas in the late 1700s, and later the area served as a lake resort.

The lake deepens about six miles south of the entrance. Two miles beyond buoy 51 on the east shore, you will find four excellent marinas, which welcome transients and are within walking distance of Union Springs. This town overlooks a natural bay on the lake. Frontenac Island, the only natural island in the Finger Lakes, lies just offshore in front of the town and offers swimming and picnic facilities. Golf, tennis, horseback riding, and the Cayuga Indian Castle, site of St. Joseph's Mission back in 1654, are nearby.

Taughannock Falls State Park is eight miles north of Ithaca on the west shore. It's a fine place to stop for sightseeing. The majestic falls plummet 215 feet over a sheer precipice; it's the highest vertical single-drop waterfall in the Northeastern United States, fifty feet higher than Niagara Falls. Hiking trails offer splendid views of this scenic place. Tie-up docks are available.

ITHACA

At the south end of Cayuga Lake, you can sample the amenities and diverse attractions of Ithaca, home to Cornell University and Ithaca College. The Allen H. Treeman State Marine Park, located one mile north of Ithaca on the west side of the lake just inside Cayuga Inlet, ranks as the largest inland marina in New York State, with thirty-nine transient berths, a pumpout station, showers, and picnic areas. In addition to the state park, there are three marinas in Ithaca, and another about seven miles north of the city on the east shore near Myers Point.

Near the state park marina, pretty Cass Park features an Olympic-sized pool, tennis courts, and picnic and fishing areas. The Farmers' Market, open 10:00 A.M. to 2:00 P.M. on Sundays, is also nearby at Steamboat Landing and Third Street from June through October. Hangar Theater is a professional regional summer theater open mid-June through August featuring drama, comedies, musicals, one-act plays, and children's programming.

Ithaca Commons on East Green Street is a downtown pedestrian marketplace adorned with fountains, trees, flowers and benches where you can sit and relax. Shop at the more than 100 specialty stores for fashion apparel, art, crafts, music and books, or dine at the many restaurants there and in the surrounding vicinity.

Only one winery calls Ithaca home, Six Mile Creek Vineyard at 1551 Slateville Road. You'll need to take a cab to see it. It's open daily from June through December. Wines include Ithaca White, Cascandilla White, and Ithaca Red. The well-kept Newman Municipal golf course on Pier Road is just off the lake. Ithaca is a fine place to tie the boat up and drive to the wineries and historic sites not readily accessible by water.

BACK ON THE CAYUGA/SENECA CANAL

Leaving Cayuga Lake, you turn back onto the Cayuga/Seneca Canal and pass through the western edge of the Montezuma Marsh to Locks 2 and 3 at Seneca Falls. This town was the site of the first Women's Rights Convention in 1848 and is known as the birthplace of the women's rights movement. Suffrage leader Elizabeth Cady Stanton and activist Amelia Bloomer lived there. The Women's Rights National Historical Park, which includes the National Women's Hall of Fame, extends into neighboring Waterloo.

Seneca Falls is one of fourteen Urban and Cultural Park communities in New York. Information about the town's attractions is available at the Information Center at 115 Fall Street, open Monday through Saturday from 10:00 A.M. to 4:00 P.M.

Between bridges S-6 and S-7 you will find a long tie-up wall with electricity and water, reported to be free of charge courtesy of the town of Seneca Falls. The wall is located within easy walking distance of the town's restaurants, stores, and historic buildings.

Waterloo, known as the birthplace of Memorial Day, was the first place in the country to have a community-wide observance for veterans on May 5, 1866. The Waterloo Memorial Day Museum on Main Street is open from Memorial Day to Labor Day, Tuesday through Friday, 1:30 P.M. to 4:00 P.M. The Seneca Country Fair is held in Waterloo the third week in July, and is reported to be a great party for the whole family.

SENECA LAKE

From Seneca Falls to the entrance of Seneca Lake, you will find a number of good marinas; some are listed in the Waterway Guide, others are shown on the canal charts and listed in the Finger Lakes Travel Guide. The other major concentration of marina facilities is at the south end of the lake in Watkins Glen. Most are listed in the Waterway Guide; other listings are included in the Finger Lakes Travel Guide.

Seneca Lake is thirty-five miles long, more than two miles wide at some points, and 635 feet deep. Seneca Lake State Park, located at the entrance to the lake, offers twenty-four transient berths in a protected basin, a picnic area with fireplaces, showers, a pumpout station, and swimming at a shady beach.

About eleven miles south of Geneva on the eastern shore, Samson State Park offers excellent transient dockage, hot showers, tennis courts, a pumpout station, swimming, picnic areas with fireplaces, and a concession stand.

WATKINS GLEN

Perhaps best known for its auto racing, the village of Watkins Glen at the south end of Seneca Lake is also a fine destination for the cruising yachtsman. The Franklin Street shopping district offers a wide variety of stores and restaurants. The Seneca Harbor Park has a 300–foot fishing pier, a marina, and the Vintage Auto Museum. In the hills above the village lies the Watkins Glen International Racing Circuit, where auto races are held on summer weekends.

The gorge at Watkins Glen State Park contains nineteen waterfalls and scenic trails along cascades, grottoes, and amphitheaters, all within a short distance of the lakefront. Walking along trails that wind through the park is both relaxing and beautiful. At dusk, Timespell, a sound and laser light show performed in the park, tells the story of how the gorge was created. The park also has scenic areas, pavilions, an Olympic-sized swimming pool, a gift shop, and a snack bar.

Following the three-mile Seneca Canal leading from Seneca Lake, a marina and park are located at Montour Falls. Here the Chequago Falls drop 165 feet, a stark contrast to the flatlands bordering Catherine Creek, famous for its trout fishing.

A cruise to Cayuga and Seneca lakes will provide enough diverse recreational activities, scenery, and history to fill even a lengthy vacation. Chances are you won't see and do everything in one visit, but will return another time to experience all the Finger Lakes region has to offer. The Finger Lakes Association reports that many visitors return repeatedly to vacation in the Finger Lakes; once you've experienced the area, a strange kind of magnetism draws you back, again and again.

Lakeland Boating, 1995

UNLOCKING LAKE CHAMPLAIN

Once known as the key to the continent, today Lake Champlain is a boater's paradise. Nestled in a deep valley between the Adirondack and Green mountains on the eastern fringe of Great Lakes country, Lake Champlain's scenery rivals Superior's vast, untamed shores and Huron's spectacular Georgian Bay, two of the most well-loved cruising grounds in the Great Lakes region.

But for Erie and Ontario boaters who don't have time to voyage to these scenic places, these western waters might as well be on the moon. Lake Champlain, on the other hand, stands nearby and ready to be explored. For Great Lakes cruisers headed up or down the Intracoastal Waterway via the Erie-Hudson link, Lake Champlain is not to be missed. On this, the country's sixth-largest body of freshwater besides the Great Lakes, boaters experience the thrill of racing across the waves with summits on either shore as a backdrop. Not all of the lake is like this however, and that's part of its charm.

In the southernmost reaches upon emerging from the sixty-mile Champlain Canal at Whitehall, the lake looks canal-like. Well to the north above Burlington, Vermont, many of the lake's more than seventy-five islands jut from the surface. The lake's larger islands, Grand Isle, North Hero, and Isle La Motte sit roughly in the middle and form an almost Y-shaped waterway with New York to the west, Vermont to the east, and Canada to the north.

Although the lake is accessible from the St. Lawrence River, most boaters will take the Champlain Canal. Along the way, quiet anchorages and small, historic towns, full-service marinas, and small cities with all the cultural attractions of their larger cousins await the inquisitive cruiser. Beyond the marshes of the upper Champlain Canal, peninsulas protrude from the shores and the lake slowly begins to widen. The narrows to the south proved invaluable during wars, an integral part of Lake Champlain's history.

Lake Champlain was once known as "the key to the Continent." Even before canals, the 107–mile lake marked the center of a set of loosely connected waterways. After a portage from the Hudson River, it provided an easy path north to the Richelieu River and the St. Lawrence River, the main link to the Great Lakes and the Atlantic Ocean before the Champlain Canal was completed almost 200 years ago. The waterways made an ideal highway for warfare between the Iroquois and the Algonkian. Europeans also used it often for bloody purposes. In fact, in 1609, Samuel de Champlain discovered the lake because of war. He and his Algonkian and Huron friends traveled up the northward flowing Richelieu River and Lake Champlain for a bit of sport with the Iroquois, who lived on the lake at the time. It was then that the Iroquois got their first taste of firearms.

Later, forts were built on the southern narrows—one at Ticonderoga and two at Crown Point. The fully restored Fort Ti, located about twenty-three miles above Whitehall, is well worth a visit. A climb up nearby Mount Defiance is rewarded with one of the most captivating vistas in the Northeast. Because of its commanding view of the surrounding waterways, it was used as a watch station during early wars. Anchorage is available off the beach south of Fort Ti and a short hike will take you to the grounds.

Beyond Fort Ti on this stretch of the western shore, the Adirondack Mountains tower above the lake. The rounded peaks are the stumps of an ancient range more than a billion years old and once possibly as high as the Himalayas. When the Adirondacks were younger, about 500 million years ago, great crustal upheaval occurred in the region. The deep Lake Champlain Valley was created, and the Green Mountains to the east rose skyward. The present lake sits ninety-five feet above sea level (Lake Ontario sits at 245 feet and Lake Erie at 570 feet), but its depths extend more than 400 feet below the surface. Way back through the annals of time, the ocean covered much of the lowlands of the region. The sediments formed on the bottom of the ancient sea are still visible today in the form of bluffs and hills.

Against the backdrop of mountains, Bulwagga Bay at Port Henry, and North West Bay at Westport offer anchorages and marinas. Westport is a good place to reprovision. Across from Westport on the eastern shore in Vermont, Button Bay State Park offers a beautiful beach and good anchorage. Beaches are part of the lake's attraction— glaciers left them behind when they receded 10,000 years ago. The lake's character stems from the many natural forces that created it, and the visual appeal is every bit as grand as Mother Nature.

Lake Champlain is famous for great fishing. About sixty species of fish swim here, including lake trout, bass, salmon, walleye and northern pike. Just one mile north of Button Bay, Basin Harbor offers a marina and the Lake Champlain Maritime Museum. The museum features a number of fascinating exhibits of maritime artifacts found buried in the lake's sediment. Its centerpiece is a replica of the *Philadelphia*, a revolutionary war gunboat. Adjacent to the museum is the Basin Harbor Club. This marina offers transient dockage, a swimming pool, showers for overnight guests, and a restaurant.

The sleepy town of Essex, famed for its well-preserved ante-bellum architecture, Willsboro Bay, and Cumberland Bay, home of Plattsburgh, rank as popular destinations. Plattsburgh, the largest city on the western shore, offers a semi-urban escape from the otherwise bucolic surroundings.

Plattsburgh has the largest freshwater beach in the country and plenty of restaurants a short walk from the harbor's marina facilities. Walking tours of the town and the old Plattsburgh Air Force Base are welcome diversions.

For museum buffs, the Clinton County Historical Museum and the

Kent-Delord House Museum are worth a visit, and the SUNY Plattsburgh Art Museum has more than 4,000 works in styles ranging from antique to contemporary. The Plattsburgh Community Orchestra and North Country Ballet Ensemble provide quality performances.

About six miles south of Plattsburgh, Valcour Lodge bills itself as Plattsburgh's only lakeside restaurant. It offers dockage and moorings for its patrons. Two other marinas are close by on Day Point: Olde Valcour Marina and Snug Harbor Marina.

Like much of the lake, Valcour Island, just off the mainland, boasts historic military significance. In 1776, under the command of General Benedict Arnold, the first American fleet to engage British warships clashed there with disastrous results for the Yanks. During the War of 1812, another naval battle occurred. This time America won, stopping an invasion of New York.

On the eastern shore, Burlington, the largest city on Lake Champlain, offers a multitude of diverse attractions. Unfortunately, the facilities at the port are limited for cruisers. Some dockage is available at the Lake Champlain Transportation Company's ferry dock or the Community Boathouse, but you won't find showers at either. Boats often anchor behind the breakwater, and there are also some moorings available.

Despite its limited marina facilities, Burlington is still worth visiting. The waterfront is just a short walk or trolley ride from the heart of downtown dining and shopping, and there's nightly entertainment at the Church Street Marketplace. The marketplace includes 130 specialty shops, twenty restaurants, street vendors, live entertainment, and festivals. Just south of Burlington are Shelburne Bay's excellent accommodations for boaters. Well protected from all but north winds, it's within reasonable taxi fare to Burlington. Above Burlington, cruisers will find some of the most scenic waters of the lake; islands and protected bays abound. Attractive ports replete with boating amenities include Malletts Bay, a nearly landlocked harbor, and St. Albans, site of a scenic state park and the Red Sandrock Hills.

Farthest north lies Missisquoi Bay, with its northern shore in Canadian territory. It's the broad terminus of the westward-flowing river it was named after and forms a lake within a lake, distinct and wild. Cruising Lake Champlain offers a combination of attractions ranging from a near wilderness experience with terrific mountain scenery and the amenities of civilization found in its towns and cities. It may not be a Great Lake, but it certainly is great in all other ways.

Lakeland Boating, 1996

The Finger Lakes region and Lake Champlain were both enchanting. However, for a fellow who enjoys sailing, the close confines of
the canal system one must take to get to each got a little tiring. The
mast must be taken down and put back up to truly take in the
beauty of Lake Champlain, not a very easy chore, nor an inexpensive one. To see the Finger Lakes, you have to keep your mast down,
unless you've got a boat that is small enough so you rig and unrig it
yourself. The only marinas equipped for transient mast work are at
each end of the Erie Canal system, effectively locking larger sailboats
out. Of course, there are plenty of big sailboats on Seneca and Cayuga lakes, but they don't usually travel on the Erie Canal, and, if
they do, they leave their home port with their mast lashed securely
to the rails of the boat or perched in a cradle built to keep the owner
from banging head and shoulders on the downed spar.

When I arrived in Oswego, New York, at the eastern edge of Lake
Ontario, I'd come through about thirty locks on the Erie and Oswego
canals. I encountered some strikingly beautiful country on my way
to Lake Ontario, and had a few adventures, too, including a close
encounter with a lock wall filled with Zebra mussels, which spit at me
as the lock drained. Seeing the big lake at last almost made me yelp
for joy. It meant I could sail once again, and, to do it on a Great
Lake after all those years of sailing boats on the ocean held a special kind of magic for me.

I lingered in Oswego, in part to wait out some nasty weather, and
in part because I found the place interesting. It looks gray and industrial, and it is. But upon closer examination I discovered the real
spirit of the port, plus its intriguing place in the history of the United
States.

OSWEGO, NEW YORK, WELCOMES BOATERS TO CANAL COUNTRY

It's easy to view the industrial port of Oswego, New York, on the east
end of Lake Ontario, as a place to stop on the way to somewhere else.
When you arrive, you're either heading to the north shore, the Thousand Islands, into or out of canal country via the Oswego Canal, or to
south shore points such as Sodus Bay and Rochester. Unfortunately,
many boaters visiting Oswego don't learn about this historic port or
its present amenities and attractions. They just pass through, quite literally, like ships in the night.

The next time you're cruising the east end of Lake Ontario, schedule a full day or two into your float plan to enjoy Oswego's fine restaurants, museums, diverse architecture and friendly people. You'll find
this an interesting and fun port of call.

The city's biggest summer event, the famous Harborfest weekend,
has been held every July since 1988 and ranks as one of the premier

festivals in the Northeast. Hundreds of thousands of people crowd the 19,000-resident city to enjoy the amusement park rides, concerts, exhibits, foods, fireworks, and much more. If you visit by boat during Harborfest (which may not be such a great idea), reserve a slip well in advance or you'll be rafted several boats deep against the east wall, or jammed at anchor in the harbor.

For the navigator, finding Oswego couldn't be easier. Vapor rising from the huge stack of the Nine Mile Point nuclear power plant to the east of the port is often visible across the lake from as far as Stony Point. Likewise, the stacks of the Niagara Mohawk power complex on the west side of the harbor can be seen many miles offshore. Strobe lights illuminate the stacks, making a splendid landmark for a night approach. An enormous breakwater hems in the harbor, however, and some say it can be tricky to find the entrance, particularly at night.

As you enter the harbor, to starboard you'll see industrial buildings, cement silos, and tanks. To port, you'll pass a large commercial dock. A little farther on is Oswego Marina. They charge $1.25 per foot for a slip inside their protected yacht basin, and $.75 per foot to tie up against the east wall—no water or electric hookups, just a plain old cleat for your money.

Many boaters tie up for free to the guard rail along the public end of the east wall just beyond the fence belonging to Oswego Marina. The downside is that you can expect to be charged $2.50 to use the bathroom. Wright's Landing, a municipal marina, is on the west side of the harbor and contains pretty shallow water. You can anchor inside the breakwater, but the harbor is subject to surge in strong northerly blows.

Another disadvantage to the free space along the east wall is that it's very public and fairly busy with fishermen using the wall around the boats. Anglers consider Oswego harbor a prime fishing spot, since it is deep and fish back up against the lock and dam. At times the water literally teems with them. If you don't mind the lack of privacy along the free wall (the marina's wall is just a little more private), you do reap a nice reward. You can easily walk to the restaurants along the waterfront and to a twenty-four-hour supermarket.

A visit to the Fort Ontario State Historic Site, only a fifteen-minute walk from the east wall, will take you back in time as you walk through the stone entryway and emerge in the courtyard of the fort. You can roam the buildings and bastions, and talk with interpreters dressed in nineteenth-century costumes. Plan on a visit of several hours, since it would be a shame to hurry and miss reading the fascinating history of the fort and region.

From July until Labor Day, daily drills and a retreat ceremony are held by the Fort Guard at 11:00 A.M., 2:30 P.M. and 4:30 P.M. The fort is open Wednesday through Saturday from 10:00 A.M. to 5:00 P.M. Visitors pay a modest admission charge of $3 for adults and $1.50 for children four to eleven. To round out your Oswego educational tour, a visit to the H. Lee White Marine Museum is a must. The museum provides visitors with a tour of the maritime history of the port and Lake Ontario through various time periods. In addition to the main building, the museum has Derrick #8 open to the public. This was the last steam-powered barge on the Erie Canal, which would have been scrapped if the museum hadn't preserved the vessel.

Another attraction on the east side of the harbor, at the commercial dock, is the *Nash*. This venerable old oceangoing tug was used to ferry supplies to troops during the D-Day Invasion of Normandy in World War II. Sailors aboard the *Nash* shot down a German plane during the invasion. After the war, the *Nash* served on the Great Lakes for forty years. Now, designated as a national landmark, the tug is open to the public. The museum does not charge for admission, but donations are appreciated.

Oswego's Heritage Foundation sponsors two self-guided walking tours that take you to the many nineteenth-century buildings throughout the city. They include the Oswego County Courthouse, Oswego City Hall, and the Oswego City Library, which are listed in the National Registry of Historic Places.

This old city is packed with historic significance not only for the Lake Ontario region, but for the nation as well. Early on, the value of Oswego as a port was evident. It was established as an official port in 1725 and was the first freshwater port in the Americas. Oswego was deemed of vital strategic and commercial value because it lay at the head of what was a patchwork of waterways that ran from the Atlantic to Lake Ontario. Explorers, missionaries, and fur traders traveled north up the Hudson River, then westward on the Mohawk River, across Oneida Lake, and on the Oneida River to a place known as Three Rivers, where the Oneida, Seneca, and Oswego rivers meet. The Oswego River flows north to Lake Ontario. This watery trail opened the wilderness to exploration. At its head, Oswego was the site of battles as far back as 1756, when the French destroyed all British defenses there. The Americans destroyed British defenses there during the Revolutionary War, and the British tried to return the favor in the War of 1812, but failed to accomplish their primary goal of capturing naval stores hidden at Oswego Falls.

From a commercial standpoint, Oswego was always a key shipbuilding port. Its prosperity increased greatly when the Erie Canal was completed in 1825 and the Oswego Canal followed in 1828. The patchwork of waterways leading from the free Oswego Canal to Oswego let shippers avoid additional freight tolls. Then goods would be loaded onto Great Lakes schooners and steamers bound for Lake Erie via the Welland Canal. When tolls were eliminated on the Erie Canal, and when newer cargo ships became too large for the Welland Canal, merchants had no choice but to ship goods west across New York State to Buffalo on the shores of Lake Erie. In 1870, approximately 900,000 tons were shipped on the Oswego Canal. In 1900, only 30,000 tons were.

Today, the port remains a transfer point for goods headed to and from industrial cities in central New York via the Oswego Canal. While not the hub of shipping it once was, Oswego is nevertheless an active commercial port. It's also an active port for recreational boating and fishing, and is a worthy destination when you next cruise the east end of Lake Ontario's south shore.

Lakeland Boating, 1995

> The south shore of Lake Ontario is much different from the Canadian side up north. For one it's a little more industrial, and for another, it's got Rochester. Sure, the Canadians have Toronto, a pretty nice place, I'll grant you. But a trip along the south shore to Rochester was well worth the time it took to get there. The big city sometimes is as alluring as a quiet cove or a secluded island.

ROCHESTER, NEW YORK

Bright lights, big city. Imagine yourself at the "World's Image Center."

Kicking up your heels in a waterfront city after a stint of secluded anchorages or small towns is always a welcome change of pace. Lake Ontario's alluring charm lies in its pleasant mix of urban and rural cruising. About fifty miles west of Oswego, Rochester is the third largest city in New York and home to more than one million residents. A booming tourist industry attracts about a million and a half people annually.

It's no surprise that boaters consider Rochester one of the lake's top urban ports of call and often stay longer than they originally planned once the city's magic takes hold. The amenities for boaters include a number of full-service marinas, yacht clubs, well-stocked marine supply stores, and markets. The theaters, restaurants, stores, art galleries, museums, beach, boardwalk, amusement park, and zoo comprise a hefty list of attractions diverse enough to entertain virtually anyone.

Situated close to Lake Ontario, Rochester is distinctly riverine in character. The city's center lies five miles up the Genesee River above two waterfalls that block navigation. Once you enter the channel between the two breakwaters at the mouth of the Genesee River, however, you'll spot the marinas that support Rochester's boating community. Voyager Boat Sales, Shumway Marine, and Riverview Yacht Basin all welcome vacationing cruisers with ample transient dockage. The Rochester and Genesee Yacht Clubs accommodate boats from reciprocating clubs. In all cases, it's a good idea to call ahead for reservations, especially on weekends.

Along with the marinas, you will notice two bridges crossing the Genesee River. The railroad swing bridge is usually open, and the Stutson Street bascule Bridge opens on the hour and half hour, except during rush hours.

You'll find provisions, marine supplies, and restaurants in the area near the harbor, and the city's attractions are only minutes away by bus or taxi. The Regional Transit System bus lines run near the marinas and make up for the minor inconvenience of a slip a short distance away from the city proper. The average bus fare is one dollar, and a "Free Fare Zone" operates weekdays between 11:00 A.M. and 2:00 P.M. within the downtown's inner loop.

After you've found a berth and settled in, hop a bus downtown and stroll through the city. You'll find big-city excitement, including trendy boutiques, antique shops, and countless excellent restaurants. This is no sleepy town, but a thriving metropolis with many large corporations. Among the big businesses stationed here are Eastman Kodak company, Xerox, and Bausch & Lomb—all of which began in Rochester and developed revolutionary imaging technologies. This bit of history has come to be one of Rochester's claims to fame; it now promotes itself as "The World's Image Center," in homage to the three giants that call the city home and have fostered its boom.

Rochester got its start in industry in 1789 when enterprising settlers saw the profit that could be earned by harnessing the power of the Genesee River. They built a mill above the waterfalls and began making flour. Eventually, flour became the city's primary industry during the nineteenth century, and Rochester earned the nickname "Flour Capital of the Nation."

The Erie Canal passes through the city, and when it was completed in 1825, the cheap transportation of goods to markets in the heartland became a reality, further laying the foundation for Rochester's prosperity. The Port of Genesee also provided easy avenues for shipping goods throughout the region.

The combination of lake, river, and canal shaped the fortune of

Rochester. When visiting by boat, it's obvious that the water has always played a key role in both the business and leisure sides of life here.

One of Rochester's prime recreational attractions is its shore, Ontario Beach Park. During its heyday between 1884 and 1915, the park was called the Coney Island of the West, meaning western New York. In addition to boasting excellent swimming and fine, sandy beaches, Ontario Beach attracted thousands of visitors to its amusement park, dancing pavilions, Japanese gardens, and concerts.

Today, the park is still a popular spot on the waterfront. It features a wide beach several hundred feet deep and more than half a mile long, a 1,200-foot boardwalk with gazebos, a 1931-era bathhouse, a historic Denzel carousel built in 1905, a concert pavilion, and much more. Lifeguards are on duty from 10:30 A.M. to dusk during the summer. If swimming isn't your cup of tea, a visit is still worthwhile in the evening to catch one of the many concerts held at the park. Last summer these performances included a Dixieland Jazz Festival, the Rochester Marimba Band, and the Rochester Philharmonic Orchestra. Every June, the Rochester Harbor and Carousel Festival draws thousands to the park.

When you make plans to visit Ontario Beach Park, allot enough time for a side trip to the Charlotte/Genesee Lighthouse on the west bank of the Genesee River near the park. The lighthouse was built in 1822, making it one of the oldest on the Great Lakes. Inside is an exhibit that traces the history of lighthouses, the Port of Genesee, and lake transportation. It's open to the public on weekends, May through October from 1:00 P.M. to 5:00 P.M.

On the east side of the Genesee River, close to Irondequoit Bay, is the Seabreeze Amusement Park. You'll find all the fun you'd expect—from wild coasters to spots to relax with a tropical drink at Paradise Island.

Moving away from the lakefront, virtually every visitor tours the International Museum of Photography at the George Eastman House. This magnificent mansion was built by George Eastman, founder of the Eastman Kodak Company. His first camera was introduced in 1888 and it revolutionized photography. The museum contains one of the world's largest collections of photographs, motion pictures, and photographic equipment, and its palatial rooms have been maintained in their original Victorian splendor.

Another popular downtown attraction is the recently restored Brown's Race Historic District, just a few blocks from Main Street and adjacent to the city's inner loop. Walk along the Pont de Rennes

Pedestrian Bridge and gaze at the beauty of the ninety-six-foot water-fall and the river gorge, or linger on a bench with an ice cream cone. While enjoying the lush scenery below, you'll see the historic build-ings of the Center at High Falls, among them the city's 1873 water-works that houses a visitor's center complete with exhibits depicting Rochester's history. The excavated ruins of an early nineteenth-century factory with its huge thirty-foot diameter waterwheel are also part of this historic district.

If you can, plan to visit Brown's Race in late afternoon. Have din-ner at the food court in the Brown's Race Market, then get ready for a treat. At dusk, colored lights illuminate the waterfall while a laser light and sound show projected on the gorge wall tells the story of Rochester. The laser show, entitled, "River of Light: A celebration of Rochester and the Genesee," has been one of Rochester's most popu-lar attractions since its debut in late 1992.

Also on the riverfront is Seneca Park, located on the eastern bank of the Genesee at St. Paul Street, just north of Route 104. The park includes picnic areas, hiking trails, and a public swimming pool. The park's main attraction for children and adults alike, however, is the Sen-eca Park Zoo, founded in 1894. The first phase of a ten-year recon-struction plan has begun to eliminate the traditional bars and cages in favor of exhibits that match the habitat of the animals, creating a more lifelike picture of how the creatures live in the wild. The zoo houses more than 500 animals, representing almost 200 species. It's open ev-ery day year-round from 10:00 A.M. until 5:00 P.M., except on summer weekends and holidays when the park closes at 7:00 P.M.

So much to do, so little time. That's likely to be your reaction when you visit Rochester. And the good news is that this city continues im-proving as a boating destination. Next time you cruise Lake Ontario, Rochester will be a much-looked-forward-to port of call for you and your family.

Lakeland Boating, 1994

Cruising partway down the St. Lawrence River was one of the high-lights of my journey through the Northeast. The mighty waterway flows northward from Lake Ontario about 700 miles to the Gulf of St. Lawrence in Quebec. Its mouth is barren, wild, and very forbidding to a pleasure boater, even one with a lot of courage. But the head-waters of the river are as kind to the cruiser as can be, and they have attracted boaters of all kinds for hundreds of years.

The Thousand Islands begin in earnest just beyond the environs of Wolfe Island, a massive piece of real estate approximately twenty miles long. The St. Lawrence Seaway, the main shipping channel leading to and from the Great Lakes, runs along the United States side of the river past a little town called Cape Vincent. Across the river on the other side of Wolfe Island is a grand Canadian city called Kingston. Both places were intriguing ports, though for different reasons which will become clear in the next two stories.

CAPE VINCENT'S FRENCH HERITAGE

Many of Lake Ontario's most scenic ports nest along the shores of rivers, enjoying both a lake and riverine ambiance. There's Rochester and Oswego, both at the mouths of northward flowing rivers, comparatively rare as rivers go. And, of course, there's the vibrant city of Kingston, Ontario, and Cape Vincent on the American side perched along the headwaters of one of the world's largest and most important rivers, the St. Lawrence.

Cape Vincent, it's as different in character from its Canadian neighbor as night and day. While Kingston bears the indelible stamp of the English, the little village of Cape Vincent, although most assuredly American in look and feel, cherishes its French heritage almost to the point of zeal. The little town just over three miles from Tibbets Point lighthouse holds many quiet pleasures for those cruising the big lake or making their way deep into the heart of the Thousand Islands farther downriver.

Turning the pages of history back more than 300 years to when the Onondaga Indians lived and hunted in the region, the first influence from the French came in the shape of two Catholic priests. Fathers Chaumonoit and Dablon preached the Word to the Onondaga. Later, a wealthy Frenchman, LeRay Chaumont, bought vast tracts of land in the newly formed United States of America, including much of present-day Cape Vincent. The Cape is named after Vincent LeRay.

Many of the landowners in the area hailed from France or could trace their roots back across the Atlantic to the land of the gay city of Paris. The residents watched keenly as the French revolted against their monarchy during the French Revolution, and not long afterward, they followed the military achievements of Napoleon Bonaparte. They even built a home for him on Real Street, the Cup and Saucer house, where he could live if ever he escaped from his island prison on the island of St. Helena.

Cruise to Cape Vincent on the second Saturday and Sunday in July and check out the town's annual French festival. You'll see Napoleon lead a parade, sample French pastries, giggle at the French puppet theater, and just have a great time. Get there a day or two early, however, since every available slip will be in high demand.

Figure 12. Boathouse and dock in Cape Vincent, New York. PHOTO BY DAVID W. SHAW.

Cape Vincent is one of the rare places where cruisers can find free dockage for periods no longer than two days. The village dock tucked behind the west end of the detached breakwater that protects the harbor can accommodate a dozen or so boats drawing no more than six feet. Additional free dockage is available at the Department of Environmental Conservation dock west of the village dock, though space is limited.

For the comforts of the town's only full-service marina in the harbor, Anchor Marina has 150 slips with ten to twenty set aside for transients at sixty cents a foot. Dockside 30 amp hookups, showers, pumpout, ice, bait, haulouts, and most mechanical, fiberglass, and wood repairs can be found there. The marina ([315] 654–2300) also sells diesel and gas.

Cape Vincent is home to the Cape Vincent Guide Association, a group of fifteen charter fishing boats operating out of the harbor. You can outfit yourself for some terrific black bass, walleye, muskie, lake trout, northern pike, and large and smallmouth bass fishing at Gault's Bait and Tackle.

Cape Vincent's main drag, Broadway, runs along the shore a stone's throw from the docks. As you walk up from the village dock, you'll find Captain Jack's on the right near the ferry dock. It's the town's only waterfront restaurant, serving a wide variety of sandwiches, pasta, and steaks. They offer dockage for guests and plan to have rooms available for the first time this year.

Aubrey's Inn serves the usual diner fare, but don't get the impression it's a greasy spoon. You'll get some good meals there. Right next to the inn you'll find Aubrey's Shopping Center which recently expanded its bakery and meat departments, making this a good stop for reprovisioning.

Two blocks down is the Cape Dairy convenience store and the Cape Laundramat. For fine dining, try the Sleepy Hollow Restaurant or for Cape Vincent's famous Friday night fishfry, Roxy's is the place to go. There's also a pizzeria, post office, and liquor store in town. The town has no taxi or car rentals, though you can rent bikes for a quick ride up to the Tibbets Point lighthouse, featuring a newly opened foghorn exhibit this year.

If you come by the Cape Vincent Chamber of Commerce on James Street near the ferry dock, you can get menus, a map, and other information about Cape Vincent. There's also a museum where you can learn more about the town and its heritage. The chamber ([315] 654–2481) is open from May to the end of October.

Lakeland Boating, 1997

KINGSTON, ONTARIO

A boating paradise fit for a king, Kingston, Ontario, has been called many different things by many different people. The Mississagua Indians who inhabited this region called it "Garden of the Great Spirit." Then the French settlers arrived and called it theirs. Later, when the American colonials banished the Brits after the Revolutionary War, Loyalists showed their obedience to the crown by settling here and changing the town's name to King's Town in 1783, in honor of the slightly mad King George III.

This last appellation is the one that would endure, though today it's not uncommon to hear locals affectionately refer to their town as Limestone City, for its foundation rests on a sprawling sheet of limestone, once the floor of an ancient ocean. The boaters who ply the sapphire waters of Kingston's harbor call this place "Freshwater Sailing Capital of the World." Once you visit this charming town hidden in the Thousand Islands, you'll call it boating paradise.

Few cruisers drawn to the unspoiled beauty of eastern Lake Ontario pass up the chance to visit Kingston. Located at the head of the St. Lawrence River, a short distance from the terrific cruising grounds of the Thousand Islands, Kingston is one of the prime cruising destinations on the east end of Lake Ontario.

All along Kingston's waterfront, grand limestone buildings built in the mid-1800s rub shoulders with modern resort hotels. This pleasing mix of the past and present, old and new is everywhere in Kingston. It's an appealing blend, and more than one million tourists visit Kingston every year to take in the sights. They often outnumber residents nearly ten to one as they walk the streets on warm summer evenings or sip Ontario-produced wines at European-style sidewalk cafes.

Kingston's cosmopolitan character comes from its international heritage. Prior to European settlement, the area around present-day Kingston was occupied by the Mississagua Indians, who called their home "Cataraqui," meaning "rocks standing in water." Then, in 1673 the governor of New France, an astute gent named Frontenac, realized the strategic importance of a settlement near the convergence of the St. Lawrence River, the Cataraqui River and Lake Ontario. The region's flat terrain, access to the three waterways and its ready supply of limestone made it a natural site for a city. Frontenac ordered his men to build a fort called Cataraqui, "borrowing" the name, as well as the land, from the Mississagua.

Soon Frontenac was proven right about Cataraqui's portentous location. The settlement became a key staging area for the exploration and settlement of upper Canada. The city's military importance lasted well after the War of 1812, which saw quite a bit of action on the east end of Lake Ontario. In 1826, the British, uneasy about the intentions of their upstart neighbors to the south, set about building the Rideau Canal to link the newly named King's Town and Ottawa. They completed it in 1832.

For a time, the canal was viewed as a key route for troops and supplies in the event of another war with the United States. But like the Erie Canal, it soon became clear that the Rideau would see mostly commercial and recreational traffic as railroads diminished the waterway's importance.

In modern times, Kingston has fared equally well. The city was Canada's first capital seat, though not for very long. It was also a bustling commercial port with a merchant fleet large enough to instill envy in other Lake Ontario cities. Today, Kingston's emphasis on lakeside sport and leisure activities is a telling departure from its former preoccupation with military, government, and commerce.

For the boater, Kingston is an easily accessible playground, with a slew of restaurants, museums, and art galleries all within walking distance of the city's lakefront.

The approaches to the city are well buoyed, but it's a good idea to follow your chart because shoals abound offshore. When approaching the city from Lake Ontario, look for the rounded dome of City Hall. This stunning building overlooks the Flora MacDonald Confederation Basin, a municipal facility with 300 transient slips. The Basin is one of four marinas that serve the area, but most cruisers opt for the Basin because of its terrific location smack in the middle of the downtown area.

The Basin may be convenient, but it's sometimes noisy, and the heads leave something to be desired. If you don't mind crowds, the marina isn't so bad—and it may be the only choice you have on a busy weekend.

Some boaters choose to anchor behind the Basin breakwater and take their dinghy to the dinghy dock to get ashore. Anchoring can be risky, however, due to industrial debris strewn on the bottom that sometimes traps anchors. Buoy your anchor just in case it gets stuck— you may be able to pull it out.

Kingston Marina is located just behind the La Salle Causeway Bridge (closed clearance is fourteen feet) in Anglin Bay on the Cataraqui River. It's not far from the action yet offers a much quieter stay, safe from the surges common during southwesterly blows. The bridge opens every hour on the hour from 6:00 A.M. to 10:00 P.M., except during rush hours, between 8:00 A.M. and noon, and between 4:00 P.M. and 5:00 P.M. The tender doesn't monitor VHF, but upon hearing the customary three-horn blast, he will open the bridge at scheduled times.

The Kingston Yacht Club has only one designated transient slip, though extra space is often available in the club's Med-style slips when members are out cruising. The club has a bar and dining room, and it's close to the attractions of the city.

The Portsmouth Olympic Harbor Marina, another municipal facility, caters mostly to seasonal boaters. Nevertheless, space is almost always available for transients, and you're guaranteed a quiet night. Its only disadvantage is you'll have to walk about a mile and a half to get downtown. Portsmouth Harbor was the site of the 1976 Olympic sailing events, and in August the Canadian Olympic Training Regatta Kingston (CORK) is held there. If you plan to visit Kingston in August, plan ahead—Portsmouth is likely to be full.

Just up the Cataraqui River, the lower reaches of the Rideau Canal make for an interesting side trip. You might want to build a couple of extra days into your float plan to go see it.

In the Confederation Park near the Basin, you'll find the Greater Kingston Office of Tourism. You can pick up all sorts of brochures and other materials to learn more about the attractions. If you haven't ordered a tourist package beforehand, this should be your first stop.

Take the fifty-minute narrated Confederation Tour Trolley ride through the city. The tour will let you cover a lot of ground without wearing down your boat shoes. It includes a swing through the Royal Military College and Port Henry, near downtown. The British built Fort Henry in the early 1800s up on the highest point of land in the area as a defense against American invasion. The fort's impressive collection of artifacts and exciting reenactments are sure to be a highlight of your trip. For a complete guide to Kingston's restaurants, visit the tourism office for a brochure, or ask the dockmaster for recommendations.

Those who wish to swig some of the best brews on the big lake should drop by the Kingston Brewing Co., known locally as "The Brew Pub." This British-style pub makes all of its wine, great food, and ale—including the famous Dragon's Breath Pale Ale—on the premises.

Other restaurants definitely worth a visit are Chez Piggy, the Clarence Street Grill, and Greco's Wine Bar and Grill. You can virtually eat your way through Kingston, trying Indian, Italian, Chinese, and Mexican restaurants, or simply by visiting family places with good food and reasonable prices. Plan on lots of dinners and lunches out when you budget for the trip. You won't regret it.

In keeping with its European counterparts, many of the establishments aren't air conditioned and beer and wine are often served warm, just as they are "across the pond." Of course, if you look around, you'll find plenty of spots that offer a blast of cold air to go with a chilled drink.

Between meals, drop by the Marine Museum of the Great Lakes. Its land exhibits and the museum ship, an ice breaker called Alexander Henry, are fascinating. The Murney Tower museum, a fortified

Martello tower overlooking the lake, and the Pump House Steam Museum are also worth visiting. All of these are right along the waterfront minutes from most of the marinas.

During July the city holds its annual Buskers Rendezvous. More than 100 magicians, jugglers, musicians, comedians, dancers, and mimes descend on the city to entertain the throngs of onlookers who gather for the event. Streets are blocked off to traffic, turning large portions of Kingston into a pedestrian mall.

Kingston combines the best of great wining and dining in a laid-back party atmosphere that also offers more cerebral activities, such as seeing a play or taking in a concert, against a backdrop of a city steeped in history and endowed with a pleasing array of architecture. Whether you fall in love with Kingston's world-class sailing, its colorful festivals, or its terrific international dining, you'll want to return soon to this town of kings.

Lakeland Boating, 1996

> Montreal was one port I couldn't reach with my boat. Its eight horse-power diesel just couldn't cut it in the swift currents downriver in Quebec. I could have gotten there easily enough; it would have been a wild ride. But getting back to Lake Ontario would have been slow going, or even impossible against the flow of the river.
>
> But I did manage to get to Montreal to check out the port, and I was happy I did. It's one of the most important ports of call for commercial shipping in North America. It's full of charm and European flavor. Perhaps someday, if I ever own a larger boat with a bigger engine, I'll go there on a yacht. If your boat is up to the trip, it's definitely worth a visit; and, if the boat can't make it, take a jet!

MONTREAL, QUEBEC

Forget Paris—this sophisticated port brings European culture to the edge of Lakeland territory.

A jetboat surges through the Lachine Rapids hurling sheets of spray over the bow and drenching the passengers decked out in their foulies. The boat seems almost airborne at times as the skipper negotiates the worst of the rapids, then returns to the Old Port in Montreal for another load of excited visitors anxious to sample the wild side of the St. Lawrence River.

The Lachine Rapids make for a great sport, pleasing thousands of people every year. In fact, they're among Montreal's major tourist attractions, a natural ride rivaling the thrills at the nearby La Ronde amusement park.

But it's only recently that the rapids have been a source of diversion. For centuries the white water was serious business, requiring city fathers to spend countless hours of labor and bargeloads of loot to build canals to bypass them. Even after the canals were completed, ocean-going vessels still were unable to reach the Great Lakes until the St. Lawrence Seaway opened in 1959. Until then, Montreal was the end of the line, roughly 500 miles from the sea. The seaway's completion prompted the development of North America's most important inland port.

Founded in 1642 by French missionaries and fur traders, today Montreal has grown to be the second largest French-speaking city in the world. Montreal is like Paris, but in many ways it's better. For one thing, you don't have to cross the Atlantic to get there. You can actually boat there up the St. Lawrence River from Lake Ontario in two or three days. Or, come via the Rideau Canal and Ottawa River, a nice, leisurely trip. When you arrive at the Port d'Escale in the Bassin Jacques-Cartier, you're right in the heart of the Old Port, surrounded by street musicians and artists, sidewalk cafes, theaters, dozens of museums, and a seemingly countless number of restaurants. You can't beat the convenience.

Before 1993, the year the Port d'Escale opened for business, most boaters visiting Montreal were either from Quebec waters or on their way south or back home to the Midwest via the Champlain-Richelieu link. It seems few boaters were willing to travel the roughly 200 miles and seven locks from Lake Ontario just to spend time in "Mon-re-all," as the French say.

Those that did come typically sought berths at the marinas on the north shore of Lac Saint-Louis. However, the marinas weren't close to a Metro stop and consequently were isolated from city attractions. Longueuil was and still is very popular because of its proximity to the Metro and ferry service to the Old Port. Even so, it wasn't like docking right in the center of the action.

The marina at Port d'Escale, built as part of a decades-long campaign to revitalize the city's waterfront, caters only to transients. It has virtually been remade, erasing part of the city's more recent history while preserving its rich heritage.

Along the waterfront you can still see the rows of limestone commercial buildings that once housed thriving port businesses. Goods were transferred to smaller craft capable of passing though the Lachine Canal, which opened in 1825, and proceeding upstream to Lake Ontario. Huge grain silos and warehouses built to store all that cargo lined the shore.

But all that is gone. Now it's an urban parklike setting with a view of the river and the Parc Des Îles. The improvements came about as part of the city's celebration of its three hundred and fiftieth anniversary. It was a great excuse to spiff things up, and Montrealers went at it full throttle, restoring old historic sites, building beaches and other recreational facilities and in general putting a new face on Old Montreal.

Just across the river in front of the Old Port is the Parc Des Îles, which consists of Île Sainte Hélène and Île Notre Dame. Chances are you'll spend some time at the Parc Des Îles while you're visiting Montreal. The site of the 1967 World's Fair, today the islands form a giant recreational center just a short Metro, bus, taxi, or water taxi ride away from the Old Port.

Not to be missed is the giant golf ball-like geodesic dome originally built to house the United States' pavilion at the World's Fair. Known as the Biosphere, the big ball just reopened in 1995 as a museum and environmental center.

The Casino de Montréal in the French pavilion offers splendid dining, entertainment, and gambling in an elegant setting with 1,700 slots and a host of games at the tables. La Ronde, the largest amusement park in Quebec, is the site of the world-famous Benson & Hedges International, a fireworks competition held in June and July that you can watch from your boat just off the amusement park.

In addition to the Parc Des Îles, the Olympic Park built for the 1976 Olympics and the Montreal Botanical Garden (the second largest in the world) are also must-see attractions accessible by Metro or cab. Ride a cable car up the Olympic Tower or check out the four distinct ecosystems reproduced in the Biodome.

On a summer day the Botanical Gardens, next to the Olympic Park, are truly spectacular. Walk through the ten greenhouse exhibits and thirty theme gardens, each adorned with some of the over 30,000 species of flora on display.

Make sure to allow time to explore downtown as well, with its array of boutiques, department stores, restaurants and museums. A particularly intriguing place to visit is the Underground City, eighteen miles of underground malls, movie theaters, museums, restaurants, hotels, and office buildings. When the winter winds rip across the streets of the city, Montrealers simply go underground. The Metro links sections of the underground into a patchwork of subterranean havens from the weather. It's possible to go from your apartment to work, and out for a night on the town in the dead of winter without ever putting on your coat.

But you won't find a sign saying, "Underground City Here." Montrealers take it for granted people know about the place and know how to get there. But it can get confusing. A great place to access the Underground City is downtown at St. Catherine Street and University Avenue near Eatons Department Store.

When visiting Montreal it's easy to forget that it's a port city, and always has been. Home to forty-four shipping companies, the port handles approximately 22 million tons of cargo every year, rivaling New York and Baltimore in volume. If you stay near the Old Port you won't see much evidence of this high level of activity. After the St. Lawrence Seaway opened, the Lachine Canal was closed, causing the Old Port to go into decline. The downward bound ships and recreational boaters now follow the seaway parallel to the Lachine Rapids, down the last lock at St. Lambert, and on behind the Parc Des Bless.

The approach to the Old Port is straightforward and well marked. However, pay attention to your position relative to the current flowing down the main river channel. It flows very swiftly, though it is tamer in the buoyed channel leading to the Old Port. Once you reach the marina basin you're out of the current and even the wind, since the floating docks are situated in an old shipping berth with forty-foot bulkheads on three sides. This gives you a little privacy from the folks ashore.

Montrealers gave themselves a wonderful anniversary present when they brought back the waterfront along the cobbled streets of Old Montreal. But they gave recreational boaters cruising Quebec's waters a real gift as well. Montreal is now one of the best ports of call on the eastern fringe of Great Lakes country. It may be out of the way, but it's definitely worth the effort to undertake such a bon voyage!

Lakeland Boating, 1996

Maritime Museums
PRESERVING THE PAST

The waterfronts along the rivers, lakes, and coast of the Northeast hold a tremendous treasure of history. It seems every place has its own story, a link to the past that somehow makes the present more meaningful through the shared experiences others went through in times long ago.

In the United States, it may appear that the people have little regard for the history that shaped the nation, if you look at how much of the past ends up in the scrap heap. An old brownstone, a classic sailing ship, a drive-in movie theater; the old tends to give way to the new, which, while it may be natural enough doesn't do much in the way of keeping alive the rich heritage that this still relatively young country can claim as its own.

But regardless of the throw-away mentality in the United States and its apparent pervasiveness, no pat generalities hold true. The trend may well be to replace the old with the new and forget about what came before as we look ahead to tomorrow, but there are those among us who cherish the past and work to preserve it. There are also those among us who take a more passive interest expressed in the simple act of going to a museum to check out what's there for a couple hours on a weekend day trip.

The following stories will introduce you to some of the more active history keepers, and to the long-forgotten world that so captures their imagination. The stories should give any who love history a bit of hope for the future, because they demonstrate that, striving together, people can and do achieve wonderful results that preserve the past, enabling succeeding generations to learn about and appreciate the people who came before and helped push the United States forward, for good and ill, to where it stands today.

A HOME FOR UNDERWATER HISTORY

The old Lifesaving Station No. 4 in Monmouth Beach came into existence to rescue victims of the sea. But the dilapidated building may find a new lease on life as a place to preserve the memory of the maritime disasters off the Jersey shore.

The center, built more than 100 years ago as one of the lifesaving stations that dotted the shore from Sandy Hook to Cape May, was abandoned in 1992 when the Marine Police moved out. Now it may see a rebirth, as New Jersey's only museum dedicated solely to shipwrecks. The coasts of New Jersey and Long Island harbor the wrecks of more than 5,500 ships, one of the largest concentrations of shipwrecks in the world.

The New Jersey Historical Divers Association plans to restore the crumbling old building and use it to exhibit artifacts brought up from the local wrecks—everything from china to cannonballs. They're counting on the several hundred members of the group and fellow divers who have been collecting bits and pieces of New Jersey's history for decades to dust off their specimens and donate them to the museum. In addition, the museum will house a shipwreck library and archive.

The genesis of the idea sprang to life in an oblique way. It all started in a little dive shop in Brielle.

Before it went out of business, the Brielle Dive Center was a favorite haunt among local divers. It was a very special place crammed with the usual diving equipment—wetsuits, fins, masks, and scuba tanks, but it had something else to offer, too. The owner, Bill Schmoldt, set aside a large portion of the store to exhibit artifacts brought up from shipwrecks off the Jersey shore, as well as books and other materials about the history of maritime disasters that occurred along the coast.

"While I waited around to get my tanks filled, I'd linger over the displays and read about the wrecks," said Dan Lieb, a graphic artist and avid diver living in Avon. "It was a real treasure for local information. Bill had plans to open a research center, but as it happened the shop fell on hard times and it closed."

Lieb took up where his friend left off and together with a core group of other divers set in motion a plan to convert the lifesaving station into The New Jersey Shipwreck Museum.

The building is owned by the state's Department of Environmental Protection, which has agreed to lease the structure to the nonprofit New Jersey Historical Divers Association for use as a museum. The group received the needed approvals from the Monmouth Beach Planning Board in June.

"We've given the association a letter of intent that indicates we're willing to enter into a lease agreement if they demonstrate the ability to renovate the building and establish a museum. The building is in pretty bad shape and has no other uses, and in all likelihood without their efforts it would have to be demolished," said James Hall, assistant commissioner, natural and historic resources of the DEP.

From a cosmetic perspective the building represents "an ugly blotch" in otherwise cosmetically appealing Monmouth Beach, said Louis Sodano, the town's mayor. "If the effort to start the museum succeeds, the building will be fixed up. It'll be neat and clean, and that's good for the town," he said.

Beachgoers are often unaware that so many ships have been lost off the New Jersey coast, according to Tom Hoffman, park ranger and historian for the Sandy Hook Unit of Gateway National Recreation Area.

"After people have enjoyed sunning themselves on the beach and playing in the surf, they often come in and ask, 'Hey, any shipwrecks out here?' When I tell them there are thousands, they seem surprised," said Tom Hoffman.

According to John Bandstra, president of the New Jersey Historical Divers Association, the architect working pro bono for the organization made a thorough check of the building and judged it structurally sound. "We believe it can be put back into shape and converted to a shipwreck museum for around $300,000," Bandstra said. "We're applying for grants and seeking donations from corporations and private donors to make The New Jersey Shipwreck Museum a reality."

On February 7, town officials, historians, local citizens, and members of the association will gather at the Church of the Precious Blood in Monmouth Beach for the first fund-raiser. Bandstra and Lieb, the association's treasurer, both said they feel optimistic about their ability to raise the money needed to establish the museum. But cash doesn't grow on trees, and they're not likely to find it in the holds of Jersey shipwrecks, either.

"I think it's fair to say they (the association) have a little bit of a tough road ahead of them," Hall said. "They've shown a lot of determination and have come a long way already. While it's not easy to raise that kind of money, it's not impossible."

"The people behind this project have put a lot of thought into it," Hoffman said. "It's not going to be a place with a few old timbers and pieces of broken china. It'll be something more than that, a place that brings together under one roof a comprehensive view of New Jersey's shipwrecks and which will continue working toward preserving an important part of our maritime history."

The Star-Ledger, 1997

COME FOR THE VIEW; STAY FOR THE HISTORY

On those cold, clear winter days when the summer haze has long vanished from Sandy Hook Bay, the north tower at Twin Lights—perched atop the Highlands of Navesink a total of 256 feet above sea level—offers visitors one of the most spectacular views on the East Coast.

Now that's a big claim. How can New Jersey stand up to Mount Desert Island or the splendid sand dunes at Kitty Hawk? Pretty easily. The Highlands of Navesink are the highest point on the coast between North Carolina and Maine. The commanding heights, combined with a unique blend of cityscape and sandy shore, attract 80,000 visitors to Twin Lights every year to take in the view and to visit the maritime museum. Winter is the best time to come since the humidity, so oppressive during the summer, isn't around to obscure visibility.

If you've ever climbed the north tower and looked out over the white sands of Sandy Hook toward Long Island's South Shore, you'll recall the strange feeling you get as the buildings on the island stretch eastward and seemingly drop off the end of the earth. They don't actually disappear, of course, just dip out of sight below the horizon. Or if you look north, you'll see the grand Verrazano Narrows Bridge, the soaring blue and gray towers of Manhattan, and even the head and shoulders of Lady Liberty, a greenish smudge of antiquity amid the shine of the Big Apple.

Twin Lights itself pleases the eye. The brownstone building that connects the two towers gives it the appearance of a castle. Formerly used for storage and a workshop and living quarters for the lighthouse crew, the brownstone now houses the museum at Twin Lights Historic Site, which became part of the state park system in 1962. Last May, the finishing touches of a long, $200,000 restoration project were completed. The museum now looks better than ever.

Part of the restoration included revamping the exhibits by weeding out the artifacts not directly in keeping with the four themes that comprise the concept behind Twin Lights Historic Site. The exhibits now cover the history of the Navesink Highlands, piloting and navigation, lighthouse technology, and the Lifesaving Service, which got its start in New Jersey and later became the search and rescue branch of the United States Coast Guard. Plenty of things to interest boaters with too much winter time on their hands.

As you walk through the museum, one of the more impressive exhibits you'll see is the Fresnel lens and the 700–pound clockwork mechanism once used to rotate the light. Invented in 1822 by Augustine Fresnel, a French physicist, the lens which bears his name revolutionized lighthouse technology in Europe. The lens looks a lot like a giant beehive. Prisms directed and focused the light into narrow beams shot through a magnifying glass, greatly enhancing a lighthouse's visibility from seaward.

The United States was slow to catch on to the advantages of the Fresnel lens. But in 1841 the Navesink Lighthouse Station, as Twin Lights was then called, became the first lighthouse in the nation to use a Fresnel lens. Its 6-million-candlepower beam was visible twenty-two miles out to sea.

Later, in 1898, Twin Lights became the first lighthouse to use electricity to power its light source. An enormous electric bivalve arc lens, which is also on display in the museum, was installed in the south tower. It produced 25-million candlepower and was the most powerful light installed in a lighthouse in the nation. The "glooming" effect, light reflecting off the night sky, could be seen as far as seventy miles out.

Many visitors wonder why the lighthouse service, which completed the present buildings in 1862, chose to build twin towers. It was thought at the time that two towers were needed to help mariners tell the Navesink Light Station apart from Sandy Hook Lighthouse five miles away. The south tower had what's known as a "first-order" lens, the brightest possible light, and the north tower had a "second-order" lens, which obviously wasn't as bright as its neighbor.

Together, the two lights marked the approach to New York Harbor and were the signposts mariners searched for as they made their way to the port. However, as lighthouse technology developed, relying more on identification via light intensity and frequency of flashes, the need for two lights lessened. In 1898, when the south tower was electrified with the bivalve arc lens, the north tower light was shut down.

Today, if you're approaching the Highlands of Navesink at night, look for the blinking north light at Twin Lights. By special permission of the Coast Guard, the museum is allowed to light the north tower as a tribute to the many lighthouse keepers who helped guide ships safely home. Twin Lights was officially decommissioned in 1949.

Outside the museum, you'll find a fascinating exhibit in one of the oldest lifesaving stations still in existence. Back when the Lifesaving Service came into being in 1849, little shanties were placed on the beach to house lifesaving equipment. The former lifesaving station now houses the museum's boat collection. It includes a sneakbox, a pilot boat, a Shrewsbury crab boat, the *Fox*, which is a replica of the first boat rowed across the Atlantic, and two life-cars. The life-cars were used to ferry passengers off stricken vessels; they're odd-looking things resembling submarines more than rescue craft.

Today, the Highlands still represent an unmistakable daymark. They're a welcome sight for boaters heading up the coast or approaching New Jersey from well offshore. Twin Lights may no longer be needed to guide shipping to and from New York Harbor, but it's a place that remains an integral part of New Jersey's maritime history. If you can, check it out; it's worth the effort.

Offshore, 1996

A REVOLUTIONARY EFFORT

Trenton. Springfield. Monmouth. Jockey Hollow. When historians speak of the role New Jersey played in the Revolution, these are the sites that often come up.

But Little Egg Harbor? Chestnut Neck?

These South Jersey locales and the part they played in the defeat of the British have been all but lost in the shuffle. But a determined handful of residents of Port Republic, Little Egg Harbor Township and other nearby towns are working to preserve the area's place in history as one of the most important American privateer ports during the Revolutionary War.

They're setting aside land for the establishment of the only privateer museum in the nation, fighting to preserve other historic sites and keeping alive the memory of patriots who died trying to stop a British attack along the Mullica River in October 1778.

Why dedicate a museum to pirates? Because the privateers' preying on the British ships helped wear down the English, explained Gary Giberson, mayor of Port Republic in Atlantic County and one of those behind the efforts to preserve the area's history.

"There is no historical site dedicated to the privateers, when clearly the ravishing of His Majesty's ships and rising costs of insuring them helped win the war," Giberson said. "A big part of it happened right here in southern New Jersey, along a great river settled by people who thought they had a right to govern their own lives."

The October engagement is known as the Little Egg Harbor Expedition, and it's an all but forgotten chapter in American history.

Upset about the privateers operating out of Chestnut Neck, a thriving port on the Mullica River in present-day Port Republic, the British sent approximately twenty warships and 1,600 men to sack the village and raid the iron works at Batsto that were turning out tons of shot for George Washington's cannons. They stormed the little fort at Chestnut Neck on October 6, driving the defenders away without loss of life, and burned the village, the shipyard, and ten recently captured vessels.

Word of approximately 1,000 Continental Army and militia troops advancing from the north turned the British soldiers back to the sea, however, before they could reach Batsto, about fourteen miles up the Mullica River at the mouth of a major tributary, the Batsto River. The shallow, meandering waterway would have presented the Americans with an ideal opportunity to ambush the British troops, so the commander scrubbed the mission.

With the fleet's departure delayed by unfavorable winds, the British continued to harass the folks living in the area, landing to loot and burn as they pleased. On October 15, they staged a nighttime attack on an outpost of the Pulaski Legion stationed in present-day Little Egg Harbor Township, bayonetting forty-five men in their sleep.

The Little Egg Harbor Expedition is largely forgotten even by historians despite the fact that Chestnut Neck was a major staging area for privateers. Some say it was the most important privateer center, with its location at the midpoint of shipping lanes along the coast.

But the sacking of Chestnut Neck and the massacre of the troops sent to protect it still resonate with the people who live near where it happened.

Just ask George Czurlanis, a seventy-six-year-old disabled World War II veteran and longtime resident of Little Egg Harbor Township. A diminutive stone monument erected in 1894 honoring the dead of the Pulaski Legion sits on a half-acre in the middle of town, looking a little out of place amid the houses and mini-malls.

Were it not for Czurlanis and a core group of about twenty volunteers, the monument and the site of the Pulaski Legion headquarters, also in the township, might not exist today. Development during the 1960s turned much of the area where the Pulaski Legion was stationed into a residential neighborhood, including fields where farmers had unearthed skeletons thought to be those of members of the legion, who were buried in a mass grave.

In 1981, Czurlanis formed the Save the Pulaski Monument Committee and spearheaded an unsuccessful court battle to block construction of two mini-malls that would mar the view of the monument. It was feared the development would destroy the monument. However, the volunteers persuaded the developer to donate a half-acre around the monument to the township, which would then deed it, along with the Pulaski headquarters site, to The Affair at Egg Harbor Society, which grew out of Czurlanis' committee.

Problem solved? Not by a long shot. According to Czurlanis, The Affair at Egg Harbor Society is stuck with paying approximately $1,600 in property taxes per year on the two sites. Its latest bid for a tax exemption failed in July.

"We were denied tax exemption on the county and state level because there was no building on the land," Czurlanis said. "But these are still historic sites and should be tax exempt." Both sites were placed on New Jersey's list of historic places in 1993, largely due to Czurlanis' efforts.

For the last two years, he's paid most of the tax bill out of his own pocket just to keep the land from being sold to developers, which he claims would happen "in a minute" if the taxes were unpaid.

Almost broke and desperate to save the sites, in August Czurlanis dressed up in a Continental Army uniform and stood in front of stores in town soliciting money to pay this year's tax bills. Handing out flags and information about the massacre, Czurlanis discovered that enough people cared, at least this year. He raised the $1,600.

Why does he care so much about the men who died 218 years ago?

"When I go down to the monument to pick up litter, I feel disturbed. I lost comrades during World War II, and I'd like to think people across the sea are taking care of their graves. These men died right here, and yet there seems to be a lack of honor for the supreme sacrifice they made for our country. I'm trying to preserve the ground they died on, that was soaked with their blood. As a soldier who's seen combat, who's been wounded twice, how could I not empathize with these men? How can I let them be forgotten?" Czurlanis said.

The citizens of Port Republic have had better luck in preserving their part of the Little Egg Harbor Expedition and the key role Chestnut Neck played in winning the Revolutionary War. Efforts to found the first museum in the nation dedicated to privateers are well on their way to fruition.

A monument to the privateers operating out of Chestnut Neck was erected in 1911 on the shores of the Mullica River in Port Republic, and it's still there, a silent tribute to largely forgotten heroes. A privateer sailor stands atop the seventy-foot spire facing seaward, as if standing guard over the port.

In 1993, Mayor Giberson was instrumental in persuading two owners of property adjacent to the monument site to sell it to the federal government to preserve the site for posterity. Chestnut Neck and its revolutionary history are dear to Giberson's heart. His family was among the first to settle Chestnut Neck back in 1637.

Giberson enlisted the help of former congressman William Hughes, who was from the area, Senator Bill Bradley, and other legislators. They succeeded in getting the Bureau of Fish and Wildlife Management to purchase the two properties in 1994 and 1995, setting aside approximately twenty-five acres for the museum.

Giberson said the museum is roughly five years from completion, assuming the money can be raised. If the effort is successful, the fort and shipyard will be restored. A full-size privateer ship will be included. Artifacts hidden away in local attics and those yet to be unearthed will go on display in the museum building, which they hope will be at the tip of the Edwin Forsythe Wildlife Refuge adjacent to the site if they are granted permission.

Before any building occurs, Giberson said, a thorough archeological dig must be completed. "Before one stone is overturned, we'll need to get a team of national historians and archaeologists to come in here," Giberson said.

"It's not right to forget the past, though many of us do. After all, if we don't look over our shoulders at where we've been, how will we know where we're going? The museum will help us remember," Giberson said.

COLONIAL CHAPTER IN BATSTO'S STORY TO GET EQUAL TIME

While two groups of volunteers continue working to preserve the Revolutionary War history in Little Egg Harbor Township and Port Republic, a third group has been pursuing the same goal at Batsto Village in Wharton State Forest.

After ten months of mediation with the New Jersey Department of Environmental Protection's Division of Parks and Forestry, which manages the site, the Batsto Citizens Committee reached an agreement with the state on September 6 that will ensure that the village's role in the Revolutionary War would not be eclipsed by an over-emphasis on the Victorian era.

The dispute between the state and the Batsto Citizens Committee, which has been working to preserve the historical aspects of Batsto since 1956, arose when the final draft of the Batsto Village Plan was distributed in 1994. It was a conceptual plan about the future operation of the village itself, not a detailed exhibit plan.

George Vail, general chairman of the Batsto Citizens Committee said, "We took issue with several of the statements regarding the emphasis on the village. We were under the impression that the emphasis as stated in the plan would focus mainly on Joseph Wharton, when we felt a broader spectrum should have been included."

Joseph Wharton, a wealthy Philadelphia financier, bought up 96,000 acres in the Pine Barrens in 1876, including Batsto Village, which he developed as a "gentlemen's farm." Since most of the buildings dated from Wharton's time, to the state it made sense to establish the village in a historic setting from that era.

The state has agreed to modify the Batsto Village Plan to include suggestions from the Batsto Citizens Committee such as establishing European settlement as a period for interpretation, which wasn't in the original plan, as well as Revolutionary War interpretations and themes.

"We wanted an equal emphasis on the colonial aspects of the village and the Wharton era," Vail said. "We didn't want the site to lose its identity as the 'bog iron village in the pines,' as it's commonly known in the history books."

The Star-Ledger, 1996

TUCKERTON'S NEW SEAPORT BRINGS BACK THE OLD

In the late 1800s, wealthy families rode the trains down New Jersey's coast to a place tucked deep in the pines and marshes known as Edge Cove in Tuckerton. From there, steam ferries shuttled them out to Tuckers Island (which has since disappeared and appears to be making a comeback) near the twin inlets of Beach Haven and Little Egg. Originally a summer retreat for Quakers, Tuckers Island suited the well-to-do as a resort with its cool sea breezes and quiet ambiance far from the frenetic pace of life in more urban parts of the state.

In the early 1900s, the railroad stopped running trains out to Edge Cove, but the spur leading to the bay still saw plenty of action. On windy days, the clammers working the flats with tongs and rakes hauled their catch to depots for shipment to market using a railroad car rigged with a sail. It rolled quietly through the marshes and woodlands without the aid of noisy steam locomotives, an odd sight to most city folks. On calm days, the clammers towed the rail/sail car with a team of mules.

Known by many names, most appropriately, Clamtown for its huge supply of clams harvested from the clear waters of the bay, Tuckerton held tightly to its traditions. A working town whose inhabitants lived by their wits and their muscles, earning a living with what the bay brought with each passing season, the changes that swept America somehow didn't make much of an impact on Tuckerton. It was, and still is, a place with its feet planted squarely in the rich soil of a simpler time, and the people there like it that way.

In fact, residents of the Tuckerton area have taken some very notable steps to preserve the heritage of those who worked the bay, and the history they unwittingly made as they carved their now-famous decoys for hunting duck and geese and built their equally well-known sneakboxes. The Barnegat Bay Decoy & Baymen's Museum, which opened in 1993, has grown into a grass-roots movement to establish a large seaport museum in Tuckerton. You won't see the likes of it unless you head to Mystic Seaport in Connecticut or The Chesapeake Bay Museum in St. Michael's, Maryland.

After four years of hard work, the more than 1,000 members of the Decoy Museum, along with hundreds of other volunteers, are poised to see their dreams for a seaport come to fruition this summer. Construction crews will begin work on a replica of the Tuckerton Lighthouse, ten other buildings, and 2,000 feet of bulwarks and boardwalks along the waterfront adjacent to Tuckerton Creek. More than $2 million dollars, $600,000 of which came from a New Jersey Department of Transportation grant for the promenade, has already been raised.

"We have tried to highlight the ingenuity of the baymen, how they were able to make their own tools, how they made a living on a resource-based economy. Even today, we have people still living in the true tradition of Barnegat Bay, people who are clammers, oystermen, who fish and hunt, or make their living as charter boat captains. The seaport museum celebrates the unique and special history of the bay and its people," said Terry O'Leary, program director of the Barnegat Bay Decoy and Baymen's Museum.

Plans for Tuckerton Seaport call for the construction or restoration of twenty-six buildings. Each structure will highlight various trades representing the way of life on New Jersey's bays. Everything from whaling, which did play a part in the early history of New Jersey's maritime enterprises, to clamming, fishing, decoy carving, yachting, boatbuilding, and much more will find a spot at the seaport. Together, the buildings and the exhibits within them will create a living village, a place where you can park your car (or your boat; the seaport will have guest slips for visiting boaters) and journey back in time.

The forty-acre site of the seaport sits on land settled long before the Revolutionary War. The early pioneers found Tuckerton Creek hospitable, protected from storms and well positioned for both hunting in the pines and fishing in the bay. The oldest house in the area, built in 1699, still stands, and, according to O'Leary, may become part of the seaport's collection of buildings.

The port of Tuckerton really bustled as the country grew. It was a major shipbuilding center, turning out all kinds of vessels, including three-masted schooners of over 200 tons in the 1800s. The old boatworks located at the site will be restored. Situated midway between Philadelphia and New York, Tuckerton was designated the third port of entry in 1791. Its midpoint location and close proximity to raw materials made it an important part of the young nation. Another big plus: it remained ice free in all but the harshest of winters.

Those clams made perhaps the biggest splash. Most of the shoreline around the seaport is full of old clamshells from catches made long ago. In some places the shell piles were twelve feet thick. Though the baymen are now scarce, there still is a clamming industry in the region.

"All of our parking areas and roadways are made from the old clam shells," O'Leary said. "They provide good drainage, a good road surface . . . what could be more appropriate for a place once known as Clamtown?"

Although Tuckerton Creek is too shallow for any but the smallest boats, funding for a major dredging project is expected to go through this year and work on a deeper channel should commence in 1998. This will make it easier for the casinos in Atlantic City to run their shuttle ferries to and from the Tuckerton Seaport, which O'Leary said is part of the seaport project.

For recreational boaters, local and those just passing through on a cruise, the next few years should see the Tuckerton Seaport as a brand new destination. A place deep in the heart of the bay, with roots that go back more than 300 years.

Offshore, 1997

ROSEMARY NESBITT: FOUNDING A MARITIME MUSEUM

Fifteen years ago, many people in Oswego, New York, talked about founding a marine museum to exhibit artifacts from the area. But the talk did not become action until Rosemary Nesbitt made a simple suggestion.

Nesbitt was a member of the Port Authority of Oswego at the time. One day at a board meeting, she pointed out a window at a building on the west side of the harbor, the former site of the Port Authority, and said, "Why don't we use that building for a museum?"

The director thought for a moment and said, "Great idea, Rosemary. You be the director."

Three years later, in June 1982, Nesbitt and scores of community volunteers celebrated the opening of the H. Lee White Marine Museum. Today the museum attracts approximately 10,000 visitors annually.

Established in 1725, Oswego was the first freshwater port in North America. It played an important role in exploration, trade, and immigration into the heartland. Oswego is also an important location in the New York State Canal System. It is the only outlet from the canal system that runs directly into Lake Ontario. The Oswego Canal connects Oswego to the Erie Canal, which in turn runs east-to-west across upper New York State from the Hudson River to the Niagara River.

Attics throughout Oswego were crammed with valuable objects from the community's history. That was until Nesbitt's efforts provided a place for these objects to be seen.

The museum exhibits include derrick boat #8, now in dry dock. It was the last steam-powered vessel on the barge canal. The museum saved it from the scrap heap in 1987. The large tugboat *Nash* floats at the commercial dock and is open to the public. The *Nash* was used to ferry supplies across the English Channel during the D-Day invasion of World War II and was designated a national historic landmark.

"I consider the *Nash* a sort of shrine, a place to honor the brave men who served on tugs during the war," Nesbitt said. "We tend to forget the important role these men played in supplying our troops as they made their way into France."

Nesbitt, sixty-nine, retired in 1993 after forty years of teaching theater, mostly at the State University of New York at Oswego and Syracuse University. She holds bachelor's and master's degrees in theater with an emphasis on Shakespeare and has directed many productions at the university level. While she worked between fifty and sixty hours every week at the university, she carved out time to make the museum a success.

"When it came to designing exhibits, I approached it as if I were directing a play. Directors need to know color, how a stage can create a picture for the audience. A good museum demands well-displayed exhibits," she said.

Contrary to advice of experts, Nesbitt decorated the museum in warm colors—brown paint with a deep-red carpet—and unlike most museums, no chains or ropes keep visitors from getting close to exhibits. Walking through the museum takes visitors on a chronological tour through maritime history.

Nesbitt continues to work as director on a volunteer basis. Seventy-nine others also work as volunteers to keep the museum going, with one full-timer who is paid to manage the operation and catalog all the objects. The Port Authority of Oswego covers maintenance and operating costs.

The museum was named after H. Lee White, founder of the American Steamship Lines Company, who was born in Oswego and included Oswego in the names of all his ships. His brother, William White, is the museum's main benefactor.

Nesbitt's insatiable appetite for history began when she was a little girl. Her father used to bring the family to Oswego and tell stories of the town's history in the dining room of the now defunct Pontiac Hotel. Seated at a table in the hotel listening to her father's tales, she admired the paintings of Fort Ontario by artist George Gray. Years later she would acquire five of these paintings for the museum, bringing the past full-circle with the present.

"Father was very patriotic and believed strongly that his children should know history, how it shapes the present," she said.

When asked if her duties at the museum imposed on her personal and family life, she shook her head and said, "To me, the museum is a hobby, a form of intellectual leisure. It's not a burden at all and it never has been."

Lakeland Boating, 1995

People of the Waters

During the course of my journey through the Northeast, I had the pleasure of meeting dozens of interesting characters. The waterfront seems to be a natural place for them to gather, like the proverbial moth to the flame. Meeting these folks, the dock hands, the old salts, the professional captains, and the fellow cruisers, all becomes part of the experience of boating, making it special and rewarding, at least that's how it was for me as I traveled. With the water as a common love, the usual barriers one finds among strangers disappear. Add a boat, and you've got a ready-made way to break the ice.

At first, the tendency of strangers to walk up to my boat and start in on a gamming, as some nautical buffs like to call it, struck me as a bit disconcerting. I was used to life in the suburbs, where people seldom look you in the eye as you walk down the street, much less say hello or acknowledge your presence in some other way. I was used to the idea that people were okay as long as they stayed in their own space and didn't intrude on mine. It's sad, really, that so much of life in America, whether in the city, suburbs, and, to a lesser extent, in the country, means keeping to one's self and not trusting in strangers. But that's the reality of it, and that's that.

But out on the water it's different, and it took a little getting used to. I soon did, however, and I found myself drawing slowly out of my shell as the days of the voyage progressed into weeks, then months. I became the person who initiated conversations with strangers, and answered the questions of others freely without any of the baggage from life ashore. In doing so, the experience of boating was made all the finer. It was the discovery of people's good sides, how interesting they can be, the giving and taking, the sharing, the trust, that contributed to those days out on the water.

At my slip at the head of Barnegat Bay, it's a little different. People keep more to themselves. They're seasonal residents at a marina, not cruisers, at least not in the real sense of it. But there is still that common bond all of us share together, since we all love the water and our boats. The casual hello, or a little fun poked, it's all there, just not as much as I've seen in other places.

The stories in this chapter will introduce you to some of the characters I met along the waterfronts whose lives I thought might interest the readers of magazines and newspapers. I couldn't possibly write about everyone I met, in part because some of the individuals were just plain, nice old folk, but nothing special beyond the basic specialness of being a kind and warm person. I couldn't write about the strangers who were rather tilted in their view of life, those who had a rough edge, for many of the same reasons. So, the people of the waters you'll meet by no means represent the lot; they're intriguing, though, and each one of them has a unique place on the shores of the Northeast's rivers, lakes, and coastline.

DIVING DEEP INTO THE PAST

Some folks love to garden; others collect stamps. Steve Nagiewicz, a dive boat captain operating out of Point Pleasant Beach, spends his spare time hunting for shipwrecks off the Jersey coast. A hobby befitting a guy in the dive trade, though some might say it's a busman's holiday.

There are thousands of shipwrecks out there—cargo ships and passenger liners, sailing vessels and schooners, tugs and barges—but only a "fraction" are very well known, according to Nagiewicz.

Contrary to common perceptions, these wrecks aren't laden with a pirate's ransom in gold. And most of them do not even resemble what they once were.

"Ships fall apart fairly rapidly after they sink. The image of an intact wreck, with tattered sails floating in the current, isn't reality. A wreck often looks more like a junkyard than the ship it once was," Nagiewicz says.

Over a short time, all that's left of a wooden ship are the anchor, some heavy timbers, and the vessel's metal fittings and anything else durable enough to stand up to the corrosive power of salt water. Eventually, it all disappears under the ever-shifting sand.

Going out to find one of these wrecks could test the patience of Job. You've got to really love it, particularly in New Jersey, where no hope exists of finding a ship carrying treasure chests, and where the water is cold and visibility nothing compared to what you find in the Caribbean.

"It was a big learning process, hunting for the wrecks," Nagiewicz says. "I'd read the local histories and accounts of the wrecks would mention towns I'd never heard of . . . like Squan Beach, which is Manasquan. I learned about the New Jersey coastline, and what has happened there.

"Knowing the history of a wreck, then going out to find it, and succeeding, it's like finding a living piece of the past."

Nagiewicz became interested in wrecks back in 1975 when he did his first deep-water dive to get his recreational dive certification on the wreck of the *Delaware*, a steamship which sank about a mile off Bay Head in July 1898.

It's a day he'll never forget. Despite the hardships, he credits the experience on the *Delaware* as the start of his love diving on shipwrecks and hunting for them when he can.

"There were four-to-six-foot seas, it was rainy and windy, and I was terribly seasick," Nagiewicz recalls. "But I made the dive anyway. I got to the bottom terrified, and then I saw something big towering above me and realized I was seeing the ship's huge single-piston steam engine. It was a marvelous, unreal sight, seeing it there surrounded by fish, rising twenty feet from the bottom."

Eleven years later, Nagiewicz bought his first dive boat, which he called *Diversion*, since he went diving primarily as a diversion from his day job in a sales position. A captain licensed by the Coast Guard, he began to moonlight in the dive charter business and eventually quit sales for life on the water.

Initially after buying his dive boat, he'd go out searching for wrecks the low-tech way, with a depth sounder and a grappling hook. Often, he'd dive down thinking he'd found a wreck only to find schools of fish.

Sometimes, though, he'd discover a wreck.

"It was just like I was an explorer. Here I'd found something I'd never seen, and perhaps something that no one had seen for a very long time. It's a hard feeling to describe," Nagiewicz says.

Nagiewicz graduated to the high-tech approach to wreck hunting by chance when a friend who owned a marine survey company bought a side scan sonar for business purposes a couple years ago. A side scan sonar looks like a cruise missile. As it's towed behind the boat, it sends echoes downward and sideways that reproduce a picture of what's on the bottom.

The nonbusiness uses of the sonar weren't lost on Nagiewicz, who asked his friend, Vince Capone, if he could borrow his new toy to go look for wrecks. "Vince laughed and said that 'toy' cost $250,000," Nagiewicz recalls. "But he thought the idea sounded fun, so we went out for a look."

The side scan sonar put serious wreck hunting within Nagiewicz's reach. The device would make it possible to locate wrecks that less sophisticated equipment would miss, making true "first" discoveries more likely.

The two wreck hunters searched up and down the coast for miles on either side of Manasquan Inlet, locating at least six wrecks, some previously known, others never before discovered. At Sea Girt, they encountered a particularly elusive wreck, more an apparition of a past ship than its actual bones.

Nagiewicz believes the remains of a Spanish sailing ship sunk in the early 1800s lie in a depression off the beach. "We never found the wreck, but the magnetometer (metal detector) indicates there is probably a wreck buried under the depression we found with the sonar."

Sometimes when a bad nor'easter blows through, Spanish coins wash up on the beach in Sea Girt, according to Nagiewicz. The coins date back to the early 1800s, providing a clue about age while at the same time lending credence to the possibility the wreck really exists.

Off Point Pleasant about thirty miles offshore, Nagiewicz discovered the wreck of an old sailing vessel in 150 feet of water. All that remained were some old timbers, and among them he found three hand-molded silver bars.

Was the ship carrying a fortune in silver? Highly improbable. Nagiewicz isn't into wrecks for treasure of the obvious kind, so the absence of additional silver bars at the site doesn't bother him.

Nagiewicz brings a pack rat's dream up from the wrecks: oil lamps, bottles, cups, ink wells, porthole fittings, and all kinds of metal fixtures. Most of it isn't worth much, but Nagiewicz thinks differently.

"I've always looked at a bottle or a glass that came from a ship lost a hundred years ago as being special because of its place in history. I think about who drank from it all those years ago, what the ship it came from must have been like," he says.

Nagiewicz keeps records of what he finds on a wreck and where it was discovered, much in the same way an archeologist excavates a dig. In this way, the ship becomes almost like a museum, only you need at least basic certification (advanced is better) and scuba gear to see the exhibits.

When he's not hunting for wrecks or taking recreational divers out to see them, Nagiewicz makes regular appearances on local cable TV shows. He also lectures on diving and marine life off the coast at local public schools.

In the younger grades, kids often ask Nagiewicz if he's ever been bitten by a shark while diving. The answer is yes.

"They immediately want to know what's missing," Nagiewicz laughs. "I have to explain that a shark can bite you without removing a large piece, and that they usually won't bite you at all unless you do something silly. It's not like *Jaws*."

The Star-Ledger, 1996

DON PRICE

When autumn arrives with its cool northern winds and kaleidoscopic colors, Don Price steals time away from his boat restoration company, St. Lawrence Restoration, Inc. He motors his 1922 Hacker design speedboat or his 1957 Chris-Craft Sea Skiff, a twenty-six-foot open fishing boat, to the island homes of friends, or fishes when the fancy strikes. It is a season Price savors, for his company keeps him busier than a one-armed paperhanger the rest of the year.

For eighteen years, Price's company has played an important role in keeping the antique and classic wooden powerboats on the river in shipshape condition. These old boats, often called woodies, once left to rot in boatyards and backyards, have enjoyed a resurgence of popularity among powerboaters since the mid-1970s. Price, with the foresight invaluable to any successful entrepreneur, saw the need for a restoration shop along the St. Lawrence River dedicated exclusively to restoring and refinishing woodies. In 1973, the year he founded the company in Clayton, New York, his was a good idea seemingly ahead of its time.

"Most of the boaters at the time were really excited about fiberglass. There were hundreds of wooden boats here . . . but not much interest in them," he said.

Price bought a store on James Street in Clayton from which he sold sundries, including boat supplies and wildlife prints. Behind the store was a 9,000 square-foot abandoned car garage that he turned into a restoration shop for woodies. "All we did was clean out the junk, paint the trim on the building, and start moving boats in," he said. "We didn't have money for other improvements."

Price became involved in the Clayton chapter of the Antique and Classic Boat Society, then a fledgling organization of several hundred woody enthusiasts who were scattered internationally. (The organization now boasts a roster numbering in the thousands.) Price, forty-four, also served as co-chairman of Clayton's Antique Boat Museum for five years in the mid-1980s and remains a committed member of the museum and the wooden boat community at large.

The interest in woodies burgeoned over the next fifteen years, providing the capital needed to move the operation from James Street across town to the only protected harbor, and to gradually build the business into what it is today. Price's current facilities include a marina and boat storage buildings in addition to the two heated shops that accommodate boats up to fifty feet and the four shops for boats under thirty feet. He expanded the services to cover fiberglass and steel, and today employs twelve people year round.

Why did Price like woodies enough to spend his life working with them? The answer lies as much in Price's appreciation for the beauty of varnished mahogany and polished chrome fittings, and the speed and maneuverability of woodies, as it does in his natural ability to work well with his hands. He'd grown to love boating in the Thousand Islands on summer visits from his hometown in Utica, New York, during his boyhood; he moved to the region after earning a bachelor of arts degree in 1970. He landed a job with a construction company and settled in with no immediate entrepreneurial ambitions, but was intent upon earning a living and enjoying boats.

Price bought his first vessel, a twenty-six-foot Hutchinson mahogany fishing boat in disrepair, and refurbished it in his spare time. "I loved the river and I loved boats, and it [the Hutchinson] was the only thing I could afford. Wooden boats were cheap then, very cheap," he said.

But as much as he loved that first boat, he sold it in 1972 to raise money for the house he was building for himself. The boat turned a tidy profit, and the business possibilities were not lost on him. One year after the sale of his Hutchinson, Price was on his way.

"I just naturally gravitated toward wooden motorboats. I like the people who are involved with them, and I enjoy the beauty of seeing an antique boat quietly motoring up the river," Price said. "I've always loved the St. Lawrence River and I wanted to make a go of a business that suited me and the area. Once I started, I never looked back."

Lakeland Boating, 1991

THE OLD MAN ON THE ISLAND

Royalties from John Keats's fourteenth nonfiction book, *The Skiff and the River*, an ode to the St. Lawrence skiff, weren't used to pay the grocer or landlord. Instead, Keats replanked the bottom of his twenty-one-foot, varnished mahogany St. Lawrence fishing launch, built in 1935 at Hutchinson's Boat Yard in Alexandria Bay, New York. Though Keats had meticulously cared for the boat since he bought it in 1954, its fifty-two ribs and strakes below the waterline needed to be replaced.

Since 1953, Keats's home during the spring, summer, and fall has been Ball Island, a two-acre rock situated among a group of four smaller isles a few hundred yards into Canadian waters between Alexandria Bay and Rockport, Ontario. They spend winters abroad and in Syracuse, New York, where Keats teaches writing at Syracuse University. Keats's book *Of Time and an Island* describes the island and the changes that have occurred on the St. Lawrence River since the turn of the century. Among the other books he has written are *You Might as Well Live*, a biography of Dorothy Parker, and *Howard Hughes*.

Living on an island makes boating a way of life, not just a means of recreation. Shopping, going to the post office, and visiting friends all require boat trips, and if the weather is bad, as it frequently is during the spring and fall, a stout boat is as essential to life as food, clothing, and shelter.

A love of boats led Keats, sixty-nine, to the island in the winter of 1952. That year, his brother-in-law bought the island to get three boats that came with the land. He only wanted the boats, and he offered to sell the island to Keats, who at the time was working as a reporter for the *Washington Daily News*. He'd been employed there since returning from duty after World War II. Keats accepted the offer, thinking that the place would be good for vacations two weeks out of the year, but he quit his job in 1953 to live and work on his island.

Keats writes at the head of Ball Island in a spartan sixteen-square-foot cottage overlooking the St. Lawrence River. The island also has a boathouse containing the family's living accommodations, a guest cottage, and a small storage building. There is no electricity and little connection with the outside world. For example, if Keats and his family—which includes his wife, their three children, and their children—want to hear music, there's an ancient wind-up Victor Talking Machine and albums of Caruso and Galli-Curci. At dusk, they light Aladdin lamps and candles.

One passage in *Of Time and an Island* sums up Keats's perception of his home: "Everyone needs an island in his life where he can go to sort things out, even if it is only an island he creates for himself in time, a sort of pit stop on the shoulder of the roaring rat race."

Lakeland Boating, 1990

SANDY HOOK PILOTS

At parties, the small talk often gets round to that most obvious of questions, "So, what do you do?"

For most, the answer is pretty simple. It doesn't take a rocket scientist to figure out what, say, a plumber does to put food on the table and send the kids to college. But for Andrew McGovern, it's not so easy.

"A lot of people, when they hear I'm a pilot, they ask what airline I'm from. I try to tell them I'm a ship pilot, but I frequently get blank stares," said McGovern, a pilot and director of training at The United New York/New Jersey Sandy Hook Pilots Association, based in Staten Island.

Those blank stares arise from the old out-of-sight, out-of-mind syndrome. Jets roar overhead, making themselves known in even the wildest reaches of the state. But ships that come into and out of the busy ports along the waterfront in upper New York Harbor don't often push their way into the public's ken of the everyday. The bananas on supermarket shelves, the cars at the dealer's lot, somehow they just appear. That they came off a ship isn't exactly at the forefront of the consumer's thoughts.

However, all the ships, roughly 9,000 of them every year, that steam into New York Harbor from ports all over the globe need the McGoverns of the world to bring them safely up to the dock without getting into mischief. The shoals off Sandy Hook, swift tidal currents, fog, and sometimes heavy seas make entering or leaving the harbor anything but child's play. And the traffic? Sometimes it's so heavy it makes the Parkway look tame.

Pilots have guided ships into the harbor ever since 1694, when the legal eagles of the time passed regulations requiring the presence of skilled local mariners aboard inbound and outbound ships. The idea was to keep ships and cargoes safe, and while that's still very important today, the pilots' first priority is to protect the public and the environment. Keeping ships off the shoals translates into no damage from oil spills or from hazardous cargoes, such as chemicals, let loose in the port.

According to the Port Authority of New York and New Jersey, the port produces approximately 165,000 jobs and $20 billion in annual regional sales. The eighty Sandy Hook pilots and eight apprentices (pilots in training) play a vital role in the port's vitality.

Sandy Hook pilots wait for inbound ships aboard a pilot boat stationed off Ambrose Light about seven miles seaward of Sandy Hook every day of the year. When a ship shows up, the pilot on call takes a small motorboat called a launch to the vessel, climbs a rope ladder hung down the side of the hull, and takes over control of the ship from the captain.

Getting aboard the 600- to 700-foot ships with main decks thirty to forty feet above the waves can give the best pilots a touch of gray hair and white knuckles.

"We haven't lost a pilot in years," McGovern said. "But we often do have injuries. Getting off the ship after you've taken it out to safe water is much harder than getting on because you're stepping backwards onto the launch from the ship. If you fall in at this time of year, you'll be dead in minutes from the cold water."

McGovern added that the pilots all wear safety gear, including floatation devices. He recalled a bad winter storm back in 1980 when he was still an apprentice that killed three pilots and sank one of the launches used to ferry pilots to and from ships. He was on station aboard the pilot boat when it happened. "We found the launch washed up on the beach a few days later, and eventually the bodies came ashore, too," he said.

In other storms, McGovern described driving the launch up forty-foot waves and seeing nothing but sky, then plummeting deep in the trough till the little craft was submerged. "I've had times when the launch rolled over to ninety degrees. I'd be standing on the wall one minute, then the deck, then the other wall the next," he said.

It takes fifteen years of training before a pilot can handle the largest of ships. Sandy Hook pilots are apprentices for seven and a half years, and it's much like a trial by fire with lots of work at a pay rate slightly above burger flippers in fast food restaurants.

Paul Klein, twenty-eight, of Clifton, took his "vow of poverty" as an apprentice with the Sandy Hook pilots in 1992. While his friends are out buying houses and cars, he's still relying on his parents for a place to crash when he's not on duty.

"It's tough sometimes, not knowing how you're going to even buy dinner," Klein said. "But I've always loved the sea and having a chance to become a pilot will give me the best of both worlds. I won't be off for months at a time aboard ships, but I'll still get to work on the water, and that's what I've always wanted," he said.

If Klein passes muster and puts in the fifteen years it takes to become what's known as a full branch pilot, he will stand to earn between $60,000 to $100,000 a year. Not a bad payoff, but it's really not about money at all, he said. It's about a lifestyle, being part of a close-knit group of people doing a unique and exciting job.

"It's a really great career for the right person," Klein said. "I have no regrets about working hard to become a Sandy Hook pilot."

A WOMAN'S WORK

Women, long absent among the ranks of pilots who steer ships in and out of busy harbors, have started to make inroads into a previously all-male occupation. Out of 1,000 pilots and apprentices nationwide, only nine are female.

But that's a big change in itself. Not long ago, nary a lady could be found on a pilot boat.

One of those nine woman is Colleen Moran, a twenty-six-year-old New Jerseyan from Beachwood, a small town on Toms River.

"It used to be the boys from the farms would follow their fathers who were pilots from the fields to the sea," Moran said. "It was a job that tended to stay in the family, but that's starting to change, particularly for women who want to be pilots."

Moran competed with more than 100 applicants for her place as an apprentice with the Pilots' Association for the Bay and River Delaware when a handful of positions opened up two years ago. Now she's on her way to becoming one of the people that safely guide the largest ships in the world through constricted, traffic-filled waterways.

"For me the challenge of using local knowledge to guide oceangoing ships in narrow channels is very exciting and rewarding. It's not the kind of job many people would like, but it's the best one in the world for me," Moran said.

Moran will "go free" in 1998, which means she'll have reached a level where she can pilot ships with drafts of no more than twenty-five feet without supervision. She'll have to spend four more years working up to vessels with drafts of up to fifty-five feet.

But the long stint as an apprentice is worth it, she said. "It's a dream come true."

The Star-Ledger, 1997

COUNSELOR TRADES COUCH FOR COCKPIT CUSHIONS

When Karl J. Koch set sail with friends for a Chesapeake Bay cruise six years ago, he didn't know the experience would inspire major changes in his life. The cruise crystallized his decision to act on a nagging dissatisfaction with his job as a mental health counselor: "I was sitting in the cockpit and admiring the sunset, and I remember turning to one of my friends and saying, 'You know, I've really got to get back to working with boats.'"

Koch quit his job that same year to find work related to boats. It was only natural. Koch had loved recreational boating all of his life, and he'd worked on the water, too.

His first job as a child had been at a boat rental dock in the Thousand Islands where he summered with his grandparents, who were avid boaters. In his early twenties, he'd worked on a police boat, and he'd served a four-year stint as an electronics technician in the Coast Guard. After leaving the Coast Guard and obtaining a degree in psychology in 1973, Koch got away from boats to what he thought was going to be a "real" career as a mental health counselor.

For the next ten years, Koch worked with mentally retarded people in prisons and halfway houses—and with bureaucrats. "In retrospect, I see now it was crazy for me to go into the mental health field. I wanted to help people, but the bureaucracy was extremely frustrating."

Now, at forty-three, Koch can look back on the last six years in boating without recalling frustration. He works as a rigger for Schrader Yacht Sales in Point Pleasant, New Jersey. He also installs electronics systems in boats and works in sales. He's well known among local boaters, especially among the 500 charter captains who he has taught in two previous jobs as a charter boat licensing instructor.

"At first times were really thin," he says. "It was tough riding it out between checks. But the way I saw it I had to be true to myself. I'm at home on boats. I love boats and it doesn't matter what kind, sail, power, rowboats, canoes, and kayaks. I love them all."

Koch owns a 1967 Celebrity, a nineteen-foot sloop that he sails on weekends and after work on weekdays. His job keeps him busy and though his home in Point Pleasant Beach is near the water, he still doesn't have lots of time to sail.

But Koch doesn't mind. "I'm back in boats for good and it feels fantastic."

© Reprinted with permission from Soundings Publications, LLC, 1989

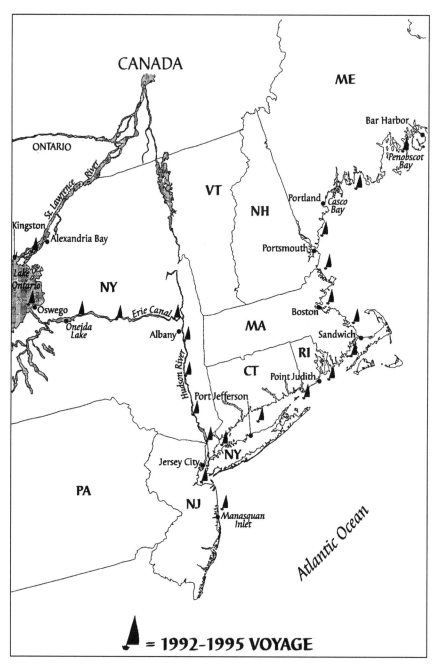

▲ = **1992-1995 VOYAGE**

Figure 13. Map of the Northeast showing the route of the author's extended solo voyages. MAP DESIGNED BY MARGARET WESTERGAARD.

The Odyssey
NAVIGATING THE WATERWAYS OF THE NORTHEAST

Most every person harbors a special dream deep inside. Each is as different as the individual, and some are more noble, adventurous, practical, simple, or complicated than others. Some are impossible, or quite near to impossible to shake loose from the abstract into reality, while others can come to fruition with a little luck, hard work, and careful planning. But they all have in common a thread, the desire for something to work toward, to hold close when time and the press of life conspire to rob hope from existence and stamp out the spark that burns in the heart and reaches for the stars.

Where a dream comes from often cannot be pinpointed, like going back over a road map to see where a path began and finally ended up. It just springs to life, almost spontaneously, almost without the conscious knowledge that something new has come to live in one's spirit; at least that was the way I found it.

The dream for me was to experience boating in a way that would take me deep into the land, the sea, the lakes, the rivers, and to introduce me to the people of the waterfront and the history behind the little towns and cities, an inland passage to a place both cerebral and spiritual, physical and emotional. It didn't come about in a series of well-planned steps, not as it often does for, say, the retired couple who own a boat and spend years planning a dream voyage around the world, or more likely, down the Intracoastal Waterway to the Caribbean Sea. Rather, it slowly took root, grew stronger, and ultimately compelled me to act.

Looking back on my voyage through the Northeast, I realize now that the dream first got planted deep in my mind during a journey aboard a sailing canoe in the heart of the Adirondack Mountain lake country. That trip took me to some beautiful places, and it was in many ways a release for me during a difficult time in my career. The recession was on; times for a free-lance writer couldn't have been worse, so the chance to sail and write for pay obviously struck me as quite special.

After I came home and again faced the reality of the times, and of my own economic and emotional vulnerability, I kept on keeping on despite all indicators that I would fail to find a way to keep on keeping on, and through it all I always returned in mind and spirit to those windswept waters of the Adirondacks, the intense colors of autumn, the yelps of coyote, the smell of woodsmoke, and the lonely cry of a loon on a moonlit night. It seemed to me that life out there in the wild was more real, more important than trying to find work as a writer. It meant more than just earning money and stacking up clips to climb a ladder that seemed to be leading down instead of up.

I suppose some of us dream of escaping from things that make us unhappy, of running away into our minds to a place that we create where we can find a dash of peace in an often troubled life. I knew deep in my heart that that was what I was doing, as I sat at my desk, nearly empty of assignments and full of novels that no one wanted, and dreamed of taking to the waters under a cloud of sail. Freedom. Adventure. Life on the edge. It all took hold of me and grew into a vision of attempting something close to impossible.

I thought maybe, just maybe, if I went on a grand voyage I would find both the spiritual and physical freedom from conventional life I wanted and at the same time find things to write that would actually see the light of day in the boating magazines. I initially thought I would somehow scrape enough money together to buy a little boat, and sail up the Hudson River, cross the Great Lakes, head south through the heartland to the Gulf of Mexico, and then back home up the East Coast. Sounded just the thing, exactly what the doctor ordered.

Of course, it was a crazy idea. I had no money, just hope. But as it turned out, I did figure out a way to put my dream into action. It took a lot of luck, and plenty of hard work. I found the recession meant no one was buying boats, so many folks wanting to sell were willing to practically give them away. I located a beautiful little twenty-four-foot sailboat, a Bristol, for those of you who know about such matters. It was perfect for cruising, a good seaboat. With the money I'd earned from a big project at an ad agency, and a loan from my wife, Elizabeth, I swallowed hard and threw all practicality out the window. I bought the boat and sailed her north in the autumn of 1992, fully expecting to complete my 5,000-mile voyage through the United States.

I made it to Lake Ontario and the St. Lawrence River. The following spring, however, record floods inundated the heartland, turning golf courses to lakes, and transforming the rivers into seething nightmares of white water. Money ran short. I turned back, but I didn't forget about why I'd started out.

Like most people who dream and fail, or at least some of us, I didn't give up, but made some compromises to bring the dream in line with reality. I decided that I would confine myself to the Northeast. Even though I was still pretty broke, I took off again in 1994 and 1995, spending as much as five consecutive months aboard the boat exploring the waterways. What follows are the stories that came directly from the voyage, though every story in this book can trace its roots back to my love of the water and many to the discoveries I made on my long journey.

> The first story will take you to that very special trip in the Adirondacks, where you, too, will catch a glimpse of the start of a dream that hasn't altogether vanished, not even now. You see, once you cruise for long periods, life ashore lacks the pull it has when you seldom leave it astern. I will voyage again, and, I hope, the paths will lead me to even more adventure and an even greater appreciation for the vast diversity of humanity and the places we inhabit.

A WIND THAT FOLLOWS FAST

SAILING IN THE HEART OF THE ADIRONDACKS

As the wind, dead astern from the southwest, filled our sail, the sheet grew taut in my hand. I looked at my sailing partner, Gregg Sterling, then glanced aft at the village of Long Lake, which bisects this aptly named, fourteen-mile-long glacial scratch. Buildings, cars, and seaplanes near the town bridge seemed to shrink in the distance. We left Whispering Woods Campground behind us on the western shore. I fondly remembered visiting there once, and I hoped that the coming five-day sailing tour of Long Lake, Cranberry Lake, Raquette Lake, and Lake Lila would provide me with equally rich memories.

I was not to be disappointed.

We were sailing a seventeen-foot Adirondack Goodboat, the *Elizabeth*, designed and manufactured by Mason Smith, of Long Lake. We moved in harmony with the wind and waves as we passed Round Island. The sound of the water under the wooden hull mingled with the luff of the sail and the intermittent vibration of the leeboard; trees crowded the rocky shores. Being on the lake under sail was like being at sea in the middle of a forest.

Gray clouds hid the sun and the wind piped up, gusting to twenty-five knots. The waves got much bigger as the lake widened. We held on and roared down the lake past rock markers, which we studiously avoided. We also kept well offshore and watched for surf or ripples, which warn of shoals. Still, right out in the middle of the lake, the leeboard, with a loud "whack," glanced off a rock hidden below the surface. Sterling and I looked at each other in complete surprise. We'd seen no clues to point out the rock. I suddenly had the uneasy feeling that we were sailing through a minefield.

Shortly after our close encounter with the rock, we noticed a shelter on the edge of the lake at Kelly's Point, about four miles from the boat ramp. Huge boulders lined the shore; the evergreens were whipped into song by the wind. With spray flying over the bow, Sterling dropped the sail and rowed us against the wind and cresting waves to a small beach. We chose a campsite off the beach, out of the wind, and pitched the tent.

As dusk fell, the wind dropped, as it usually does in the evening and early morning, and the glassy lake reflected the stars and moon. Sterling and I remained silent as we watched the campfire flicker against a giant boulder behind the fireplace. Somewhere nearby, coyotes filled the quiet night with yelps and whines, and they made me think of Jack London's *Call of the Wild*.

As expected, the next morning was calm, a perfect time to scoot back up the lake before the prevailing southwest wind made the return trip difficult. Our boat came equipped with a little outboard motor, and we were glad to have it. It would have been a long row, and we were pressed for time to move on to Cranberry Lake.

Cranberry Lake is big water, covering 6,976 acres, and creeks and bays greatly extend the size of the main waterway. The advantage offered by this type of topography is that once you're sailing on the main reaches of the lake, there are many course options to campsites on points of sail that fit whatever course the prevailing weather makes possible. (Long Lake, on the other hand, has much more limited course options.)

Unfortunately, in some instances, heavy weather can make any point of sail dangerous, and such was the case this day on Cranberry Lake. When Sterling and I launched the *Elizabeth*, we had no idea that trouble was just minutes away. We planned to beat our way southward four miles down the west shore of the lake, to avoid shoals indicated on our topographic map, then reach east to Joe Indian Island. We wanted to enjoy the solitude of an island site far from the usual crowded camping spots.

It didn't quite work out that way.

I thought about shaking out the reef in the seventy-square-foot lugsail, a squarish configuration of dacron suspended from a spruce yard at the masthead and attached to a spruce boom. Reefing (folding up part of the sail and tying it securely) reduces the sail area by 30 percent, slowing the boat. We had needed to reef on Long Lake in the twenty-five-knot winds, but it didn't look rough now, and I wanted to sail fast.

"Let's shake out the reef," I suggested.

"Let's wait till we get out there first," Sterling said. "We can always shake the reef out then."

Sterling rowed the boat into deeper water and shipped the oars. While I lashed the rudder in place, Sterling lowered the leeboard. (The leeboard was mounted forward on the starboard side, a yard back from the mast, and was attached to the boat with a solid-brass gizmo that allowed lowering or raising as needed—much like a centerboard. Leeboard and rudder extended eighteen inches below the surface of the water to provide a lateral plane for steering.) Sterling hauled the sail up, secured the halyard and down haul, and we were off on a pleasant beam reach.

As we reached open water, the wind hit us like a freight train. Gusts reaching thirty knots slammed into us, driving two- and three-foot whitecaps over the bow. The lee rail nearly dipped under every few minutes, and it took all our sailing skill to avoid capsizing.

It was a thrilling experience that reminded me of sailing in mildly rough weather at sea, but, since we were in a seventeen-foot-long open boat, the weather conditions were beginning to make me nervous. A granddaddy wave reared up and broke over the bow, drenching Sterling and shipping water into the bottom of the boat. We decided to head to Long Pine Point, past Dog Island, to a campsite near the Cranberry Lake State Campground. Beating all the way down the lake to Joe Indian Island would have been dangerous as well as time-consuming.

The waves grew larger and the wind increased as we sailed farther out on the lake, past Chipmunk and Matilda bays. Then, during a fearsome gust, the rudder lifted out of its gudgeons. I managed to grab it before it washed away, and I released the sheet to let the sail flog in the wind while I put the rudder back on.

Shortly after we nearly lost the rudder, Sterling and I came to the same decision: it was time to head back to the boat ramp. Dark clouds loomed to the southwest. A real snotty blow thundered toward us. In the mountains, squalls can hit so fast that a craft doesn't have time to get off the water. We didn't want to get caught in treacherous weather.

I slowly fell off the wind, spilling air from the sail as I turned. The boat rolled violently, shipping water over both rails as it surged through the crests. We rapidly closed with the rocky lee shore, and I realized we would have to gybe to turn west on a reach toward the shelter of the boat ramp.

I was just making my turn when a huge crest boiled under the boat. To my horror, the rudder lifted out of the lashings, which must have come loose again, and floated off the stern into the whitecaps. I watched it for a few seconds, then lost sight of it as I let go of the sheet.

"Drop sail?" Sterling asked as we rolled beam to the seas.

"Yes!" I shouted into the wind.

Sterling released the halyard. The rig snagged and fell into the water.

The rocks on shore drew closer by the second. Crests broke over the windward rail, and the boat began to fill with water. Sterling cut the snagged lines away and brought the rig aboard. (The need to cut lines does not arise often, but most sailors keep a good knife handy just in case.) It was good that Sterling had reacted so quickly; otherwise, we could have swamped.

Now we had rocks to worry about. Sterling unshipped the oars and held us bow to the wind, stabilizing the boat. He guided us past the rocks to the beach of a summer cottage; nobody was home. Relieved to be off the water, we watched as the sky became grayer and more threatening.

Sterling walked to the ramp and got the car. While he did that, I went back to the beach to start unloading the boat so we could put it back on the trailer. And, lo and behold, I found our lost rudder in the surf, not three feet from the stern of the *Elizabeth*! I just couldn't believe our luck. The odds were good that the rudder would wash up on the lee shore, but not right next to the boat.

We dropped the Goodboat back at Mason Smith's shop and drove to Paradox for a night's rest at Sterling's home. We also took the opportunity to dry our gear. On this sailing excursion, we had brought along what we normally would have brought on a canoe trip: a four-man tent, stove, lantern, two backpacks, sleeping bags and pads, and a cooler. We also packed plastic bags, to prevent spray or rain from soaking everything, though, as it turned out, water got to the gear anyway. One other concern helped determine what we could bring along on this trip. Under sail, we would have to shift nimbly from one side of the boat to the other in order to act as live ballast when beating to windward. This meant that we had to be sure to leave a fair amount of room to move around in, more so than would be necessary on a canoe trip.

On Wednesday, we headed to Raquette Lake, a large body of water full of shoals; they're well marked, as are the channels, with red and green buoys. We launched the boat at Burke's Marina late in the afternoon. It was calm, so we decided to motor to Tioga Point, where we planned to camp. I checked the topo map and figured we'd head around the east side of Big Island, round Strawberry Island, then head eastward across the lake to Tioga Point. It seemed so easy that I didn't bother to chart a course with my compass—a big mistake.

In the waning light on this unfamiliar water dotted with islands and full of points and bays, the land masses blended together. Beautiful mountains provided the vistas I'd longed to see, but, scenery aside, it was hard to figure out where we were, even by checking the topo map.

"Where the hell are we?" I asked. Sterling shrugged. As dusk came, the map fell into the water, and it ripped when I grabbed it from the smooth, dark surface of the lake. I vowed never again to neglect using my compass and topo maps in unknown territory. Eventually, we pulled up to a boathouse and saw a sign that said "Bluff Point." We'd overshot our destination, so we motored back to Tioga Point.

Our campsite was beautiful but rocky. We built a fire from driftwood and watched the moon slowly inch across the sky. A fox in the woods behind us gave its distinctive bark. On our way across the lake, we had passed many private homes, some big sterndrive powerboats, and sailboats more than twenty feet long, but from our vantage point it appeared that we had the lake to ourselves. The next morning, we left Raquette Lake in a dead calm and moved on to Lake Lila.

The Lake Lila Primitive Area is comprised of 7,215 acres and includes Mount Frederica, a five-hundred-foot summit that can be reached by taking the short trail to the top. The lake itself is fourteen hundred acres, with a maximum depth of sixty-four feet. However, many unmarked shoals and rocks fill the lake and limit access to the seven islands there, four of which have designated campsites and natural white sandy beaches.

We cartopped the boat to the parking area, strapped it onto a special dolly used for portages, and pushed it over roots, rocks and narrow trail bridges on the trek, about a third of a mile, to the water. (A dolly will help move heavier sailboats, but the trail is rough, and anything bigger than a Sunfish or a sailing canoe would be too difficult to portage. Also, trailers and motors are prohibited, further necessitating a small, light sailboat with which to ply this lake.) The wind blew from the southwest, which meant we had to beat to windward from the northern end of the lake, but the sail was quite pleasant in the light air. Mountains exquisitely carved by the glacier seemed even more beautiful from the sailboat, with its wing of white contrasting with the blue water and the trees on the rounded slopes; loons called as we sailed by. We then reached west to Canada Island and made camp at one of the prettiest campsites I've ever seen. The land had been cleared under the tall white pines, which had shed a carpet of soft needles, and firewood had been left near the fireplace.

After dinner, Sterling and I walked along the little trail leading from the site, at the interior of the island, to the beach. We sat on the glacial rocks strewn everywhere and watched the full moon climb slowly into a pale-blue evening sky; the haunting sound of a great horned owl came from somewhere in the woods. The sun set below Mount Frederica in shimmering red, outlining the summit. Trout splashed circular ripples in the calm water, which reflected the white moon like a giant mirror.

As I sat and allowed the peace of the place to wash over me, I thought that this kind of serenity was a good end to our misadventure-punctuated adventures. The next day, our sailing tour of North Country lakes would be over. I felt a twinge of regret, but not for long. I would return to it in memory, as I would the pages of a favorite book, and savor these moments again when I was far away from the Adirondacks and from sailboats.

Adirondack Life, 1991

HUDSON RIVER ODYSSEY

Despite a lack of funds solo sailing the inland waterways of North America was not a dream to be deferred.

Cloaked in a gauzy haze, the Tappan Zee Bridge arched just ahead of me. A light wind formed ripples on the gray-black water, which undulated from the natural chop of the river and the occasional wake of a passing boat. Sweat had soaked through my T-shirt. I sat down in my sailboat's cockpit, dizzy from the heat, and looked up as my boat passed under the bridge. I'd never seen the Tappan Zee from the water, and as I stared at the enormous concrete caissons and the acres of pavement above me, I felt humble.

I had begun the voyage on my sailboat *Elizabeth* (named after my wife) last September from Point Pleasant, New Jersey. From there I sailed up the coast to New York Harbor and proceeded to the Hudson River on the first leg of what would be a 5,000-mile odyssey through many of North America's inland waterways. I'd spent my scanty life savings and borrowed money to finance my journey.

A wave of self-doubt and fear hit me as I passed under the bridge. Was I being courageous in following my heart, or a fool? I pushed the self-doubt away as I left the Tappan Zee astern. Too often I'd heard of people waiting till retirement to "live life," only to get sick or die before they reached their so-called golden years. I didn't want to defer my dream and risk never seeing it come true.

The wake flattened the river behind the boat. It formed a band of reflected sunlight that appeared to reach back miles toward the furrowed browned basalt of the Palisades and the glass and steel towers of Manhattan. To my right, the silvery glint of a passenger train caught my eye. The gentle breeze carried the clackety-clack sound of its wheels across the water and mingled with the gentle slap of wavelets against the hull as I sailed on to the lakelike water of Haverstraw Bay.

Figure 14. Sailor-author David Shaw catching the wind on Long Lake in the Adirondacks. PHOTO BY GREGG STERLING.

I gradually grew tired from the heat and the hours of piloting the boat. Where to stop for the night? I hailed a man aboard a little sailboat out for a late afternoon sail. "Is there a marina around here?" I shouted. He sailed close to my boat and pointed north toward Stony Point. "Why not try MYC," he said, referring to the Minisceongo Yacht Club, "that's where I keep my boat." I followed the man into a protected yacht basin, a beautiful facility founded by the descendants of Irish immigrants who flocked to Haverstraw Bay in the last century to work in the brickyards which once lined the shores. The dockmaster, a friendly man wide in girth and quick to smile, greeted me. "Yes," he said, "you can tie up here for the night. Once you get settled, come on up to the Snack Shack if you want some company or a good supper." He pointed at a building on a little hill overlooking the bay.

I spent some quiet hours in the boat, but then loneliness cast its shadow over me and I headed over to the Snack Shack. There, dockmaster Frank Skala took an interest in my voyage. "Just a second," he said, rising from the table. "I'll be right back." He reappeared carrying a green booklet, a history of MYC. "I thought you'd like to read about our club," he said, giving me the book as a gift. He turned to a page that sported the photographs of past commodores, and pointed to his own portrait. I smiled. In his younger years, Skala bore a striking resemblance to the skipper on the TV show "Gilligan's Island."

Skala autographed the photo for me, and wrote: "Good luck to David and his sailboat." Skala, well-liked and well-known among the boaters along this section of the Hudson, was the first of many people I met who offered the hand of friendship to a complete stranger.

I spent three days sailing on Haverstraw Bay, then moved on to the Chelsea Yacht Club above Newburgh, where I'd been invited to stay as a guest by members I'd met at a regatta held by MYC. Just north of Stony Point, the Highlands rose to heights of more than 1,000 feet. The steep, rocky banks formed a gorge through which the Hudson River ran fast and deep, passing stretches with ominous names like the Devil's Horse Race and World's End. The Hudson is sometimes called the "Rhine of America," and as I craned my neck to take in the incredible scenery I found the description quite fitting.

I arrived at the Chelsea Yacht Club tired and ready for a meal, but I remained in the cockpit for a little while to watch the sun sink below the trees on the western shore. Scarlet and purple and orange light, soft with the coming of dusk, bathed the many sailboats swinging with the tidal current at their moorings. Soon, however, hunger drove me below to fix supper. I turned on the radio for company and discovered that the Highlands cut off reception from Manhattan-based radio stations. I listened to unfamiliar stations from Poughkeepsie and thought of my home in Westfield, New Jersey. The sound of trains and the throb of tug engines pierced the otherwise silent night. In the morning, I again listened to the radio, and smiled at the stage name of the traffic reporter, Gridlock Gordon. It struck me that each region featured its own cast of radio personalities; they become part of our daily lives and, after a time, seem like old friends. Passing through one region into another, I was the outsider, almost an intruder, yet once I became familiar with the Gridlock Gordons on my voyage upriver, I felt as though I had made new friends, and felt just a little sad when I lost the station.

The radio was my link to the communities along the way, but it also reminded me that I was always on the move. At Kingston, I encountered my first storm. Gusts of wind more than thirty knots blasted downriver from the north. Three-foot waves slammed into the boat, driving sheets of spray aft. Off the bow, the extensive shoals north of Kingston surged white with breakers. I motored past the historic Rondout II Lighthouse into the protected waters of Rondout Creek, happy to find shelter from the angry water.

That night, thunder boomed overhead as I sat in my cabin and watched the windows flash white with each bolt of lightning. Wind lashed the rain into whirling, nearly horizontal blasts that drummed on the deck and roof above me. The severe thunderstorm evoked a primal sense of awe at the strength of nature, and illustrated with each violent roar and terrifying flash how insignificant a lone person aboard a little sailboat is. I remained awake long after the storm passed, and thought of many things as I listened to the wind's soft whisper through the stays and shrouds.

Several days later, I reached Troy. A Canadian yacht shared the dock near me, and, as is the custom among boaters regardless of nationality, conversation ensued. I informed the couple aboard the yacht that I planned to sail up Canada's Trent-Severn Waterway, a 240–mile watery highway that connects Lake Ontario to Lake Huron. The man's face lit up. "We live along the Trent-Severn," he said, his accent distinctly British. "You're in for a beautiful trip. I like your New York State, but I have to say you'll find the Trent-Severn even more beautiful." Not taking issue with him over which region was more handsome, I responded: "I understand the country is pretty wild up there." The man nodded, "Don't take any unnecessary risks." He gave me navigation advice and told me he was headed south for an extended cruise. "We're seventy locks from home already," he said. "By the time you get done with your trip, God knows how many locks you'll have passed through. You'll have had your fill of them, I expect." I laughed, allowing that he was probably right. Never having traveled through locks, however, I looked forward to the novelty of the experience.

The next day, I passed through Troy Lock and reached the junction between the Hudson River and the Erie Canal. While I waited to lock through, I thought back on what defined the Hudson River region—the sights I had seen and the people I had met on my way up the river. The Taconic, Ramapo and Catskill mountains, the blue water sometimes wide and sometimes narrow, the dense forests, the palatial homes perched atop verdant hills, the pockets of industry, the wineries, and the succession of passenger and cargo trains and grand bridges.

The two enormous gates of Lock 2 opened, and I motored slowly into the dark rectangular chamber. Water dripped from the slimy rough walls. Out of direct sunlight and encased in deep shadows, it was quite cool. I looked over my right shoulder to catch a last glimpse of the river. But I was seconds too late; the gates had closed, and all I could see was a steel wall.

The Erie Canal carried me west to the Oswego Canal, where I headed north to meet with the eastern end of Lake Ontario. I crossed the lake to the Thousand Islands, where I left my boat for the winter.

This summer I expect to resume my odyssey. I'll start at the Trent-

Severn Waterway, cross Lake Huron and Lake Michigan and sail down America's heartland waterways to the Gulf of Mexico. I'll finish this journey, which began on the Hudson, by sailing the Okeechobee Waterway across the Florida panhandle, and then back up the East Coast to home.

Hudson Valley Magazine, 1993

LOCK-STEPPING TO THE GREAT LAKES

In late September, I took an autumnal voyage from the Big Apple to store my boat in Clayton, New York. It was a journey that would follow the Hudson River-Erie Canal link to Lake Ontario, up the St. Lawrence River to the Thousand Islands. It was also a journey that many lakeland boaters are likely to take at least once in their cruising lifetimes, heading south for an Atlantic holiday or perhaps bringing a boat to the lakes for the first time. This link to the Great Lakes, open for business since 1825, has always been a venerable highway for pleasure and commercial craft. Nowadays, though, as history, scenery, and fine amenities accumulate along the shores of the Hudson-Erie Canal link, this path has become prime powerboat country.

The Hudson is known as "the Rhine of America" because of its mountainous scenery and wide water vistas. The Mohicans, who lived on the Hudson's shores, called it the "river-that-flows-two-ways." Tides ebb and flow inland fully 154 miles to the Federal Lock at Troy. And, depending on where you are, currents run fast.

Sometimes called a fjord, a more precise description of the Hudson is a drowned river. As sea levels rose after the last Ice Age, ancient river valleys filled, submerging the centuries-old rapids, rocks, and waterfalls. The Hudson River became an estuary, with ocean tides sloshing in and out at an average range of three to five feet. Hudson River boaters are cruising across the tops of ancient mountains, a trail bordered by several of the most scenic areas in North America.

As I motored upriver away from the five boroughs of New York, the Statue of Liberty faded to a green smudge obscured in the thick, smoggy air before finally disappearing in the haze. Even though I had just begun my Hudson River journey, the frenetic pace of city life was already a world away. Almost immediately, the brown basalt cliffs of the Palisades topped heights of 500 feet or more above the west shore. The river widened into the Tappan Zee, a bay almost two-and-a-half miles wide and twelve miles long. I slowed to idle and craned my neck as I passed under the Tappan Zee Bridge, one of the many grand bridges I would admire on the way upriver. A tug and barge overtook my craft, then faded into the haze ahead.

The Highlands reared skyward to the north of Stony Point, as I motored across the wide expanse of Haverstraw Bay. I enjoyed the contrast of a lakelike water vista set against a backdrop of lush hills colored purple and blue in the fading afternoon light. The next morning, I left Stony Point with a minimum ebb tide and entered the Highlands.

Upriver, I encountered a fast, narrow stretch of water called The Devil's Horse Race, and World's End, a place where the U.S. Coastal Pilot warned of dangerous eddies at a sharp turn in the river. One local man told me that he went into this section with his sailboat when the moon was full and the tides were high and his boat spun three hundred sixty degrees several times. I kept a sharp eye on the heavy pleasure boat traffic while I admired the 1,000–foot mountains, some with pointy summits, others capped with gentle curves. The Taconic and Ramapo mountains hemmed the gorge in on both sides. These ranges are part of the Appalachian chain, and reminded me of youthful hiking trips on the Appalachian Trail, which crosses the Hudson on the Bear Mountain Bridge. I passed West Point Military Academy, and navigated World's End without incident.

The river narrowed again above Newburgh Bay, but flowed north without many turns all the way to Troy. I set the autopilot, kept watch for shipping, and relaxed. Dense forests lined the shores. Occasionally, a city crowded both banks, spoiling the bucolic ambiance.

Hours ticked by and a south wind kicked up whitecaps. A fair tide sped me to Rondout Creek and the historic town of Kingston, burned by the British during the Revolutionary War. I hiked up and down the steep hills of the town, and visited the Hudson River Maritime Museum, where the exhibits look back on the days of steamboats and Hudson River Sloops with their giant gaffed mainsails and wide flat hulls. If you want to learn about the Hudson's history, this is the place to go.

The wind shifted to the north during the night and blew up to thirty knots. When I cleared the protected waters of the creek I'd anchored in, the full fury of the wind struck and the boat suddenly slowed in the gusts. With three-to-four-foot waves blasting spray over the bow, I turned right around and went back up the creek, content to let the angry Hudson rage till its mood improved.

After Kingston, the river narrowed still more. Shoals along the shore and flats in mid-river required close attention. Wise navigators keep a sharp eye on the well-marked channel between Kingston and Troy, and don't stray into unknown waters. At Troy the beauty of the Catskill Mountains gives way to tank farms, commercial docks, and high-rise buildings.

The next day, I turned west off the Hudson at Waterford. I had reached the first locks of the 348-mile Erie Canal. Locks 2 through 6, the famous "Flight of Five," provide a watery elevator ride to 184 feet above sea level in less than two miles. It took about two hours to get through.

The canal opened trade with the western territories and funneled immigrants to foster the growth of inland cities such as Cleveland, Milwaukee, Detroit, Buffalo, Chicago, and Toledo. Mules and horses towed barges along the canal, bringing supplies to the Great Lakes and into the heartland, playing a key role in the Union's western campaign during the Civil War.

The first stretch of the canal twists and turns on the Lower Mohawk River and it was impossible to use the autopilot. A strong wind gusting to thirty-five knots kicked up short, steep two-to-three-foot waves on the nose. The wind lasted for three days. Trees hemmed in the shores and the houses perched on the banks. The smell of wood smoke from the homes, cow dung from the fields that open on either side of the canal, and rotting vegetation filled the air. Surprisingly, the odor did not offend, but rather added to the rural atmosphere.

I left the river and followed landcuts, straight paths that lead due west to Oneida Lake, a shallow body of water known for its steep waves. Crossing the twenty-one miles of open water with no trouble, I proceeded to Three Rivers Point, where I left the Erie Canal and began a twenty-four-mile journey north through the seven locks of the Oswego Canal to Lake Ontario.

I motored into the last of the thirty locks I'd passed though since Troy, 186 miles away, and brought the boat up to the ladder inside the chamber. As I stepped out of the cockpit onto the deck, I stopped short, drawing a quick breath. Before me stretched the broad blue expanse of Lake Ontario, oceanlike in its enormity. The water in the lock drained, the gates swung open and I motored out into Oswego Harbor. As I gazed past the jetties at the inland sea I would cross to the Thousand Islands, the lock swung closed behind me.

Lakeland Boating, 1993

Take a look at the world's greatest cities and you'll find no two are exactly alike. Each has its own unique personality, its own claim to fame. But the common link among most of them centers on the water. Water for drinking, growing crops, transporting goods to and from the cities; without the lake, river, or coastal harbor, most of these hubs of humanity, so full of nightlife and glamour, fashion and culture, would not exist. This notion makes itself plain to anyone who studies such things, or merely observes the obvious.

When cruising in the Northeast, you can't help but run across cities. They're scattered throughout the region, dotting the rural hinterlands with pavement and poking the sky with high rises. Coming upon a city by boat brings with it a strange kind of romance; it sweeps you back in time to when boats were the main means of transportation. Sailing to the cities represented yet another subtle way in which long distance cruising can enrich the soul by putting it in touch with the larger picture, quite apart from the experience of seeing another place for the first time.

SAILING TO THE CITIES

When casting off for an extended cruise, whether it's around the world or within the home waters of one's own country, the usual objective is to get away from the frenetic pace of life in the big city. Out on the boat sailing with a fair wind and smooth seas, smoggy skies, traffic jams, crime, and the press of business represent a life left happily behind in the wake.

In 1992, I began a voyage through the waterways of the Northeastern United States and southern Canada with similar goals. I couldn't afford a big boat and a couple years away, but a series of limited journeys of three or four months at a stretch was feasible. During the last four years, my travels have taken me through most of the major waterways, fresh and salt, in the oldest settled region of North America.

To my surprise, sailing to many of the biggest cities on these waterways was an experience every bit as exciting as weathering storms, braving fog, dodging ships, and enjoying quiet anchorages and brilliant sunsets. From Kingston, Ontario in Canada, to Portland, Maine, approaching the waterfronts of major Northeastern cities under sail held a kind of magic I hadn't expected; I suppose that's why we go voyaging—to stumble on the unexpected pleasures, urban or otherwise. The works of civilization can rival nature's, which may seem obvious but wasn't something I thought much about until I sailed to the cities.

As I sailed my twenty-four-foot sloop up the lower bay of New York Harbor, winging along with a fair southwesterly on the first leg of my voyage bound for Lake Ontario, I admired the grand sight of the Verrazano Narrows Bridge and imagined what it must have been like for my sailing predecessors to approach the harbor when no bridge existed. All the early accounts of those who sailed there first speak of

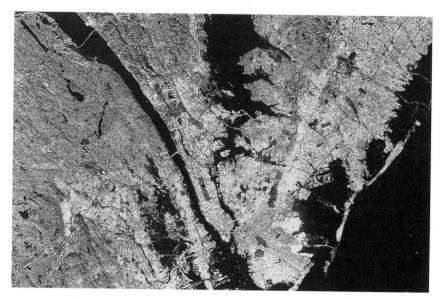

Figure 15. Spaceborne radar image of the New York City metropolitan area. The island of Manhattan appears in the center. Long Island, New Jersey, the Bronx, and lower Westchester County can also be seen. The Hudson River, the Long Island Sound, and the Atlantic Ocean surround the land masses. COURTESY OF NASA.

breathtaking beauty and the fragrant scent of trees and flowers wafting off the shores.

Now, of course, the scent is not so pleasant. Yet, despite the distasteful presence of civilization in the air, the span towering above me, one of the world's largest, was beautiful. It counterbalanced, in a small way, the negative results of our impact on nature.

The blue and silver skyscrapers perched on the bedrock of Manhattan became fully visible shortly after I passed under the bridge. Verrazano, the first sailor to see New York Harbor in 1524, called this portion a lake. Later, an Englishman named Henry Hudson, sailing for the Dutch in 1609, took his vessel, the *Half Moon*, beyond Manhattan to the present site of Albany. I would follow his path, as I did later in the wakes of John Smith, Samuel de Champlain, and others.

At anchor in the old Morris Canal basin adjacent to Liberty State Park in Jersey City, soft orange light reflected off the buildings across the river which bears Henry's last name, and with the dusk came a splendid show of lights. It was a curious blend of natural and unnatural beauty I found repeated at every city, though each had its own distinct personality, an ethos as unique as each of us.

Albany, one of the oldest cities in America, bears this out. It's not like Manhattan at all. For one thing, it's a lot smaller. But that's not what sets it apart from its big brother downriver. After days on the

Hudson, with its mountains and forests on each side, I emerged from the bucolic to the urban. Manhattan's buildings all smacked of the new while those of Albany revealed an architectural tapestry of many time periods. Art Deco mingled with plain brick facades; the shiny modern with the delicate, subdued face of the last century.

Although the mast was unstepped in preparation for my transit of the Erie Canal, and the noise of the engine robbed me of the quiet I had experienced sailing past Manhattan, the old port of Albany was a pleasure to see from the water. I'd visited there before, as I had Manhattan. In a car, I was in the thick of often depressing city life. But passing by on a sailboat, whether the mast was up or down, I felt apart from the unappealing aspects of urban life and was able to see the cities from a new, pleasing perspective.

Twisting up the Mohawk Valley on the Erie Canal to Lake Ontario via the Oswego Canal, I arrived at Oswego, New York, the first freshwater port established in the United States. Today, huge tanks of an industrial complex give the place a gray look. The buildings don't inspire much, though many are historic landmarks.

In the past, the port was alive with sailing vessels of all kinds. Forests of masts were the dominant feature. Oswego, at the mouth of the northward-flowing Oswego River, was a major crossroads for shipping goods west and east well before the Erie Canal was completed in 1825; commerce soared after that, and immigrants flooded into the heartland along this route.

I was happy to have the mast stepped and to be on my way. Some cities, while they are home no doubt to people who love them, are best left astern.

The vast expanse of Lake Ontario stretched out before me. The prevailing westerlies blew strong and ocean-size rollers marched across the sweet water. Great Lakes sailors know how dangerous these bodies of water can be; saltwater sailors who have never been there, I've found tend to underrate them.

My little sloop is a good seaboat, full-keeled and heavy. I was glad to have such a vessel on my crossing from New York to Canada, and many other times during the voyage, too. After the tame Hudson river, Lake Ontario put the boat through its paces. Double-reefed main with the clew of the roller-furled genoa forward of the shrouds, sheets of good-tasting spray that left no film on the decks flew wildly. Ahead of me I saw no land, only a vague outline to the east off the starboard beam.

The waves turned the minutes to hours, as Gordon Lightfoot so aptly said in his song, "The Wreck of the Edmund Fitzgerald." I was alone on the inland sea bounding like a racehorse to the shores of another nation.

The city of Kingston eventually became visible. Even from afar, it looks nothing like any American city I had seen or would see later. The domed City Hall looked like a European estate fronted by a picturesque park on the waterfront. The limestone and brick buildings, complete with turrets, ornate ironwork, and balconies high above the streets lacked the sometimes harsh, utilitarian lines of American architecture.

I felt as though I'd sailed from a land of factories and tanks at Oswego, Albany, and New York City to Europe. I'd crossed an inland sea, not the Atlantic. Yet I'd still crossed an invisible threshold to a completely different land. Hearing French on the radio, the paucity of air conditioned restaurants, as I hear is quite common in Europe, and the colorful Canadian currency added to my feeling that I'd traveled farther than I really had.

Like most cities, Kingston drew its strength from the water. It sits at the head of the St. Lawrence River on the northeastern corner of Lake Ontario. Like Oswego, but to a much larger extent, it, too, was a crossroads, serving as a staging area for the settlement of upper Canada. As early as 1615, Samuel de Champlain visited the site, then known among the Mississagua Indians as Cataraqui. First the French, then the British occupied the site, and after the upstart Yanks to the south won the War of Independence, Loyalists flocked across the St. Lawrence River to start new lives in King's Town.

I sailed down the St. Lawrence River a short distance among the granite islands which made the region a playground of the rich from both countries. But I did not reach Montreal, which I regret. (I did, however, get there via jet to check out the waterfront and the wonderful city life after the voyage.) Time, so precious, had run out. I'd spent two seasons on inland waters, keeping mostly to quiet places with visits to the cities as forays into a more hurried existence I left behind. Turning away from the freshwater, I sailed back to the sea the same way I had come anxious to sail down east.

Sailing eastward, I followed the same path that jets, trains, cars, and trucks take in transit up and down the Boston-New York City corridor. Although the land from seaward holds great beauty, it is still part of the vast megalopolis; sprawling suburbs dominate. The north country, which is untamed, especially in Canada, was far different and more to my liking. The coastal settlements from New London to New Bedford, all very old, revealed a similarly gray feel to what I experienced in Oswego. These places all share a rich historic past; it's the present state of economic decline I found unappealing, so I kept as much as possible to the quiet places until I reached Boston.

Approaching Boston from the sea for the first time once again summoned back the same enthusiasm I had felt when I first passed under the Verrazano Narrows bridge and saw the buildings of Manhattan. As I sailed offshore, Boston became visible a long way off, a bluish blur at first, its tallest buildings slowly took shape. The outer islands drew into view, making the approach different from those of other cities I'd sailed to. The undeveloped offshore isles, kept almost in their natural state, contrasted with the monument-like skyscrapers at the head of the harbor and formed a pleasing mosaic.

Heeled to a strong southwesterly breeze, I guided the little sloop through fleets of sailing boats darting among convoys of huge ships. Sun bathed the islands in a warm, hazy light. The city lay before me, grand and clean from afar. Ashore, traffic was probably crawling along, as it usually does. But out on the water, the city took on an almost fanciful appeal—like Oz until you find the wizard is a fake, the vision an illusion.

I was happy to keep my illusion and put into Winthrop, where the roar of jets landing and taking off from Logan Airport was a constant reminder that I was immersed in civilization. Strangely, though, it wasn't unpleasant. As in other urban settings on the water, Boston Harbor holds its own unique appeal. Riding to a mooring, I was an observer rather than a participant in the frenetic ambiance, which was how I preferred to keep it.

Sailing eastward, ever eastward, through thick New England fogs, blustery southwest winds, the occasional thunder storm, I left the megalopolis astern. The character of the settlements along the coast changed from the new to the old, like I was turning pages back in time the farther east I went.

Off Cape Elizabeth, Maine, I turned the boat northward into Casco Bay. The city of Portland lay off to port. My approach was less dramatic than in Kingston, but the beauty was just as impressive. Portland is like an urban island set among the pure, pristine isles of the bay. It sits on the mainland blessed with a particularly fine front yard. Its inhabitants can still lead rural lives, if they wish, for the land all around remains less developed than that farther south. Walking along the revitalized streets of the Old Port, I was struck by the lack of litter, graffiti, and street people. If Portland has dirty laundry, they don't air it in public.

Out on the water again, headed as far east as I could get within the time allowed, I left Portland astern. No other major cities awaited me, for I did not intend to brave the tidal currents of the Kennebec River to see the famous port of Bath.

Reflecting back on it now, I realize in retrospect how important my visits to cities were to the overall experience of voyaging. How can one enjoy the quiet places without a contrast once in awhile? Sailing to cities, as our predecessors did, brought me into a continuum as old as the settlements themselves, and made me feel part of the bigger picture, the vast scheme of time that harkens back to the days when intrepid explorers and pioneers first came to the shores of North America.

Sail, 1997

While in Boston on my way down east to Maine, I had the pleasure of lingering for a week or so at a little yacht club in Winthrop. My uncle is a member, and he kindly found me a mooring and smoothed the way for me to use the club's facilities. It was in Winthrop that I began to be aware of a response among the boaters I met which was similar to what I experienced up on the St. Lawrence River: the surprise that registered in their eyes and voices that I'd come so far in such a little boat, and that I was from New Jersey.

It seems boats from New Jersey are seldom seen in the far north country of the St. Lawrence, which, I admit, didn't really surprise me much. I got a kick out of spinning stories of my voyage up the Hudson River, through the canals, and across the big lake. But in Boston, a mere hop from New Jersey, the surprised response made me wonder.

"Where are you heading?" I'd be asked.

"Oh, I thought I'd go up to Acadia National Park," I'd reply.

"You're going all the way to Maine? That far into Maine?"

One guy actually crossed himself. Though he was only kidding, the truth is often cloaked in jest. I asked my uncle about why people would be so surprised that I'd sailed a twenty-four-foot boat from New Jersey to Boston, and intended to keep on heading eastward with it. He explained that Maine's waters were challenging, and that the marinas with nice electric hookups for the microwave and TV and refrigerator were few and far between, that the time it took to get there seemed not worth the effort for many boaters. That I would do it in a little cockleshell boat with practically no electronics, and definitely no radar, made them fancy me a soul with a bit too much nerve.

"You can get in big trouble out there," they'd say.

I was pretty sure they were right. Already, I'd had my share of close calls, including almost getting run down by a barge in New York Harbor. I made a stupid mistake and nearly paid with my life. I fell overboard trying to dock the boat back in 1992, when I was starting up the Hudson River and still hadn't gotten the hang of solo cruising. Fortunately, only my dignity suffered from that little mishap.

Had I known what was ahead of me in Maine, I probably would have thought twice about going. I'd like to think I would have gone, anyway, but I'm not so sure I would have. In a little harbor in southern Maine, I found myself caught in a fierce tide rip running at about six knots. Foolishly, I tried to pick up a mooring, missed it, and smashed into a beautiful classic sloop a very wealthy blue-blood Mainer had just spent $30,000 to have meticulously painted.

Both boats suffered damage, though mine ended up crippled with a mashed rudder while the rich gent's wasn't, which, I suppose, was a good thing. If you're going to get into an accident with your boat, it's best to ruin your own rather than someone else's. You'll note an oblique reference in the next story about a marina which was known for doing good repair work; I needed the expert craftsmen to put the Bristol right, and while they were at it, I had them work over the engine, too.

Even after the accident, I still wanted to keep going. I wasn't prepared to quit, though I tell you I thought about it quite a lot. Ultimately, I decided that I'd best keep on keeping on; to not finish what I'd started was too much. I'd already had to turn back from the larger voyage and I'd be damned if I'd fail again.

A CRUISE TO MAINE—SOLO!

I've spent most of my time aboard boats messing about on the protected, shallow waters of Barnegat Bay, New Jersey. Boating in Barnegat Bay has its pleasures. The many rivers and creeks that drain into the bay make wonderful gunkholes, and the bay itself plays host to hundreds of vessels of all sorts on busy summer weekends.

Yet, after a time the familiarity of home waters can dull the boating experience. It's not boring, but I wanted the excitement of new experiences.

As a consequence, in 1992, I set off on a four-year voyage through the waterways of the Northeast. I'd wanted excitement and I got plenty—sometimes far more than I desired. My travels took me to Lake Ontario via the Hudson River and Erie Canal link to the Great Lakes, and up the East Coast to Maine and back.

Since 1992, the boat has wintered in far away places well to the north and west of Barnegat Bay, such as the frozen, gale-swept St. Lawrence River in Clayton, New York. In 1994, the boat once again in saltwater, I turned east and headed for Maine. I got as far as Cape Elizabeth. I left her at Brewer's South Freeport Marine in Casco Bay for the winter, a place that can be as cold and tempestuous as the St. Lawrence River.

With its close proximity to Portland and easy access by highway, plus the marina's reputation as a fine place to have repairs done, the choice to leave the boat at Brewer's was an easy one. Besides, most people familiar with Maine waters say that Casco Bay is the first place you really get to experience what it's like to cruise in Maine. It was a great place to continue my trek eastward in 1995.

I steered the boat out of the Harraseeket River against a flooding tide. The green cans tilted northward, leaving frothy wakes that looked as though the buoys were steaming along at three or four knots. They reminded me of the buoys off Sandy Hook, where the current also runs quite swiftly. Earlier that week, lobstermen reported that the spring tides, made all the stronger with a full moon, had actually sucked the cans under. I proceeded with caution as I rounded Pound of Tea. Once around the little island, the beauty of Casco Bay spread out before me in a visual feast.

Sparkling blue water dotted with large and small wooded isles, the cool breeze, the occasional tingle as spray blew back over the bow into my face, the thrill of being out there on the water again after a long, though mild winter swept over me. I was back to cruising and happy at the prospect of seeing places I'd only been able to view from photographs or read about in waterway guides.

As I made my way down Broad Sound to the open sea, my thoughts drifted back to the quiet pleasure of the previous evening. I'd watched harbor seals dive and surface off the stern, blowing for air. The pogies, which had come in on the flood tide, splashed around the boat. An osprey trilled and a cormorant dived for its supper. The lowing of cows on Wolfe Neck reached the boat. It was a fine evening, one imbued with the specialness of Maine, and I looked forward to many more of them.

The passage down Broad Sound and out to sea began in a peaceful, relaxed way. But as soon as I got offshore, fog rolled in, a real pea soup. My boat was equipped with only a loran and a compass. I also have an ancient VHF and my one big investment, an autopilot.

It's not that I'm a purist. I'd love a depth sounder, GPS, radar, speedo, log, chart plotter, and any other gadget to make life easier, but such is not my reality. If you want to cruise on a shoestring budget aboard a small boat, you pretty much have to do it by the seat of your pants.

If I want to know how fast I'm going, I estimate my speed through the water based on the throttle setting (I don't have a tachometer, either), and on the loran, which may or may not give me an accurate reading on my speed over the bottom. And, I take current into consideration, too. But I've no exact means to really tell what's going on at a given moment, just a sense of the boat and past experience to guide me.

If I want to know how deep the water is I take out a length of line with a sinker on one end and do a Mark Twain impersonation. Slinging the weighted line well forward of the bow, with the engine in idle, I watch the knots in the line till the sinker hits bottom. Not very convenient, but the old lead line has worked for centuries and it still does, if you know how to use it properly.

Up and down the coast, other mariners have given me strange looks when they see me use the lead line. I can imagine what they're thinking: "Is this guy nuts or something?" You see all kinds on the water, and not everyone has the luxury of a complete battery of electronics.

So, when the fog rolled in off Cape Small at the east end of Casco Bay, I was a bit nervous. Should I turn into the New Meadows River and head for the basin? Since I could see absolutely nothing, I toughed it out in the relatively safe offshore waters instead, favoring an easier harbor to enter down the coast. I cruised blind mile after mile from waypoint to waypoint along my dead reckoning track. This led me from one noisemaker to the next until I reached the wide entrance to Boothbay off the Cuckolds, which look nasty when you can see the swells break on the rocks.

Gingerly, I turned the boat almost due north into a harbor I couldn't see. The fog hung thick and heavy as an old winter coat. Squirrel Island lies at the entrance to Boothbay, and I pointed my fog horn where I thought the island should be and fired off a short blast. I listened for the rapid echo which would mean it was close. One blast . . . then the count: "One Mississippi . . . two Mississippi . . . Echo!"

"It must be real close!" I thought. More blasts. I drew closer to the shore of an invisible Squirrel Island.

Some time ago, safe at home, I'd read with mild amusement about the lore of how Mainers in thick fog supposedly stationed a guy perched on the bow with a sack of spuds, which he'd toss out ahead of the boat. When he heard a thud instead of a splash, he'd signal the skipper to turn. I had no intention of getting that close to shore, but the story of the potato thrower did enter my mind.

When I got close enough to the land, the fog scaled back a bit, revealing the cove, then closed in again. Relief flooded over me. I knew for sure where I was, that I wasn't going to run smack into Squirrel Island, and headed slowly into the inner harbor of Boothbay. I was fogged in for two days, but happy anyway, since Boothbay is a very nice place to visit with its many marinas, shops and good restaurants.

Pressing on ever eastward, I cruised past the formidable headland of Pemaquid into Muscongus Bay. The warm, friendly sun, puffy fair weather cumulus, and a light southwest wind were signs that Maine isn't all fog and gloom. I passed Western Egg Rock, where puffins were reintroduced to the area, though I didn't see any of the cute little birds.

The character of the land seemed more rugged than the rounded isles of Casco Bay. I'd been told that the farther east you go, the more wild the land and waters get. On such a beautiful day, the ruggedness still was apparent, as was the obvious decrease in the number of recreational boats I saw along the way.

I cruised past Port Clyde into western Penobscot Bay, and the purple humps of the Camden Hills soon filled the horizon. I knew at last I'd come far enough east to get a feel for Maine waters as I made my way through Muscle Ridge, one of the more beautiful and well-known passages along the coast.

Penobscot Bay is home to the famous Outward Bound School on Hurricane Island off the big island of Vinalhaven. I couldn't resist poking around those waters to see if I might spot Outward Bound students either sailing their tiny craft or camping out on one of the islands. The students attend the school for reasons of their own. The rigorous routine of exercise and learning how to live off the land is meant to build character, though the idea of eating kelp and sea gull eggs, swimming miles in that frigid water, and being marooned on an island on purpose didn't sound like much fun.

Not far from Hurricane Island, on a tiny knob of rock with a couple spindly trees clumped together, I noticed a plastic tarp formed into a crude tent. I scanned the island for signs of life and discovered a man on the shore dressed in jeans and a long-sleeved shirt. Even though it was a warm summer day, he also wore a stocking cap. He didn't look very happy.

He must be doing his solo trip, I thought. Not far from the island were a bunch of beautiful summer homes set back from the shore. Inside those homes was comfort and good food, but the buildings might as well have been in outer space, so removed were they from the reach of this dejected-looking guy seated on his private rock.

Heading back from Vinalhaven to the bustling city of Rockland, the restored 1930s J-Boat, *Shamrock*, cut through the water under full sail. It was a magnificent sight even a diehard powerboat enthusiast would find exciting. The decks were full of people, who paid large sums of money to go for a sail. They waved and cheered as they passed a modern racing sailboat heeling to the wind.

Suddenly, the report of a cannon rang out. Gray smoke hovered about the *Shamrock's* stern for an instant and blew away seconds later. In the old days, captains of sailing vessels used to honor one another with a cannon salute. I watched as the skipper aboard the racing sailboat disappeared below decks and emerged with an assault rifle. He pointed the muzzle skyward and fired a round, which I assumed must have been a blank, to return the honor of receiving a salute from the captain of the venerable *Shamrock*. The sharp crack of the gun made me jump. The people on the *Shamrock* cheered all the more.

You don't see that in Barnegat Bay, I thought to myself as I shook my head and smiled at the spectacle. Only in Maine do you see something like that on the water . . . only in Maine.

I had been bound for Mount Desert, Maine, from the outset of my slow voyage up and down the Northeast coast. The mountains, the fjord that cuts deeply into the island to form Somes Sound, pristine waters, and a coast that grew more rugged the farther east I went, were just over thirty miles away from Pulpit Harbor. I'd put in there two nights before after making an easy day of it across the west side of Penobscot Bay from Rockland to the island of North Haven.

A cracking southwesterly blew up to twenty-five knots the next day, so I decided to stay put and avoid a thrashing. I rode quietly at anchor in complete solitude, reading, watching osprey in a large, old nest, and just enjoying while the wind howled outside the harbor and made music in the pines.

As I left Cabot Cove, a scenic stretch of water to starboard as you enter Pulpit Harbor, I felt certain this could be the day I reached my final eastward port, Northeast Harbor on the southern shore of Mount Desert. Anticipation and excitement at reaching the halfway point of the saltwater leg of the journey was almost palpable. Even the somber mood of the weather didn't intrude—at least not yet.

Light fog shrouded the island. A two-foot chop kicked up the occasional whitecap, creating patches of white on the gray water that caught the eye for a fleeting moment and disappeared. Although it was mid-July, I wore blue jeans, a long-sleeved shirt, and a sweater against the chilly wind, and my foulies were within easy reach below in case I might need them.

Back home in New Jersey, people sweltered in record-breaking heat, and out in Chicago, the heat was actually killing. Quite a contrast, one that helps show how in many ways Maine is really a different world. I'd come from a beach coast in New Jersey to the opposite extreme, and the change was welcome.

A group of small islands flank the northeastern shore of North Haven. I wove my way through them out of the lee of the land, and the chop became waves. The wind blasted toward me over the large fetch of East Penobscot Bay.

"Are we having fun yet?" I muttered. I looked over to port, where

Deer Isle should have been, and found it missing. Way down the bay, fog began to swallow everything. I sighed and plotted a return course for the Fox Islands Thorofare, which bisects Vinalhaven and North Haven. The thorofare itself and the islands were full of places to anchor and wait out the fog.

Even after becoming better accustomed to piloting the boat in fog, it's never something I would do if I had a choice. My passage east to Mount Desert would take me through the Deer Isle Thorofare, which winds around past the granite quarries on Crotch Island and the town of Stonington. Ledges and lobster pots litter the waterway. Try it in the thick o' fog my first time through? Not if I had a choice. I dropped the hook in Vinalhaven's quiet Perry Creek and waited for conditions to improve.

The next morning, the fog was gone. I could see Deer Isle! Beyond, the hills merged together into a panorama of purple and blue.

Closer, the unbroken coat of evergreens on the white splotches of granite seemed within arm's length. At full speed, I raced out of the Fox Islands Thorofare across the eastern bay with the wind in my face and a bone in the boat's teeth. Almost in no time I'd crossed what the day before was a barren waste of impenetrable gray, as though all else on earth no longer existed—only the nothingness of empty space. A feeling of loneliness settles over me in times like that. More often it's when the fog rides on no wind, but sometimes even when it's carried along sideways at twenty knots, the disconnected feeling comes on.

Not on this day, though, I thought happily.

To the east of me as I entered the channel lay the islands comprising Merchant Row. They are supposed to be beautiful, and indeed they were. Yet the beauty was not fragile or tame, nor was it grand. The granite tailings in old quarries on Crotch Island (a distasteful yet somehow fitting name for it), the thick expanses of pine, the dark water punctuated with patches of weed covered ledges, made for an impression of how rugged life must be for those who call this place home and earn their wages from the sea.

I passed the town of Stonington to port. It's a scenic village and until recently it was largely ignored by cruising boaters. It is an old fashioned fishing town situated on a granite hillside overlooking a colorful harbor chock full of commercial lobster and work boats.

Right there in plain view as I went by was the Stonington Opera House. I wondered who went to see the operas, whether they had any. (I'm sure they must; otherwise, why have an opera house?) I wondered why, if they had an opera house, the town didn't encourage boaters to come from other ports. I wondered similar things at other places in Maine, too.

The east end of the Deer Isle Thorofare opens up into Jericho Bay, and at that end are a number of channels between ledges, most of which are charted but unmarked. I was bound for Casco Passage, a twisty little jaunt through ledges off Swans Island.

I was moving merrily along through a particularly ledgy spot when the fog returned. I'd seen the early warning signs, that white cloud, seeing your own breath, and I'd willed the fog to stay away—apparently without success. This was one spot I feared getting caught in, and, of course, that's when the fog bank decided to pay me a visit. This was no offshore run to Boothbay; very precise navigation and a cool head were needed here.

That lonely feeling settled over me. I got nervous, again. I'd charted a course to a can sitting on Whaleback Ledge, and timed my run to it. I had to make the can to know when to turn into the wide-mouthed shallow cove where I planned to anchor. Only problem was I'd run out my time. I should have arrived at the can by now! I had an uneasy feeling I might find the ledge the hard way.

Suddenly, the can loomed out of the fog about fifty feet off the starboard beam. It was a mixed blessing. Yes, I had a firm fix on my position, always a comfort when you can't see anything. Unfortunately, however, the can should have been to port. I made a slow, ninety-degree turn, and as I passed the can the black hump of what looked like a whale in the process of sounding emerged from the gloom for a few seconds and disappeared again into oblivion.

I changed course and headed for the cove, again using my fog horn to feel out where the land was. When the elapsed time for the run into the cove indicated I should be inside, I got out my trusty lead line. Just as I was about to heave it, the fog scaled back a tad, giving me the true gift of seeing where I was . . . right where I should be. It promptly closed in again a few minutes later.

I made sure the anchor was set properly and opened a well-deserved beer. Thirty miles or so might sound like an easy run, but as I was finding out during the course of the voyage nothing is ever what it seems. What looks easy can tax you to the limits; what appears a hard passage can be easy.

That night, I sat on deck and looked out into the moist shroud of fog, completely alone in the large cove. Celtic music on the public radio show "Thistle and the Shamrock" seemed quite a fitting accompaniment and added to the primal aspect of the scene . . . afloat in space; it could have been the beginning of the world.

Just off Casco Passage, on my way to Bass Harbor Bar off Mount Desert, a creature of some sort surfaced ahead of the boat. By this time seals had become a common sight. At first, my reaction was "Oh, wow! A seal!" Now, I simply muttered, "Get out of the way, seal."

It dived and surfaced closer and revealed itself as a dolphin. I watched it play off the bow with the same enthusiasm I'd felt when I first encountered seals in Casco Bay. It's a beautiful sight to see a dolphin play off the bow of your boat, and I never did see another during the voyage. I suppose if I had, I'd have become as blasé as I was about the seals, but since I never saw another dolphin the moment retains much of its magic.

I crossed Bass Harbor Bar, which I'm told is usually foggy, in crystal clear conditions. The spectacular view of Mount Desert's rounded back, blue and purple near the summit, a lush green closer in, was what I had traveled so far to see. It was a seascape of true splendor. The Western Way, a passage into Northeast Harbor, provided an even grander vista than near Bass Harbor. How different the coast looked now than it did even in Casco Bay. The feel of a different world was never so apparent as it was then. I'd arrived at last, and the sense of satisfaction was as sweet as the scent of pine wafting offshore from the heights of Mount Desert Island.

Cruising the Maine Coast Magazine, 1996

After the freshwater adventures early in the voyage, I found my times on the coast even more packed with thrills, some of which I have already mentioned. On my way home in 1995, I got another scare. I don't make much of it in the following story, because its main purpose was to focus on what fun it is to cruise to Block Island, Rhode Island. But if you read between the lines, you'll catch a glimpse of my anxiety. The next story after that, which tells about how serious the hurricane season of 1995 was, will provide further insight into just how bad things could have been.

RHODE ISLAND RETREAT

The hull of a sailboat a mile or so ahead of me disappeared behind the swells in the slow, easy-rolling rhythm of the sea. Horizon hiders, I call them. You'll find those rolling swells off Block Island, Rhode Island, even during calm conditions, although on the day I visited they seemed a little bigger than usual.

Those swells kept me up much of the previous night at anchor in Sachuest Cove, near the mouth of the Sakonnet River. It's a picturesque spot on the eastern edge of Narragansett Bay. All night the hiders refracted around Flint Point and roared against the beach on its windward side. As I watched another hill of water roll toward me, there was no doubt that we in New England were already feeling the impact of distant Hurricane Felix. In the trough of the roller all I could see was water, and once on top, I had a great view of Block Island as the bluffs of Clay Head came in and out of the haze off to port.

Although not as rugged and towering as their counterparts on the southern edge of Block Island, the Clay Head bluffs are a part of the identity of this eleven-square-mile island. Shaped like a pork chop with its tip pointing almost due north, the island is part of the glacial moraine that built the twin forks of New York's Long Island, the Elizabeth Islands south of Cape Cod, Martha's Vineyard and Nantucket.

Rolling fields, deep hollows, ponds, dunes, cliffs, and miles of sandy beaches give Block Island's terrain a distinct look. The lay of the land, the smell of the sea, the slow pace of life on the island are some of the reasons I visit often.

Despite the summer crowds, for me there is an overriding attraction to Block Island: its sense of isolation. The island's distance from the mainland sets it apart from the hustle and bustle of suburbia, preserving its character. It sits ten miles off Point Judith, Rhode Island, and eighteen miles from Montauk Point at the tip of Long Island's southern shore. It's so near the chaos of the mainland, but the water surrounding the island acts as a moat, keeping out the frenetic pace of modern times.

WHERE THE PRESENT MEETS THE PAST

Like much of New England, Block Island enjoys a rich and colorful history. Adrian Block, a Dutch explorer, was the first European to come ashore on the island in 1614, earning himself lasting fame in this section of New England. Settlers arrived in 1661 and began to carve out an existence in what was then a very wild place. The island turned out boatmen renowned along the coast for their skill at handling small craft. Far from being simply a mariner's locale, the island also had its share of farms. As the settlements grew, so did the tales of the island and its residents. Today you can still hear stories of witches and wreckers who lured unsuspecting ships aground with false beacons. One popular story tells of an immigrant ship wrecked and burned off the island with a terrible loss of life. It's said you can sometimes see the apparition of a ship afire on calm, dark nights.

Ghost stories aside, the island holds many memories for me, and I turned them over in my mind as I rounded the northern tip of the island, passing a sinewy band of sand that stretches well offshore. Many a boat from the past (and even a few from the present) has found that sandbar the hard way; more than 200 ships have been wrecked off the island's shores.

Not long after rounding the bar, I came upon the channel entrance to Great Salt Pond, a landlocked harbor a mile long and about a half-mile wide. The pond, also known as New Harbor, nearly bisects the middle of the island, cutting its north and south sections. I rode the flood tide in through the narrow passage, past the Coast Guard station to starboard.

Ahead, the panorama of the harbor spread before me like a postcard of New England. Boats of all sizes and shapes rode to moorings or at anchor in the southern end of the harbor. Hundreds more filled the slips at the marinas. Water taxis darted around, picking up and dropping off boaters amid plenty of other traffic. A typical summer weekend sees as many as 1,000 boats crammed into the harbor. I don't mind the crowds, though, because once you get off the boat and head into the island, it's not too hard to be by yourself.

Although the pond itself is a natural body of water, its function as a harbor is the result of man-made influences. Before 1895 (when the narrow passage was carved out of the sand to open the pond to the sea), the only harbor on Block Island was a little cove on the eastern shore. The islanders tied their boats up to poles set in the shallows behind a tiny breakwater, and the harbor soon became known as Pole Harbor.

Today, a fine breakwater system encloses the cove, which is really only an indentation in the island's coastline. Pole Harbor is now known as Old Harbor, and by today's standards it's small and offers limited facilities for recreational boats, which is why almost everyone goes to the pond.

Once ashore, I walked along the quiet roads leading through moors, past ponds and summer homes on my way to Old Harbor. The hundreds of stone walls running throughout the island, nearly 400 miles of them, served as reminders of the past. I wondered how difficult it must have been to farm such rocky land.

The Victorian architecture in Old Harbor also took me back in time. The harbor, listed in the National Register of Historic Places, began to bustle as a haven for tourists in the late 1800s. It still looks much as it did at the turn of the century. As I relaxed and became accustomed to the laid-back Block Island mode, I recalled many early mornings at low tide when my family and I would come down to the pond to dig for clams. We'd wade out a short distance and poke our toes deep into the sand until we felt a clam, then into the bucket it went.

The clear waters of the pond still produce good-quality clams, which you can dig yourself once you've obtained a permit from the town. Despite all the visiting and native boats permeating the area, the islanders have maintained the shell fishery through various conservation methods. Among those are the designation of the pond as a no-discharge zone, providing free pumpouts for boaters and prohibiting anchoring in the clam beds.

PRESERVING THE ISLAND'S ENVIRONMENT

The islanders have set aside 20 percent of the land as protected open space, and efforts continue to set aside even more. In 1991 the Nature Conservancy, the largest land-conservation group in the nation, designated Block Island and Peconic Bay in Long Island as two of the twelve Last Great Places in the Western Hemisphere.

Among the creatures sharing space on Block Island are rare species of birds that nest in the moors, on the beaches, and in the occasional stands of dwarf pine. Many, including the grasshopper sparrow and the upland sandpiper, are found nowhere else in Rhode Island, and in the fall, migrating birds arrive in such numbers that they sometimes black out the sky.

I continued my land-based exploration, heading toward the south end of the island to see the 200–foot clay cliffs known as Mohegan Bluffs. Strategically placed stairs let you partially climb down the bluffs at designated spots. You can walk to the bluffs from Old Harbor, but I preferred to ride. I rented a bike and took off for an afternoon of exploring and swimming.

Perched atop the bluffs is Southeast Lighthouse, a beacon some say can be seen as far as thirty-five miles out to sea. Built in 1874, it once sat 100 yards from the lip of the cliff, but over the years erosion has eaten away the bluff and threatened to topple the lighthouse into the sea. In 1993, the lighthouse was literally picked up and moved a safe distance back from the bluff.

I was lucky to have one of the scenic views at the bluff's edge all to myself for a few moments. I stood at the edge, gazing out to sea, taking in the buzz of an insect, the song of a bird and the sound of distant surf carried on updrafts of wind ascending the cliffs. For miles on either side of me I saw nothing but the bluffs—old, weathered, and topped with scraggly bushes. Below me was the flat beach with its band of white at the surfline.

Before my trip to Block Island ended, I was also treated to a glimpse of the island's darker side. I listened to the incoming weather reports about Hurricane Felix, and became increasingly anxious. The storm was a real monster, packing top winds of 140 knots, and was expected to arrive in only three days, but there was no reason to push on to meet a schedule.

Bright and early the next morning, I made arrangements to haul the boat, just in case the storm reports were accurate. The big cruisers in the harbor had already departed, and the mooring field and anchorage were virtually empty. The contrast to how it looked a few days earlier when I came in was striking and a little spooky.

For the next five days I stayed put, while Felix hovered off the mid-Atlantic coast. The island took on an even slower pace, the way it gets after Labor Day when the majority of the tourists go home for the winter, leaving the 800 year-round residents to enjoy the autumn in solitude. Although eager to get on my way down the coast, I had to congratulate myself. If I had to pick a place to get marooned in the Northeast, this was it.

Trailer Boats Magazine, 1996

THE KILLER WIND

Jerry Immel, a longtime resident of St. Thomas, U.S. Virgin Islands, will never forget last September 15. As Hurricane Marilyn slammed into the island with sustained winds of 115 miles per hour late that Friday night, he stood on the bridge of his ninety-six-foot tug in the midst of the worst storm he had witnessed in his thirty years as a licensed captain.

Before 10:00 P.M., Immel's anemometer pegged its top reading of 100 knots and stayed there—until it blew away. Suddenly, the blackness disappeared and a ghostly white glow lit the harbor. It wasn't lightning or St. Elmo's fire. What Immel had witnessed was a rare phenomenon, one meteorologists theorize was caused by moonlight shining at an angle through the hurricane's eye some distance away.

Despite a massive amount of study, hurricanes still are not completely understood. Last year's Atlantic hurricane season was the most active since 1933, when twelve tropical storms and nine hurricanes formed. In 1995, a total of eleven hurricanes and eight tropical storms lashed the Caribbean and Atlantic, setting a new record for the total number of full-fledged hurricanes in one season. Yet in the Eastern Pacific, hurricane activity was well below normal. There were seven hurricanes and three tropical storms—six named storms short of the annual average of sixteen in the Pacific. Why did so many Atlantic hurricanes form last year? Why were there so few in the Pacific?

The nation's leading hurricane expert, Dr. William Gray of Colorado State University, whose record of hurricane prediction is unsurpassed in the last decade, had at press time in mid-July forecast an "average" hurricane season for 1996, predicting ten tropical storms, six of which were expected to become hurricanes. A normal Atlantic season sees an average of nine named storms, either tropical or hurricane. A normal Pacific season breeds sixteen storms.

What were the causes of last year's Atlantic storm bloom? Why did Dr. Gray and other meteorologists predict much less action this year? Let's start with the basics.

Hurricanes and tropical storms form under precise sets of conditions. In order for such storms to form, the sea surface temperature (down to about 200 feet) must be eighty degrees or above. Heat with high moisture in the lower atmosphere and an upper-level high pressure system must be present. Prevailing winds outside the storm must blow in the same direction as the storm itself.

A cyclonic disturbance requires another ingredient: rotation. Beyond 250 to 300 miles on either side of the equator, the air flowing upward into a fledgling tropical storm with its low-pressure center will begin to spin, due to deflection from the Coriolis effect caused by the Earth's rotation. In the Northern Hemisphere, the motion is counterclockwise: in the Southern Hemisphere, clockwise. But regardless of the direction, when the circular motion starts, it's a cause for concern.

As the storm develops from a depression, the low induces warm air at the sea's surface to rise, forming clouds and squalls—releasing heat and creating a low-pressure center at sea level. Air from outside the center starts to flow inward, then upward, at increasingly higher speeds.

The rising air further reduces the pressure at the center. The storm starts to spin, the inward flow of air increases and flows upward even faster, and an eye forms with cloud walls that can reach 40,000 feet to the base of the stratosphere; calm air from those great heights descends into the eye.

No other storm packs a punch as powerful as, in some cases, 500,000 atomic bombs on the order of those dropped on Nagasaki in World War II. Fortunately, even when conditions are perfect for the formation of a cyclone and when a system begins to "live," only 10 percent actually develop into dangerous blows. When a hurricane hits land, it loses heat and moisture and weakens. This is also true when a tropical cyclone travels over areas of cold water.

Back to the question, why was 1995 such a bad year? Statistically, the answer is straightforward: there were more depressions than usual from which hurricanes could form. Also, sea surface temperatures in the Caribbean and Atlantic were well above normal. Climatic anomalies also had a bearing on last year's busy season. In West Africa's Sahel, a semidesert on the Sahara's southern fringe and the site of persistent droughts for most of the last twenty years, above-average rainfall fell in 1995. This is important, because many of the worst cyclonic storms are born on "easterly waves" originating in this region or in the Gulf of Guinea to the south. These are upper-level low-pressure troughs that travel westward and combine with other ingredients needed to breed a tropical storm. The warm rains give strength to easterly waves.

Another key factor last year was the waning of El Niño, a periodic, abnormally warm sea surface current, and the waxing of La Niña, a periodic, abnormally cold sea surface current, both in the Eastern Pacific. El Niño, brought about by a change in prevailing winds on the Pacific side of South America, was originally identified around Christmastime (hence its name, which means "the boy child"); however, every few years a warmer than normal El Niño supplants the cold and weakened Humboldt Current. An abnormally strong El Niño can raise sea surface temperatures by as much as nine degrees. A strong El Niño also lowers the pressure in the Eastern Pacific. Strong El Niño periods also reduce African rainfall and create upper-level winds traveling from west to east that shear the easterly waves headed the other way. None of this makes a tropical storm happy; fewer storms form in stronger El Niño years.

La Niña ("the girl child") exerts the opposite effect: cold water returns to the Eastern Pacific, the shearing winds cease and rainfall in West Africa increases. This produces conditions favorable for tropical storm development. At such times, Atlantic tropical storms and hurricanes breed profusely and travel westward from Africa as they did last year.

So far in 1996, African rainfall has dropped back to normal, reducing fuel for the easterly waves. La Niña hasn't strengthened; it may even weaken or disappear altogether.

Another factor that likely will mitigate hurricane development in the Atlantic this year is something called the quasi-biennial oscillation, a shift in upper-level winds, which will not favor a spate of storms like last year's.

Hurricanes, while often capricious, stick to fairly predictable patterns dictated by the season. In June, a time of fewer storms, most develop in the Gulf of Mexico and western Caribbean. These storms often target the southeastern United States.

In August and September, the height of the season, formation activity extends from the Gulf of Mexico to Africa. In these peak months, storms can strike anywhere from Mexico to Maine. Toward the end of the season the action returns to the Caribbean.

Monthly Pacific hurricane activity coincides with that of the Atlantic. The danger area ranges from Central America to Mexico and west to the Hawaiian Islands. Most Pacific storms move in a northwesterly direction and die in cooler waters. Occasionally, they recurve to the northeast and affect Mexico and Southern California.

Any passage maker that is inevitably and unwisely caught out at sea in or near a hurricane should understand "translational winds." If a storm is heading due north in the Northern Hemisphere at a typical fifteen-to-twenty-knot speed, for example, the forward speed on the northeast and easterly side of the storm will combine with the sustained winds spinning in a counterclockwise motion.

A boat caught on the east side of the eye of the hypothetical storm with average sustained winds of seventy-five knots will find itself faced with southerly winds at speeds equaling the storm's sustained wind speed, plus the speed of its forward motion, or in this case, ninety to ninety-five knots, more if the forward motion is faster. (The great New England hurricane of 1938 traveled forward at astounding speeds of up to seventy miles per hour!)

The closer to the eye one gets, the higher the winds will be, because they accelerate in a manner similar to water running down a drainpipe. In addition, swirls of wind near the eye wall can reach speeds estimated to be in excess of 200 knots. These are not tornadoes (which sometimes do form in hurricanes) but awesome cells within the hurricane's structure.

The unlucky cruising boat facing a storm has a few options. The rule of thumb is to determine the boat's position relative to the forward track of the eye, then set a course at right angles away from the deadly center. This sounds fine in theory. But taking another look at the hypothetical storm it becomes clear that a boat caught on the edge of the southeasterly quadrant would have to turn eastward to establish a right-angle course. That would mean dealing with wind and seas dead off the starboard beam—not wise. Yet running downwind with the storm would gradually find the boat sucked in toward the danger zone.

One more problem of major concern is that storms don't often steer a straight course. Upper-level wind flows, determined by the presence of high- or low-pressure systems, move hurricanes one way or the other. A major high or low in the storm's path will block or "steer" the storm, but highs and lows generally are themselves in motion, accounting for the often erratic tracks of hurricanes.

Hurricanes are among the world's deadliest storms. Although climatic anomalies that caused the intense 1995 season in the Atlantic have largely gone, even a "normal" year can spell trouble for anyone unfortunate enough to be in a hurricane's path. During the busiest month for hurricane development on both coasts, keep a weather eye out and be prepared to batten down the hatches.

Cruising World, 1996

> My home waters of Barnegat Bay are some of the friendliest on the entire East Coast. Sure, they're crowded on the weekends, as are many others. For example, anyone who has run the Annisquam River behind Cape Ann in Massachusetts on a busy summer weekend will agree. But subtract the crowds and you've got calm water even when the wind howls and the surf roars against the Jersey shore's barrier islands.
>
> Outside those barrier islands, the coast can challenge the best of boaters. It can even sink you, if you're not careful. Many of the folks I met who planned to cruise south regarded New Jersey with a healthy dose of respect, and they asked me many questions about how to best navigate and avoid the dangers. In the nation's most densely populated state, few of the residents realize just how nasty the cruising can get beyond the glitz of the boardwalks.
>
> The following story tells a bit about the coast's hazards, and it also ties in the last of my many trials during the coastal leg of the voyage. After cruising for so long, and within a stone's throw of Manasquan Inlet, the sea still wasn't done with me.

THE SHIPWRECK CAPITAL OF THE WORLD

Back in the days of sail, the Jersey shore was known as the "graveyard." It's a nickname hard to imagine on a sunny day at the beach when you're lost in a sea of umbrellas.

But when the wind pipes up and waves crash ashore during a cracking nor'easter it becomes far easier to imagine the coast as a fearful place for sailors. Driven before wind and waves, sailing ships, like pieces of driftwood, often get pushed toward land. Sailors call this a lee shore, and in the days when ships headed to and from New York were powered by sail, New Jersey was one of the worst on the East Coast.

Heavy shipping traffic set the stage for decades and decades of death and destruction along the Jersey shore any time the wind roared in from the east. More than 3,000 wrecks litter the ocean floor off the coast, silent reminders of a dark side of the shore's past. In Manasquan, Deal, Spring Lake, Island Beach, Long Branch, Brigantine and many other locations, sunken ships rest in the shallows just beyond the breakers.

The years between 1839 and 1848 were particularly bad for sailing ships. During that period 338 ships blew ashore on the coasts of New

Jersey and Long Island. One winter storm in 1846 sank ten ships and killed forty-six people.

The loss of life and property might have gone on unchecked until today's mighty tankers came along if not for one influential New Jerseyan.

William A. Newell, a physician, set out to turn the tide in favor of the sailors and their ships, and he succeeded, laying the foundation for a lifesaving system and service that eventually became the United States Coast Guard. Newell made a lifelong commitment to the U.S. Lifesaving Service after watching an Austrian brig break up off the coast of Long Beach Island in 1839. Newell and other onlookers stood by helplessly as the captain and crew were forced to abandon ship, only to be swallowed up by the sea.

So moved was Newell, he got himself elected to Congress so he could persistently lobby for funds to establish a series of lifesaving stations from Cape May to Sandy Hook. As a result, Congress finally allocated $10,000 in 1848 to form eight lifesaving stations.

The lifesaving stations were equipped with surfboats fashioned after the famous Sea Bright skiff, a craft indigenous to New Jersey built to enable fishermen to launch and land right off the beach. They also included mortars for firing lifelines to vessels, and an airtight, unsinkable, walnut-shaped metal thing known as a life-car, invented by Joseph Francis.

This was all state-of-the-art lifesaving back then. Mariners off the cold, dangerous coast of Great Britain had long traditions of volunteer lifesaving, as did New Englanders. However, New Jersey's was the first organized, fully equipped, and federally funded effort to create a search and rescue service.

The life-car was an example of just how serious Newell and others were about rescuing people from stricken ships. A life-car was a metal airtight and watertight enclosure run along lines secured to the beach and the ship. Four or five people climbed inside and rescuers pulled them ashore over the pounding breakers.

In 1850, the *Ayrshire*, a British immigrant ship, ran hard aground on Chadwick Beach during a January nor'easter. Conditions were too rough for surfboats. More than 200 passengers crowded the decks of the *Ayrshire* cut off from the safety of the beach by the breakers. The lifesaving crew rigged the life-car, rescuing all but one of the passengers.

Newell's faith in the newfangled contraption paid off handsomely. During its use at the Squan Lifesaving Station, 1,493 lives were saved in that one life-car.

In its heyday during the late 1800s New Jersey Lifesaving Stations were spaced at intervals of no more than three miles apart along the entire coast. New Jersey served as a model for the rest of the country. The life station concept was expanded to all United States waters and dubbed the United States Lifesaving Service. In 1919, the United States Lifesaving Service merged with the Revenue Cutter Service to form the United States Coast Guard; its search and rescue arm got its start right here in New Jersey.

Advances in shipbuilding have largely neutralized the threat of a lee shore. The swift tides and shifting shoals seldom cause any problems for commercial mariners. The state hasn't been called the "graveyard" in close to 100 years. However, the New Jersey coast still poses the same challenges and dangers for modern-day sailors as it did in the past.

The lee shore, the lack of natural harbors easy to enter from seaward, the shoals, the few good inlets; these factors come together to make the coast of New Jersey a place worthy of respect.

During my travels over the last four years aboard a twenty-four-foot sailboat on Lake Ontario, the St. Lawrence River, the East Coast from Manasquan to Bar Harbor, Maine, I sailed some challenging waters. None of them outdid New Jersey, not even Maine with its blasted fog and multitude of rocks. At least in Maine you can find a good harbor, even if you can't see it; not so in New Jersey.

Homeward bound from Maine last year, the swells from Hurricane Felix cut me off from my home port of Manasquan. Huge breakers across Manasquan Inlet closed the passage to small craft, so I waited in safer waters until the seas subsided. When I finally reached New Jersey waters, strong east winds penned me behind Sandy Hook for two days while the boat tossed about in the waves at anchor.

As I sat waiting out the easterly blow, I thought about the many skippers who had come to grief on the Jersey shore. I was anxious to get home from my long voyage, but I waited for the wind to shift and the seas to go down. History, at times, can inspire prudence.

The Star-Ledger, 1996

With the voyage now over and my schedule far busier than I'd ever thought possible back in the dark days of the recession, I found I had to content myself with cruising my home waters. I'd become like most of the other boaters, tied in with the press of business and the lack of time.

There is much to be said for the long-distance cruise, and I've got every intention of heading off into the sea for more adventures. But the home waters hold a special place in my heart, for they provide the food for thought which fuels my desire to venture forth from them and the basis of comparison when I do explore new cruising grounds. This last story is a celebration of my home waters, and, quite possibly, yours, too, no matter where they are.

CRUISING THE FIRST SOUTHERN STATE

The fellow was an odd duck. You might even have called him a boat bum, one of those waterborne hoboes with nary a penny in his pocket, no visible means of support or the inclination to secure any. He'd been living on a raggedy looking twenty-three-foot sloop, which didn't even have a head (he used a bucket), for three years loping from port to port up and down the Intracoastal Waterway from Maine to Florida, following the seasons like a bedraggled snowbird.

He'd eaten kelp, gathered mussels, fished, and bought day-old bread at the local grocery store just to get by. When the pickings were slim, which he said was nearly always, he'd add what he caught or mooched to box after box of mac 'n' cheese. But he loved his life, the freedom to cruise to his heart's content alone with his boat and the beauty of the Eastern seaboard.

I'd met him in Mattituck, Long Island, while on a cruise to Maine from my home waters of New Jersey's Barnegat Bay. Like him, I was alone, enjoying the challenges, the solitude, the new experiences that can only come when cruising. Whether it's in your home or unfamiliar waters, taking off on the boat for a cruise, no matter how short, brings with it a special kind of feeling.

"So, how do you like New Jersey?" I asked, half expecting to hear him poke fun at the state, as many skippers I'd met from other places seemed inclined to do.

"It's really beautiful," he said. "It's your first Southern state, with its sandy islands, marshes full of birds, places you can hide away from the world."

The first Southern state . . . he'd hit the proverbial nail on the head. Down past Toms River, the huge expanse of the Pine Barrens laced with rivers and creeks and dotted with sleepy little towns marks a regional divide, a sort of unofficial demarcation between the frenetic North and the more laid-back South typical of the Chesapeake, Albemarle and Pamlico sounds, the islands off Georgia's semitropical coast.

Cruising to these waters, if you know where to go (see fellow *Offshore* writer Don Launer's *A Cruising Guide to New Jersey Waters*), and when (during the week is better than on weekends), transports you into a frame of mind that makes you think of blue crab as opposed to lobster, sand instead of rock, marsh grass instead of bluffs. Even in the upper reaches of Barnegat Bay, about ten miles from Manasquan Inlet, you can find a quasi-wild place in Silver Bay. It's a bit of a stretch to compare it to the more southern hideaways, but when watching the sun set over the bight in the south end of the bay at Cattus Island County Park, you still get the flavor.

I recall sitting in the cockpit one warm summer night last season. A soft southerly breeze carried the scent of the nearby land across the water. The band of orange lights along Route 35 on Island Beach glowed to the east. Suddenly, fireworks blazed over the bay to the west, putting on quite a show. At my slip at the south end of the Point Pleasant Canal, I'd often watched the weekly Thursday night laser lightshows put on at Jenkinson's South on the boardwalk, but seeing the pyrotechnics from Silver Bay remains one of those special moments, a cruising memory, even though it originated a mere jump from the marina where I keep the boat.

Farther down Barnegat Bay, past the twin bridges that link Island Beach to the mainland, Toms River ranks as another fine spot to drop the hook. You'll see plenty of local boats rafted up near Money Island and the Toms River Yacht Club. If you're lucky, you'll catch a glimpse of an A-Cat, a Marconi-rigged, twenty-eight-foot catboat built to race for the Toms River Challenge Cup, America's oldest challenge cup regatta which began in 1871 with the founding of the Toms River Yacht Club.

(The America's Cup doesn't hold the distinction of being the nation's oldest challenge race. Originally known as the Queen's Cup, a Sandy Hook pilot named Richard Brown, skipper of the schooner *America*, won the famous race of 1851 around the Isle of Wight and brought the prize home to the United States.)

The eastern end of Toms River runs fairly straight, but upriver toward Beachwood, it starts to snake. Few people realize that the waterway flows across nearly a third of the state through dense stands of pine and cedar at an average rate of five knots. Local lore has it that pirates rowed their longboats up beyond the brackish zone to replenish their casks with pure, tangy cedar water.

As you cruise farther south, the creeks running from the mainland into the bay contain a rich brown color from the cedar trees and the bog iron that once supported a thriving industry in the area. Hence the name of the next waterway down from Toms River, Cedar Creek.

Tices Shoal, as long as the wind blows from an easterly direction, reminds me a little of Biddeford Pool, Maine. In both places, you can hear the sound of surf breaking on a nearby beach while you sit in quiet water. Tices Shoal, it's no secret hideaway, but it's absolutely beautiful to watch the sun set across the bay after spending the day swimming or walking along the shore of Island Beach State Park.

In a west wind, I nose up close to the mainland north of Forked River, or cruise up the waterway to one of the many marinas that welcome transients. At the far end of the bay, Conklin Island offers a pleasant anchorage in southerly winds. You can look northward across the wide open expanse of lower Barnegat Bay at night and clearly see the darkness that marks the protected state park area, an island within an island, one of those wild places in the nation's most densely populated state.

Offshore, 1997

Index

About the Author

David W. Shaw has been cruising northeastern waters since his childhood. He graduated from Syracuse University's Newhouse School of Public Communications with a degree in magazine journalism. Much of his writing—both fiction and nonfiction—is inspired by his love of the sea and the outdoors. Shaw is a feature writer and columnist for *Offshore* magazine and *The Star-Ledger*. He has written more than 700 articles for many regional, national, and international publications, including *Sail, Cruising World, Lakeland Boating, Hudson Valley Magazine,* and *Adirondack Life*. He is the author of *Daring the Sea* and *The Cheapskate's Guide to Weddings and Honeymoons*.